For
Cubs Fans
Only!!!

Page Two. In 1941 the news director at a small radio station in Kalamazoo, Michigan, hired Harry Caray, who had been employed at a station in Joliet, Illinois. The news director's name was Paul Harvey. Yes, *that* Paul Harvey! "And now, you know the rest of the story...."

For
Cubs Fans
Only!!!

This is the year that the Cubs absolutely, definitely, without a doubt will win the World Series—maybe.

Rich Wolfe

The Lyons Press
Guilford, Connecticut
An imprint of The Globe Pequot Press

To Thaddeus,
who has gone from a little boy
to a grown man in about twelve minutes

The Lyons Press is an imprint of The Globe Pequot Press.

All text and photos submitted for publication by die-hard Cubs fans.

Text design by Sheryl P. Kober
Cover artwork by John Kovalic

Cover concept by Dick Fox
Author's agent T. Roy Gaul
Author Rich Wolfe can be reached at (602) 738-5889.

Library of Congress Cataloging-in-Publication Data is available.
ISBN 978-1-59921-338-5

Printed in the United States of America

10 9 8 7 6 5 4 3 2 1

Chat Rooms

Preface

You are about to be swept into the brilliant minds of Chicago Cubs fans, awe-struck by their farsighted scheming, stricken dumb by their wonderful stories as they lay bare their sordid love affair with the Chicago Cubs.

There had never been a book like this until *For Cubs Fans Only*, volume 1, a vehicle for fans to share their funniest stories, saddest memories, happiest times, and craziest moments. Every story was a reflection of their personal Cubs memory bank.

The first edition of *For Cubs Fans Only* happened quite by accident.

On October 14, 2003, I received a call from my largest distributor, the distributor for Sam's Clubs, Costco, and Borders. He said, "We want a Cubs fan book for Christmas." I told him, "Well, I'm not a Cubs fan, I'm a Cardinals fan. My brothers are Cubs fans, many of my friends are Cubs fans, and my younger son is a Cubs fan. You have fourteen months before Christmas. You can certainly find somebody to do it."

He said, "No, we want it for *this* Christmas, and we want you to do it with your format because the Cubs are going to the World Series tonight or tomorrow night." I said, "You're in California. You don't know the history of the Cubs very well." When they told me how many they were going to order, I said, "You'll have them within a month." Literally, twenty-eight days later, *For Cubs Fans Only* was going down the turnpike. That book sold three times the number of copies of any book in Cubs history.

There, I said it: I'm a St. Louis Cardinals fan. Cue the apocalypse. You may feel that's a whole bowl of wrong, but authors are accustomed to criticism. Occasionally, some of that criticism even comes from outside our immediate families. As mentioned, three of my older brothers are Cubs fans as is my younger son. The former I attribute to some sort of 4-H experiment that went haywire, and the latter to a possible mix-up at the hospital.

Actually, I'm a Cardinals fan for the same reason many of you are Cubs fans: Harry Caray. While I was growing up on an Iowa farm, Harry was magnetic when broadcasting games over KMOX in St.

Louis. Harry was aces until he had one Busch too many in St. Louis and headed to Chicago to repay that debt to Satan.

While I was signing Cubs books at Nordstrom's in Oak Brook several years ago, a yuppie was surveying pictures of other books that I've done. He said rather loudly, "Hey, this author did a book on Harry Caray. Harry was terrible his last few years." I looked up at him and replied, "Harry Caray could be drunk on his ear while suffering from Alzheimer's and still be more exciting than any announcer on the air today. Plus, he was a great, giving man who loved baseball and baseball fans to his toenails and probably signed more free autographs than anyone in baseball history." To me, Harry had magic.

Furthermore, even though I'm a Cardinals fan, I abhor Tony LaRussa, so I want you Cubs fans to remember that old adage: "The enemy of my enemy is my friend."

Since the age of ten, I have been a serious collector of sports books. During that time, my favorite book style has been the eavesdropping type where the subject talks in his or her own words without the "then he said" or "the air was so thick you could cut it with a butter knife" waste of verbiage. Thus, I adopted the style of these books when I started compiling oral histories of the Mike Ditkas and Harry Carays of the world. I am a sports fan first and foremost—I do not even pretend to be an author. I really do not care what the publisher, editors, or critics think. I am only interested in Cubs fans having an enjoyable read and getting their money's worth. Sometimes, a person being interviewed will drift off the subject, but if the feeling is that Chicago fans would enjoy the digression, it stays in the book.

Finally, my Cardinals friends would be extremely upset that I'm doing volume 2 of a Cubs book before writing the second edition of the Cardinals fans book. I'm not going to tell them, so it's entirely up to you: Speak not to a Cardinals fan about what I've done. Not to anyone from St. Louis. Ever.

Thanks. Go now.

—Rich Wolfe,
Falmouth, Massachusetts

\

Growin' Up a Cubbie

John Mocek

Twelve Years Old Forever

Rootin' for the Cubs Is Like Flying Delta for the Food

Joe Bartenhagen

 After growing up in the Midwest, namely Muscatine, Iowa, Joe Bartenhagen, 40, moved to Salt Lake City, Utah, where he insists everything is "fine." His job in advertising has afforded him many luxuries—chief among them is his wife Kristen.

N o one chooses to grow up a Cubs fan. How could you choose something like this? Who would choose something like this? All fumbling, fit-inducing, and completely painful Tim McCarverisms aside, choosing to grow up being a Cubs fan would be like choosing to have a brain embolism, or choosing to have a comically minute penis, or choosing to listen to **Tim McCarver**—no one in his or her right mind would do it. . . .

Unless he or she was cursed.

The curse comes in the form of hope—though you don't know this when you're young, and older Cubs fans won't explain this to you. When you're young, it feels like certainty. But, older Cubs fans know this as pathological, unending, malignant, stupid, stupid, never-to-be-paid-off hope. By the time you begin to suspect the truth, say in 1984, back when you were fairly sure that Keith Moreland was a legitimate everyday player and that Gary Matthews's lunging, plunging coverage of the leftfield was merely, ahem, unorthodox, it's too late.

Growing up, all the other kids were Cowboy fans, or Lakers fans, or Yankees fans. They were all reasonably well adjusted—except for

Tim McCarver: Brent Musburger was the home plate umpire when Tim McCarver made his pro baseball debut for Keokuk, Iowa, in the Midwest League in 1959.

Allen Steckman, an ardent Thurman Munson devotee who threatened to break all of my pencils if I didn't call him Wild Man—and good-looking kids. I was, even though I didn't realize it at the time, already a mess. I was a bad dresser. My hairstyle never progressed much beyond simply being combed. Oh, and I was hopelessly, hopelessly chunky. Looking back, I realize this. At the time, I thought I was fairly cool. By no means a Fonzie but certainly a steady, if not periodically flashy, Richie Cunningham.

The reality that I was actually 100 percent Ralph Malph—only chunkier—dawned on me about the same time that I realized that being a Cub fan indicated some unfortunate things about myself:

Her dad—the source of her Cardinal fandom—was a dour little troll who spent his evenings parading around in his sagging JCPenney briefs and hating me

1. Being a young Cub fan meant that I was comfortable with underachievement. Losing didn't really faze me, in fact, it felt like home.
2. "Wait till next year" wasn't just the mantra of my team; it was that ethos that guided my personal development. While young Yankees, Dodgers, and Cardinals fans were winning spelling bees and kissing Katie Reardon, I found myself biding my time, waiting for the right moment and telling myself that Katie Reardon wasn't worth kissing anyways—though she was totally and undeniably the Hottest Thing to ever walk the halls of Hayes Elementary; not only was she worth kissing—she was worth some sort of coerced marriage.
3. Like my favorite Cub, Dave Kingman, I had little range, streaky power, an amorphous strike zone, and a penchant for, when faced with one of life's little, rolling groundballs, falling down for no reason and watching remotely as the ball trickled down the line and into the bullpen—as my cap slipped down over my eyes, a little.

My first real girlfriend was a Cardinal fan. She had no patience or sense of humor, though the Cubs—and I—amused her a little. Her

3

dad—the source of her Cardinal fandom—was a dour little troll who spent his evenings parading around in his sagging JCPenney briefs and hating me, not necessarily for being a Cub fan, but for exhibiting the qualities of my team. He was no prize, ensconced in his not-as-tighty-as-one-might-likey whiteys, but he made his admiration of the Cardinals seem like the result of an elegant though completely rational and obvious algebraic equation. Lou Brock was the symbol of all that was right with his team and all that was wrong with mine.

Invariably, I would counter with my theory that, while Ryne Sandberg was my generation's symbol of grace and power, Tommy Herr was my generation's symbol of why grown men should never, ever get a curly perm.

The relationship—with my girlfriend and her badgerish father—did not end well. Which is fitting since it neither started nor continued well.

In the end, I wonder: Do I have any advice for young Cub fans of today? Yes, yes, I do. . . . It is this: Cherish every moment you spend in Wrigley Field as a child—it is the most special place in all of sports. It will never change. And when you visit it thirty years from now, you will remember the very first time you walked in—how it smelled, how old it seemed. . . . It is the best reason for being not a Cubs fan, but a fan of anything.

Most importantly, and in addition to all these things, work as hard as you possibly can to become interested in **soccer** or something else. Because being a Cub fan is the worst thing in the world—worse even than being forced to listen to Tim McCarver trying to speak English.

That brings me to the incredible 2003 season. I was watching the 2003 NLCS Game 6 and Steve Bartman commits what will forever be known as *The Act*. It probably won't be forever known as that. I'm still working on what it will forever be known as. Frankly, I doubt my power to make something be known forever as something unless it is

soccer: More U.S. kids today play soccer than any other organized sport, including youth baseball. Perhaps, the reason so many kids play soccer is so they don't have to watch it.

something minor and intensely personal like the time my wife caught me looking down the checkout girl's blouse and gave me what will forever be known as *The Awful Look of Rebukement.*

So, Bartman commits The Act—reaching for a foul ball and interfering with Moises Alou's ability to put another nail in the Marlins' figurative, postseason coffin . . . who would've thought that they would have won the World Series the way they did! And, comically, I scream. I scream, "Ahhhhhh!" My wife says, "It's no big deal, it's just a foul ball." And I—again, comically—say, "You don't know! You weren't there in 1984 when Leon "Bull" Durham let the ball roll between his legs, helping to finalize three straight Padre wins! You weren't there in 1989 when the Pacific Sock Exchange hit .800 versus Cub pitching! You weren't there when the Cubs were righteously paddled by the Braves and actually nothing particularly unexpected happened! This is a tide-turner! This is a momentum-shifter! The Cubs have lost the pennant!"

I really need to stress that I said this all very comically, even though the frequent use of exclamation points and complete absence of traditionally "funny" words, phrases, or sentiments might suggest something less comical—more like ranting or whining.

As it turns out, I am right. Soon after, the Marlins score eight runs in an inexplicable torrent of offense. An incomprehensible beating as if God himself has descended from on high and administered it himself. The Cubs' World Series hopes? In tatters. Blood-speckled, tear-ridden tatters. But where am I? Watching it on TV? No. Listening to it on the radio? No. Again, *comically*, I am driving around in my car, numb to all the feeling, a whirring in my ears. It is the whirring of the universe exposing itself to me, opening up and showing its inner workings that somehow involve the Cubs never making it to the World Series. Inner workings that, while consigning the Cubs to eons of nothing, involve giving the Yankees everything; ensuring that Yankee fans will go through their stunted, ursine lives with a profound, chronic sense of entitlement. By the way, all Yankee

All Yankee fans are terrible, terrible louts; blathering scum; they know nothing of baseball.

5

fans are terrible, terrible louts; blathering scum; they know nothing of baseball—only that they win constantly. No Yankee fan ever has won an argument of any kind and yet, I believe, walks around under the distinct impression that they have never lost anything! I have never ever, not even by mistake, made friends with a Yankee fan, because they are all, to a person, *Everything That is Wrong in America*! They're easy to spot in a crowd, but they're easier still to uncover in casual conversation—in that they invariably reveal how genetically weak and averse to pain they are. They are awful, awful people.

Later, I am home again, throwing my two Cubs hats into the garbage and my wife is watching me. The 2003 postseason tired her out, too. My Tourette's-like bouts of swearing, my furniture-kicking, my obsessive, superstition-following—I did burn an old Cubs ticket stub and rub its ashes on the TV—to no avail. . . . It's all been too much. And she has, what will forever be known as, *Had It with Me.* "Won't you need those next year?" she asks. And I shake my head, a little comically, but probably not very. "No," I say. "Never." And this time I mean it. On the other hand, if we don't win it all in 2008, we will in 2009 for sure.

On the *Late Show with David Letterman* the host has a nightly Top 10 List. Following are some of the Top 10 "messages left on Steve Bartman's answering machine" after the NLCS:

You owe me $7.50 for the beer I threw at you.

I'm with Century 21—heard you might be moving.

Hey, I just got back in the country—how was the game?

Don't worry; I'm sure we'll get another shot at the World Series in 2098.

Hey, it's Don Zimmer. Thanks for taking the heat off me.

Hi, this is Mike from Hasbro. I'm calling to verify some information for your Trivial Pursuit question.

Hey, it's Bill Buckner. Want to hang out?"

The Son Also Rises

Rich Dozer

Just about every American male has wanted to run a professional sports franchise or own a sports bar . . . and wouldn't want to do either if he knew how difficult it would be. Chicago native Rich Dozer got to do the former when fellow Chicagoan Jerry Colangelo made him head honcho of the Arizona Diamondbacks. Dozer's father Dick Dozer was a well-known, longtime sports writer on the Chicago scene for over three decades.

When I was a kid, I got to leave school in Chicago and go to spring training with my Dad. I would go to school on this Florida island called Siesta Key near Sarasota. The pitcher that had pitched the day before would pick me up for school every morning because they'd have to go to the park early. I had Rich Gossage, **Terry Forster**, Wilbur Wood—these guys picking me up from school and taking me to the park because my dad was already there. I'd be waiting outside the private school; they'd pick me up, take me to the ballpark where I would put my little uniform on. I was the envy of those kids.

When I was doing it, it was those great years—'69 through '71—some of those pretty good years with Ron Santo. Players were really close friends with the media in those days. My dad was buddies with those guys. Today, they'd never let a kid of a baseball writer be a batboy. It just wouldn't happen. It wouldn't make sense at all. The players were totally normal towards me. They'd lose their temper and swear. It wasn't like they treated me with "kid gloves." The way they treated me, I was like a seventeen- or twenty-year-old batboy to them. They were themselves. It was a really classy group. The guys that were on those teams—Banks, Kessinger, Becker, Santo, Ferguson,

Terry Forster: Pitcher Terry Forster has the highest career batting average for players with over one hundred at-bats.

7

. . . the guys they
called the Million
Dollar Infield because
they were paying the
whole Cubs' infield a
million dollars.

Jenkins—were just really, really classy guys. Those were the guys they called the Million Dollar Infield because they were paying the whole Cubs' infield a million dollars—think about that in today's day and age! So, I had the envy of every kid's life.

My favorite Cub was Ernie Banks. He was always really nice. I hung out with his kids, who were just a little bit younger than me. They used to live near us during spring training. Santo was always really nice. Kessinger was very nice. Fergie Jenkins was always teasing me as a little kid. I remind him about it now—he spends time in Phoenix.

I never got in trouble for screwing up as a **batboy**. Every once in a while you forget to go out there; you don't get the balls out to the umpire when he needs a couple extra balls. When you're a little guy, the manager would look over and say, "Hey, need some balls." It was more about making sure you didn't get killed. Batboys used to kneel next to the player that was in the on-deck circle. Not now with what happened with the Cardinal player getting hit in the face. My mom and dad were always petrified that I was going to get hurt . . . that the player in the on-deck circle would be swinging and hit me in the head or a ball would ricochet back there.

Most of the times I was a batboy it was spring training. I was a batboy in Comiskey Park and at Wrigley as a kid—but very little at Wrigley. Just occasionally, when some kid went on vacation with their parents. Those were mostly paid jobs. There was a guy there then that is still with the Cubs named Yosh. As of last year he was still working at Wrigley Field in the visitors locker room. He used to be the head clubhouse guy for the Cubs.

The players were such good friends of my dad. They used to tease him. My dad in 1969—the year that the Cubs were way ahead and had

batboy: When Lou Piniella played minor-league baseball in Aberdeen, South Dakota, the team's batboy was Cal Ripken Jr.

The Son Also Rises

the big flop—came over to the Cubs at the All-Star Game that year from covering the Sox the first half of the season. The players used to tease him that he jinxed them. They'd say, "Hey, we were playing good until you got here." My dad was the first one to talk about the theory that the Cubs have trouble winning because they're tired out at the end of the year because they play so many games during the day. What happens is that the day games sap it out of you in one way plus the players have more time at night to go out and get in trouble and less time to sleep in, so it tires them out. In other words, the game is over at five o'clock, go out to dinner, go out in town, and get to bed late . . .

I worked for eight years at a CPA firm in Phoenix. One of my clients became the Phoenix Suns basketball team. When I was working on their account—after a couple years—the business manager of the Suns decided to leave and Jerry Colangelo, the Suns general partner, hired me to be his business manager. A year later he made me vice president and chief operating officer of what was then America West Arena while it was under construction. I was in charge of helping design the building and getting it built. My dad and Colangelo were good friends when I was growing up because my dad covered Big Ten basketball in the winter and Colangelo played Big Ten basketball. Colangelo was a star basketball player in Chicago Heights—same era as Jim Bouton pitching there—and Colangelo went to Kansas to play with Wilt Chamberlain. When Chamberlain left for the **Harlem Globetrotters,** Colangelo transferred to Illinois. They stayed friends for years. I was working for Colangelo, and in 1993 we start to get the baseball team, the Diamondbacks. I was Jerry's right-hand guy for the basketball team and also to help get the baseball team. When we got the baseball team, Colangelo asked me, "Which team do you want to

Harlem Globetrotters: Bob Gibson played basketball with the Harlem Globetrotters several off-seasons . . . In 1972 Bill Cosby signed a lifetime contract with the Globetrotters for one dollar per year. In 1986 the Globetrotters gave him a nickel raise. Cosby made several appearances with the team and is an honorary member of the Basketball Hall of Fame.

run? The basketball team or baseball team? You think about it and tell me in a day or two." I came back to him a couple days later and said, "I'll do whichever one you want, it's an honor for me to let you choose. My selection, if you don't care, is baseball. I grew up around baseball. I would like to start some brand-new team from scratch. I'd like to build another facility." So he made me president of the baseball team and they became the Diamondbacks. I was in charge of building the whole team from the ground up—building the stadium, building the minor leagues, and everything else. Of course, Joe Garagiola Jr. was an integral part of that.

I remember the first time the Cubs came to Phoenix. It was an unreal thrill—as a Chicago native—to be president of a team that was playing the Cubs. We tried to have a real classy organization. To treat everybody well—that was our motto.

Colangelo and I were both Cubs fans. We would go every year when the Diamondbacks went to Chicago. We'd take sponsors and advertisers on those trips. Billy Williams was the first base coach for the Cubs. He'd look over at Colangelo and I, wave, and just smile. I saw Santo sometimes and Steve Stone. . . . Bill Veeck was Barnum & Bailey—he was amazing. He was an absolutely amazing guy. I can still see him sitting in the Bards Room at Comiskey Park—a big bar and dinner place where the media and the executives would come before and after the game. He'd be sitting there with his wooden leg, and then he'd go back to his office. Roland Hemond used to say, "This is pretty funny, I was the manager of the Chicago White Sox and you were batboy. You worked for me. Then I worked with Colangelo at the Diamondbacks and now I work for you." He used to laugh about that. I helped Jerry out for two years and then thought it was time to go do something else. Now, I'm working with the Diamondbacks owner—Ken Kendrick—as my partner, in real estate development.

Walt Moryn Baseball Cards Are Selling Like Hot Cakes, $2 a Stack

John Mocek

John Mocek was raised in White Sox territory at 28th and Pulaski even though he went to Schurz High School, which is 4 miles from Wrigley. Upon graduating from the University of Texas at Arlington in 1977, he played minor-league baseball in Appleton, Wisconsin. He returned to Texas where he is now the associate athletic director at his alma mater after being the assistant baseball coach there for sixteen years.

I became a Cubs fan subconsciously from my mom and dad. My first memory is walking into Wrigley Field with my Cubs hat on with the white stripe. It was a circa 1957 Cub hat, so it was probably the 1958 season when I was four years old. As I later found out, the Cubs wore the hat with the white stripe only in 1957.

In 1959 the White Sox went to the World Series. I actually got to go to Game 6 of the World Series. My dad was a typical city guy. He was in the middle of the action. He had World Series tickets. There's a picture of me with my White Sox cap on. As a matter of fact, I was actually in the newspaper with Andy Frain's wife in 1959. I had a jacket with all the baseball logos on it and a White Sox cap. Andy Frain was the usher person of Chicago and a lot of the other major cities. My mom, dad, and I were sitting on the first base side, and Andy Frain's wife was a very beautiful lady. They wanted to take a picture of her at the World Series and because I'm sitting there, a five-year-old boy in the typical baseball jacket, they just put me in there. I never met Andy Frain. If he did come by that day I have no remembrance. My love for the White Sox started and ended with Ted Kluszewski.

My first favorite Cub was Walt "Moose" Moryn. His baseball card and autographed baseball are here in my den with some of my other great players. Walt Moryn is there because in 1959 we go to Wrigley Field in the afternoon with my mother and Walt Moryn walks over and signs my baseball. He is the first Major League player that ever signed a baseball for me. I'm five years old. There was Walt Moryn signing my baseball, the Great Moose. From that moment on it was all about Moose Moryn. Dale Long, Sammy Taylor, George Altman and Bob Anderson all signed that baseball. Those were all '59 Cubs. Most of them were starting players. To this day, those five guys are the core of my love for the Cubs. Of course, along with Ernie Banks. Everybody loved Ernie. Ernie was the Hollywood star. He was "the guy." Those five cards are enclosed in the case, but Walt Moryn is in front of the other four because he was the first.

Even if it's an exhibition game, and the Cubs beat them, then the Cubs are better than the White Sox.

Growing up on the South Side, I got a lot of grief from my friends. In the school yard, the park, and at the Little League games, we were 90 percent White Sox fans in our neighborhood. Throughout the early '60s when I was growing up, the White Sox were having a lot of success. They're knocking on the door of the Yankees. Second place, third place—they never overcame the Yankees—except in '59—but they were always in the pennant race. The Cubs were a floundering mess up until 1967. With my buddies, it was just hoping that the White Sox wouldn't win the pennant.

The big thing for us on the playground was when the Cubs and White Sox met one game a year. It was always at Comiskey Park and it was called the Boys Benefit Game—later the **Mayor's Trophy Game**. It was an exhibition game. When you're a nine-year-old kid and the Cubs got to play the Sox, that was a big deal. It was always a big point of contention on the playground. Even if the White Sox were higher

Mayor's Trophy Game: In 1994 the White Sox recalled Michael Jordan from Double-A Birmingham to play against the Cubs in the Mayor's Trophy Game at Wrigley Field. Jordan singled and doubled against the Cubs.

up in the standings than the Cubs, as a ten-year-old kid you're think-ing, "Well if they do play, even if it's an exhibition game, and the Cubs beat them, then the Cubs are better than the White Sox." That exhibition game started way back in the Black Sox era and was always postseason. Then, it used to be a preseason game where they would play three games. What I'm talking about is one game and it wasn't called the Mayor's Trophy. It was called the Boys Benefit Game. It was played exclusively at Comiskey, one night during the year. It led to what became the Mayor's Trophy. The Cub–White Sox exhibition series has been going on through many reincarnations through the years. In the '60s it was a night game at Comiskey Park. We'd go to it the majority of the time. I've got some old movies of the guys warm-ing up. One cool one is circa '63. It is before Major League Baseball put a limit on how large the catcher's gloves could be. That was when the White Sox had acquired Hoyt Wilhelm. The White Sox catcher at the time, Sherman Lollar, has this humungous glove compared to what the catchers have now.

Cub fans took a lot of grief growing up in the early '60s. As a kid, I hated the White Sox. I went to a White Sox game in 1960 with our church group, which was almost exclusive White Sox fans. They were playing the Baltimore Orioles. A pinch hitter came up for the Orioles, Bobby Boyd. He lined a single to give the Orioles the lead. I immediately loved Bobby Boyd. He was one of my favorite players, even though he was nothing but a halfway washed-up pinch hitter for the Orioles in the '60s. He has a special place in my heart because these are the thoughts that made me a baseball fan. I have Bob Boyd's card up here and it all stems from him getting a base hit on a church night at a White Sox park and the Orioles took the lead. I was the only one cheering for the Orioles while the other forty-nine of fifty people were cheering for the White Sox. Boyd had played for the White Sox for just a few years before that season. . . .

Not that it was weird, but the Cubs back in the '60s had the net that went from right behind home plate all the way up to the press box. When I was a kid that was always something I waited for. When a foul ball would be hit behind home plate, it would be up on the net.

You could not catch a foul ball behind home plate because of the net. It would get up on that net about press box high, but then it would roll all the way down until it met with the net that was right behind home plate. When that foul ball would hit up on the net, as it was rolling down, the crowd would always go, "Wooooooooooooooo!" When it hit that edge, where it would meet with the home plate netting, you'd go "Whooooop!" That was the weird thing that only Wrigley Field had. When you're a kid, a foul ball is a big deal. It was a lot of fun. The upper deck was almost never open when I was a kid in the '60s. The Cubs didn't draw that well. There were many, many days—outside of Saturdays and Sundays—they never even opened the upper deck stands. They wouldn't even sell tickets to the upper deck. I knew by time I got to be old enough, that if the upper deck was opened that it was a good crowd. Brickhouse would even make mention of it on the television, "Wow, the Cubs are having a good crowd today. The upper deck is open." The Cubs for years and years had 22,000 seats available every game at the ticket window. Those are quirky things about Wrigley Field.

The down payment on my house was paid for by my baseball card collection.

That slowly started to stop in '67 when Leo Durocher started to turn the club around and they started drawing better. Just look at the attendance. It's amazing to remember how many games there were just 5, 6, 7,000 people in attendance. Even now as I start getting older, I start looking back, I can remember things very passionately before I was ten years old. As a young Cubs fan, it had absolutely nothing to do with winning. . . .

I'm a baseball card freak. The down payment on my house was paid for by my baseball card collection. A lot of mine were in "collector's condition." I wasn't into mint. I started buying packs of cards in '59. Basically, I had the complete set of **Topps** in '57 and forward.

Topps: In the early 1990s there were over 8,000 sports collectibles stores. Primarily because of eBay, there are now fewer than 2,000.

I played all kinds of games with my cards. I played spinner base-ball. I played Strat-O-Matic baseball. I would hold my baseball cards through the course of an evening while I was watching TV. It would always be my twenty-five or thirty Cub players. Or it would be my twenty-five to thirty favorite players. I could memorize the back of my baseball cards and did that throughout my childhood. My mother never threw them away. We always knew where they were. I get out of college and pick it back up. I bought the complete sets, in the box, mint condition from '71 forward. In '81 Topps, Donruss, and Score start showing up. It started being more of a crazy business than fun collecting. My passion was really gone in the '90s. We moved into a new home in 1998 when the market was way down. My cards weren't in the greatest condition, but they helped secure the down payment on the house.

The card that I had the toughest time getting was a Billy Williams late season series. The Billy Williams in '66 or '67 late-series high-number card I did not get, and I had to secure that on my own to finish up my Cubs collection. A 1963 Cuno Barragan, who hit one home run in his career—his first big-league at-bat—was also a tough Cubs card for me to get. My most prized cards that I have are the **Ted Williams** 1954 #1 and #250. He was the first and last card in the Topps set in '54.

After I came down to Texas and started working full time in '78, I also started working for the Texas Rangers. I worked in customer relations and services. I was a security guard and dugout guard. In 1979 they moved me upstairs and I was trained to be the bartender. We would open at 5:30 and we had sixteen suites at Arlington Sta-dium. Season-ticket holders and club holders could go into this club

Ted Williams: Former astronaut and senator John Glenn was Ted Williams' squadron leader in Korea. Ted Williams was John Glenn's wing man. . . . Ted Williams and his son, John Henry, are among the 161 frozen bodies worldwide awaiting a cryogenic rebirth . . . 157 are stored in three U.S. facilities. The two Williams men are in Scottsdale, Arizona. . . . In real life, many are cold, but few are frozen.

area and get a big buffet. Back in the '70s, that bar also served the press box area, which included the radio and television broadcasters. When the '79 season begins, I'm stocking my bar one afternoon before a game. In walks Harry Caray. As good as can be, "Hey, kid, what's going on?" I say, "Hey, Harry Caray, I'm from Chicago." Harry would announce my name over the air those couple of years. At 5:30, it was time for Harry to get down to game-time drinking. We would start Harry out, most of the time, with a couple of screwdrivers. He was a good guy always. No matter how big he was, he would stand at the end of the bar, people would come in and talk. He'd say hello. He would not leave the bar for the thirty or forty minutes that he'd be there. I'd take care of Harry—mix him up three screwdrivers before he goes off. He'd go do the pregame and then he'd start drinking a beer. He'd leave with a "to-go" cup—which was a double—then he'd go to the first beer that he'd drink for the day. We had a deal with Harry—and Harry knew and he tipped well—that we'd make sure that Harry was loaded up in the first, third, fifth, seventh, and the ninth. We'd make sure we got him a screwdriver and another beer. After the game, he'd do his wrap-up, and he was right back up at the bar. Now we were in the postgame drinking Scotch. He'd knock back a couple. Piersall would drink club soda and, of course, he was a little bit of a whack job. They would be there thirty minutes prior to the game and thirty minutes after the game. Harry would always announce on the air, "John Mocek is taking care of us here and wants to say 'hi' to all of the folks back in Chicago." The encounters I had with Harry were great. He was a great guy.

Then I started working as official scorer for the Texas Rangers. I was put into a three-man rotation in 1997. I do about thirty-five games a year—almost half. I said I would never walk away from it until I got to be an official scorer for a Chicago Cubs game. The Cubs never made a trip in here until a year or two ago. Maybe now I can walk away. I worked a Tuesday and Thursday game. In Texas there are three official scorers. One of the other ones—Steve, a senior one—

We'd make sure that Harry was loaded up in the first, third, fifth, seventh, and the ninth.

is a die-hard White Sox fan. He grew up in Arlington Heights. Whenever the White Sox are in town he would take two of the three Sox games and I may do one. When the Cubs series came on, Sammy was sitting on 599 home runs. Steve goes, "Hey you want to work all the games in case Sammy hits the homer?" I'm a huge Sammy Sosa fan. I don't care about everything else. What he meant to the Cubs. What he did, to me, Sammy is always going to be one of my favorites ever. I said, "Well, let's just see what happens." So Tuesday I get to work for the Cubs, it's my 285th game I've ever scored, but I finally get to have my name on an official scorecard for the Cubs. Sammy doesn't hit the homer that night. The next morning, Stevie calls, "Do you want to take tonight? I don't care. You always let me work all the White Sox." I said, "That's bad karma. I don't want to do it. If this is the way it's scheduled, you just go ahead and take it." Of course that's the night Sammy hits No. 600. The nice part of it is that my wife and I got to share the great Sammy moment. . . .

I do community theater. I starred twelve nights in the production of *Bleacher Bums* in 2000."

When I get down there, the director has me read a card or two. He said, "You've got the Chicago mannerisms, the Chicago talk." They cast me. I was Marvin, the bad-guy gambler, in *Bleacher Bums* . . . the antagonistic one saying "the Cubs aren't going to win, they're losers." I was the resident Cubs historian and that was really cool. There was a cast of twelve people. I was able to bring a lot of my Cub quirks and explain to them about Cubdom. I had to tell them some of the Chicago inside jokes. It was really funny. Of course the funniest thing about it was I told them, "You people don't understand that I go to rehearsal three hours a night and we do this performance two and a half hours, twelve times, I am Mr. Anti-Cub in this play. I have to brush my mouth out with mouthwash all the time. I am truly acting in this deal. Everything I am saying or doing is the exact opposite because I am the sympathetic Cub fan. I am the guy hoping and praying it's going to happen. I'm not this bad guy." A lot of my friends would come to the play and bring their friends. Then, they don't even want to meet me in the café afterwards because I was such a nasty guy in the play.

That was a neat experience, being in *Bleacher Bums*. It was a really great experience because it just solidified the love I have for the Cubs. For twenty-six consecutive years I have been to Wrigley Field. I have dreams of retiring and doing nothing but being at every Cub game in a season or being at a specific place for every Cub game—for the eighty-one home games at Wrigley. If I'm not at the ballpark, I watch the game at Bernie's, Cubbie Bear, Sluggers, Murphy's, or at the Corner. I would be involved at Wrigleyville for all eighty-one games. That is my retirement dream.

> I have dreams of retiring and doing nothing but being at every Cub game in a season.

> Tony LaRussa is one of the greatest managers of all time—and I think I'm quoting him correctly on that.

I Saw It on the Radio

J. R. Russ

How would you like to work at a company that broadcasts every Major League game? Former New Buffalo, Michigan, resident J. R. Russ has that enviable job. He commutes from his home near Philadelphia to Washington where he is a sports board operator for XM Satellite Radio.

A s a kid, I remember **Jack Brickhouse** calling the infield, "Santo, Kessinger, Beckert, and Banks with a battery of Ferguson Jenkins and Randy Hundley." That sticks in my mind. The first time I ever saw graphics on television was when Jack Brickhouse was yelling, "Hey Hey!" when they hit a home run and they flashed little primitive white HEY HEY letters on the screen.

One of the first television broadcasters of the Cubs was Harry Creighton. He retired in Grand Beach, Michigan, which was the next town over from us. My father had been the mayor in New Buffalo and had known Harry Creighton. When I decided I wanted to go into broadcasting, dad set up an appointment for me to visit Harry at his home. Creighton gave me some of his nuggets of wisdom and what help he could. I wanted to be a rock 'n' roll DJ, and Creighton came from the sports and talk genre. I noticed as I went down

The caption said, "Hi, everybody, this is Harry Creighton on WGN." And it was signed "Walt Disney."

a hallway in his home he had lots of memorabilia, plaques, and photos. The one thing that really struck me was a drawing of Mickey Mouse standing with a press hat on at a WGN microphone. The caption said,

Jack Brickhouse: The first voice heard when WGN-TV went on the air in 1948 was Jack Brickhouse.

19

"Hi, everybody, this is Harry Creighton on WGN." And it was signed "Walt Disney." Even at that age I knew Walt Disney's name, and I was pretty impressed by that. Creighton was a very nice man. An older gentleman. He was in his late seventies or eighties by that time. This was 1968 or '69. We talked more about the technical side of broadcasting and what you needed to do to break into the business and some of the things to try and learn. . . .

I happened to see this ad a few years ago, after I had pretty much been out of radio for about ten years. After I owned and sold an auto business, I decided to go back into freelance voice-overs. The technology made it affordable to try and market my voice-over services. I happened to see an ad online that was looking for sports board operators in Washington, D.C., at XM Satellite Radio. I responded and I was hired along with thirty other people. First, it was to do college basketball games. Then, the following spring, they got the MLB contract and started doing every baseball game. You could work as much as you wanted. I vary between three and six days per week. You're at the mercy of the clock.

You can go in there and do a three-up, three-down, two-hour game, or you can get in there and have it run eighteen innings and be in there for seven hours. You're in charge of bringing the game feed in, filling any commercial breaks, and playing the station IDs. I don't physically talk. However, they were in need of a one-second station ID that says, "MLB on XM," and as it turned out, I'm heard on virtually every game on XM. It's only one second, but I can put it on a resume. That's my claim to fame. If it works with the schedule, I try and get the Cub game versus one of the others, just to listen to Pat and Ron.

I'm the happiest with what the team has been in years. Lou Piniella has got everything together. I'm not a big fan of Carlos Zambrano, even though he's our ace. He's given up some meatballs when he shouldn't. He's got a good record, and they signed him for $90 million, I don't know whether I would have signed him or not. I've seen them make the trades over the years of Lou Brock for Ernie Broglio

. . . losing **Greg Maddux**. . . . The Cubs seem to get them at the earlier part of their career and at the end, but they always blossom somewhere else.

I didn't like Harry Caray at first, when he came over. Somehow he endeared himself to me. I also liked Chip Caray. I didn't care for Harry's son Skip, who is in Atlanta. I don't like his sound. I do like Chip, he's great. He's back in Atlanta as well. I like listening to Pat and Ron. I don't usually like "homers" but Ron Santo, the way he lives and dies with the team. . . . They'll be ahead three runs and the opposing team will hit a home run and Pat will be calling the actual play, and you'll hear Ron in the background going, "Oh, no!"

XM just reran the 2003 game of the NLCS where Bartman interfered with the ball. I sat on my floor in my bathroom at 4:30 in the morning waiting to hear the conclusion of the game. I had to relive and suffer through that eighth inning again. It was amazing how the downfall of that whole series turned on that one play, the subsequent error by the shortstop, the pitching collapsed . . .

My sister, Jeanine, just died a month ago, and she was an avid Cubs fan. I did her eulogy. One of the lines I used to brighten it up a bit was, "And now she can truly join all those millions of Cub fans that said, "Not in my lifetime."

Greg Maddux: Ron Darling won the National League pitcher's Gold Glove in 1989. Greg Maddux won the next 13.

Craig's List

Craig Crotty

Craig Crotty, 66, has retired in Falmouth, Massachusetts. He grew up on a farm west of Chicago listening to any Major League Baseball game he could find on his old Motorola radio.

Most baseball fans of my age, when they talk about baseball cards, they always talk about the '52 and '53 Topps sets . . . and their desire to get the **Mickey Mantle** card. Mickey Mantle was not my quest in those cards. It was a bonus baby, a Yankee first baseman from Holyoke, Massachusetts, named Frank Leja and the Cubs' Hank Sauer. We would buy dozens and dozens of Topps baseball packs trying to find this Frank Leja or Hank Sauer.

If I had a dollar, I could go into town to the B&F Grocery and buy a whole carton of Topps baseball cards.

Finally, one day, I had a plan. My parents were away for the day, and I would borrow an idea I'd seen from the comic strips—that was to set up a lemonade stand. I went down to the basement, got a frozen can of lemonade, thawed it out, mixed it up, made a cardboard sign, took a card table and a seat and went down to a corner where two gravel roads intersected near our farming community.

About twenty minutes later, the first vehicle came by. It was a tractor driven by an old farmer named August Stender who was taking a load of grain to the mill. He saw my lemonade stand and stopped. He jumped off and said, "I need some cold lemonade." I said, "Well,

> **Mickey Mantle:** Between walks and strikeouts, Mickey Mantle went the equivalent of seven full seasons without putting the bat on the ball.

August, today's your lucky day." Then he saw the sign I had made up. The sign said, LEMONADE. ALL YOU CAN DRINK FOR $1. In the comics, it was usually 5 cents. My goal was to make $1 because if I had a dollar, I could go into town to the B&F Grocery and buy a whole carton of Topps baseball cards. I knew for sure that if I did that, I would be able to get the Frank Leja or Hank Sauer card. August stopped, hesitated, pulled out his wallet, gave me the dollar and drank about half a glass of lemonade and left. I quickly took the card table, the sign, and the leftover lemonade back up to the house one quarter of a mile away. I rode my bike into town to get my carton of baseball cards. I got the carton, but once again, absolutely no Hank Sauer or Frank Leja cards. About three days later, my father came looking for me—as irate as heck—and said, "Hey, young man, you need to give August Stender his dollar back." I said, "Why? I had a deal that was all the lemonade you could drink for a dollar. I've already spent the dollar." Of course, he knew what I had spent it on. I just got a good strappin' in the meantime. Today, I could have him arrested for child abuse. . . .

People my age were born at the right time! When we grew up, we would go to the ball diamond every spare moment we had and play ball until dark. We didn't need coaches, umpires, or soccer moms yelling at us or yelling at umpires. My kids grew up, went to Little League practice, threw the ball ten times, swung the bat ten times, and went home. **Little League** has ruined baseball.

Furthermore, in those days, we'd appreciate the one baseball game a week we might be able to see on TV. We all remember the first time we got TV in our house when we'd get up early in the morning to watch "test patterns." Our parents may not have liked our music, but they listened to it nonetheless. Maybe once a year, we'd be able to get a ride on a train. When we eventually started dating girls, they didn't dress like a tart, and we treated them like a lady. My sons will never know any of those things. . . .

Little League: At the Little League World Series in Williamsport—for $16 total—a family of four can each get a ticket, program, hot dog, and soda.

Remember a Yankee pitcher named Bob Turley—Bullet Bob, they called him. The Yankees got him from the St. Louis Browns. When I was a freshman in high school, everybody was raving about how hard Bullet Bob Turley threw. My high school baseball coach said, "Listen, if you batted against Bob Turley long enough, after a while, you'd hit a foul ball. Then, after another while, you'd hit a fair ball. Eventually, you'd get a base hit. You keep on batting against him long enough, and you'll hit it out of the ballpark." He said, "That's true about life. If you get experience and you have perseverance, and you never quit, sooner or later, you can accomplish all you goals." So, Bullet Bob Turley was responsible for one of the greatest lessons I ever learned in my life. . . .

Both books were free, and they were worth every penny.

Remember how we used to get the *Famous Slugger Yearbook*s at sporting goods stores put out by Hillerich and Bradsby, the Louisville Slugger people. In the fall, we'd get the *Converse Basketball Yearbook* put out by The Converse Shoe Company. Both books were free, and they were worth every penny. . . .

I'm glad I was born when I was 'cause everything has gone to hell in a handbasket lately . . . I weep for the future. The worst things that have happened to baseball are Bud Selig and Donald Fehr. How the media keeps giving these two guys a free ride is totally beyond me. Selig has screwed up everything from the '94 World Series to the All-Star Game to contraction to expansion to player salaries and, perhaps, worst of all, the total destruction of baseball records. The day Brady Anderson hit his 50th home run was the day that all baseball records became meaningless.

Under Selig's watch, drugs have become rampant—steroids, of course . . . salaries have gone through the ceiling . . . records have become worthless. The only thing his supporters have to say is, "But attendance has gone up." Why wouldn't attendance have gone up? Since I was born in the early '40s, the population of this country has tripled. There are twice as many Major League teams as there used to be. There are more games being played every year—eight more every year by each team. Selig has brought in so many gimmicks that it's going to turn into the World Wrestling Federation pretty soon. Gimmicks like interleague play, and the wild card. Next, we'll have free beer, naked cheerleaders, and the Beatles singing during the seventh-inning stretch. We've turned baseball into a circus with no concern for the records or traditions of the game.

What does the commissioner do all day long anyway? *Seriously*, what does the commissioner do all day long? I don't think he does anything. He doesn't even hand out the fines. He doesn't punish the players. Selig gets paid $14 million in basic "hush money" as I like to call it. He's a total "stooge" for the owners and is one of the worst things ever to have happened to baseball. Just before Roger Clemens embarrassed baseball during the 2008 congressional hearings, the owners—the so-called stewards of the game—give Selig a three-year extension.

Then, he had to embarrass the game further before the congressional committee on St. Paddy's Day in 2005 when he sat there and said that he had never heard of steroids until July 1998. Well, in 1995, he was quoted in *The Sporting News* as saying he wanted to convene a special meeting of the owners back in 1992 to discuss the looming steroid problem. The most galling thing about Selig, besides his pathetic looks, is his continual ignorance of the drug-testing laws in this country. Until they start testing for HGH—the human growth hormone—there is *no* drug testing policy. Who are they trying to kid with this malarkey they maintain that they have this terrific policy? They say there is no such test—guess what, there is. Just ask the WADA (World Anti-Doping Agency), they've been nailing people in the Olympics with steroids since the 1980s. There are three tests for HGH—one of which is very, very effective. It's called a blood test.

What Selig and these other baseball owners don't seem to recognize is the economy goes in cycles. For the last twenty or so years, we've been riding a wonderful crest of a great economic cycle. When the economy starts to go south, which it eventually will, perhaps sooner than later, you're going to see attendance in Major League Baseball drop like you never dreamed possible before. You might even see teams going bankrupt. It was only a few years ago that teams were already going bankrupt, such as the Arizona Diamondbacks. Selig is just a pathetic loser, and he's dragging baseball into the muck along with Donald Fehr, who is just reprehensible in his conduct. It's no wonder you never see either of them in public unless they're surrounded by a huge entourage.

The best baseball fans are on the East Coast. They're the most passionate baseball fans besides being the most knowledgeable. The further west you go in this great country, the less passion people have for anything, whether it baseball, or their jobs, or for life in general. There are only about half a dozen baseball teams that have really great fans. The Cubs of course, the Red Sox, the Mets, the **Phillies,** the Cardinals, and the Yankees . . . and that's pretty much it. Name another Major League Baseball team that has incredible fans. You can't do it.

A friend of mine suggested that other than Mike Scioscia, there may not be a single good manager in Major League Baseball today. Dusty Baker and Tony LaRussa certainly don't fit that category. I'm starting to think he's right. Why do managers use a five-man pitching rotation? It's absolutely stupid that you would take eight starts from your best pitcher and give them to your fifth-best pitcher. It's equally stupid to take eight starts from your second-best pitcher and give them to your fifth-best pitcher. Why would anyone want to take eight starts away from Zambrano and give them to Jason Marquis?

The fundamentals in baseball today are so bad . . . so bad . . . that I'm not even sure they spend any time at all coaching these guys. There are only about five outfielders in the whole game who can throw hard and accurately. Catchers have just about lost all sight of fundamentals. They don't block the plate anymore. They reach for balls coming into home plate rather than waiting for the ball to come to them. On plays at the plate, they try to catch a lot of balls in foul

Phillies: P. K. Wrigley and Milton Hershey were bitter business rivals. When Wrigley bought the Chicago Cubs, Hershey tried to buy the Philadelphia Phillies . . . and sell chocolate gum. Hershey failed in both efforts.

territory. It's just a joke. Outfielders don't catch the ball over the proper shoulder.

You can call me an "old goat" if you want . . . and I am one—I'm old enough to be a greeter at Wal-Mart. But I love baseball the way it was when I was growing up—sneaking transistor radios in the school to listen to the World Series game, collecting baseball cards for fun—not as an investment—doubleheaders, the special "smell" of the new baseball magazines every spring. There are many people my age who can name the starting lineup for the '54 Cubs, the '69 Cubs, the '84 Cubs that couldn't name you half of the starting lineup for the '99 Cubs.

> *You can call me an "old goat" if you want . . . and I am one—I'm old enough to be a greeter at Wal-Mart.*

> *I only wish the White Sox were still in Chicago.*

1969—The Year the Mets Turned the Cubs Upside Down

Doug Feldmann

Doug Feldmann is a professor in the College of Education and Human Services at Northern Kentucky University. He's written numerous books on baseball, including *Miracle Collapse: The 1969 Chicago Cubs.* He lives near Cincinnati.

There was a rhythm to living as a child in Chicago in reference to the Cubs: What I mean is with all the day games. In the last several years I've noticed every year the Cubs seem to schedule more and more home night games, whereas before they had lights they were all during the day, and that's what I knew growing up. They put in lights right after I graduated from high school, in June of '88. In August of '88 they had the first night game.

It just seemed like there was a great rhythm to life, when you structured your baseball viewing around what you knew were day games all the time. In April, you'd hustle home from school to see the last couple innings of Opening Day. During the summer, you'd be out playing ball with your friends, and you'd hustle home by three o'clock if you wanted to watch the last few innings.

It was great because it felt unique as an eight-, ten- or twelve-year-old as opposed to a kid in St. Louis or Cincinnati who was accustomed to night games and living with night baseball and probably having to go to bed before the game was over.

I was born in '70. When I was about four or five years old, I started collecting baseball cards. I'd first organize them by year. Then I'd organize them by team.

My first Strat-O-Matic year was 1975. I was five years old. My brother, who was eight years older than me, and I would put all the cards from the league in a paper bag and mix them up. We'd each pick out twenty-five players, and we'd play a seven-game series with whoever we picked out of the bag.

On two different occasions when we did this, the first player I pulled out was Bill Madlock. Don Kessinger was my first favorite Cub, but Madlock, winning those two batting titles in '75 and '76—I couldn't have pulled out a better player for my draft.

When I met Kessinger, I asked him, "Would you be interested in writing a foreword for a book on the '69 Cubs?" He said, "Sure." I told him in the midst of our conversation, "You have to understand what a rejoining of the circle this is in life for me." I told him he was my first favorite Cub when I was growing up.

The '35 Cubs were the last Cubs team to win 100 games in a season.

It was my third book and really probably should have been my second because I wanted it to be a sequel to the Gashouse Gang book—the '34 Cardinals. I've always been interested in Great Depression history, and that's what led me to doing research on the Gashouse Gang and the '35 Cubs. They were the last Cubs team to win 100 games in a season. They were 100–54 that year, winning twenty-one games in a row in September to take the pennant, including a doubleheader sweep of the Dean brothers in St. Louis toward the end of September.

That, of course, was Phil Cavarretta's first full year with the Cubs. He's a great story in itself because he was a nineteen-year-old kid from Lane Tech, right down the street, and later in the season they had **Phil Cavarretta** Day at Wrigley Field and a lot of students and teachers came down. He was still nineteen in that summer of 1935. They lost to the Tigers in the World Series.

My interest in getting involved with the '69 Cubs was being born in '70 and being a kid in the '70s. I have an older brother, and through him and his friends and people older than me the '69 Cubs were pointed to as the poster child for Cubs teams that collapsed.

Phil Cavarretta: The only managers ever fired during spring training are Phil Cavarretta of the Cubs in 1954 and the Blue Jays' Tim Johnson in 1999.

The title of the book is *Miracle Collapse*, and half of the title refers to the Mets. If people want to decide that the Cubs collapsed, that's their decision, but I wanted the book to be a celebration of the Cubs and the Mets, because the Mets won four out of every five games for the last month and a half of the season.

It was such a memorable summer, with the moon landing in July . . . Chappaquiddick the same weekend, the Manson murders, the My Lai Massacre . . . Woodstock in August of '69. Also, the Cubs were in first place for 155 days in 1969, basically from the beginning of the season until the end. For 149 of those days they were in first place by themselves, not even tied with anyone. People said, "This is the year." The incredible fact that they collapsed makes them the most memorable of all.

Kessinger told me this. When they played the big series in New York in the first week of September of '69, he said when they were getting dressed in the locker room they heard a murmur outside and they thought it was a plane going over from LaGuardia, but it was just a frenzy that the full house at **Shea** had been whipped into. They had these white rags that people were waving. There was a full house even a half hour before the game started.

They finished up the season at Wrigley. The Mets had already clinched a couple of days before, but they still had a couple of games to play with the Cubs at Wrigley Field. It was very unfortunate what happened with the Bleacher Bums the last couple of games. It really got ugly, and people were hanging from the outfield wall and jumping down on the field. A group of them, twenty or thirty, would make their way to over behind the dugout and they'd jump on top of the dugout. When one of the games was over, they were still on top of the dugout. The ushers couldn't get these guys off the top of the dugout. One of the Bleacher Bums was pulling or pawing at a player, and he said, "Well, you guys were good, but you weren't good enough."

Shea: During a 1979 Patriots game against the New York Jets at Shea Stadium, a remote control model airplane crashed into the stands at halftime, hit a Patriots fan, and killed him.

About the Don Young incident in New York, when Santo blew up at him in the Chicago papers, that affected Young. He only came to bat sixty-nine more times in the '69 season after it happened. Kessinger told me Young was so embarrassed by that one game that when he would go out at night along Lake Shore Drive or Rush Street in Chicago he would put on fake glasses and a beard so no one would recognize him.

Young was so embarrassed he would put on fake glasses and a beard so no one would recognize him.

I went to a lot of Cardinal games when I was a kid because of visiting family who lived in southern Illinois. Of course, we went to many Cubs games when I was a kid, driving into Chicago from the suburbs, and you always felt like you were going into somebody's house or neighborhood to play a pickup game.

It was a friendly atmosphere around Wrigley Field. It was different from going to a Cardinal game. I love the Cardinals—and it's strange for a kid to grow up loving the Cardinals and the Cubs—but you go downtown for a St. Louis Cardinals game, you park in a big garage, and there's no restaurants around. You just walk across the street to the game and then get back to the car in the garage. There was more of that true neighborhood feeling for a Cubs game. That memory is very strong from childhood, the community feel to the ballpark.

Fanecdotes

I grew up in a very small town in southern Illinois. You know the cliché, "everybody knows everybody." It was the kind of town where you weren't afraid to leave your house unlocked when you left home . . . the kind of town where moms would send their young children to the four-aisle grocery store to get a gallon of milk and a loaf of bread without worrying about their safe return. Back then, the only thing there was to do during the summer was play baseball or watch it on TV. You could always count on the Cubs playing on WGN. There's no telling how many Cub fans there are now because of WGN broadcasting games nationwide.

Some of my earliest childhood memories were watching the Cubs at my great-grandmother's house when she would babysit me. I thought we watched because I wanted to watch . . . turns out she wanted to watch as bad as I did. Like most other young Cub fans, I grew up idolizing Ryne Sandberg. He was one of the most consistent, fundamentally sound players ever. He made me want to play for the Cubs when I grew up.

One of the most memorable days in my life was my first trip to Wrigley Field when I was twelve years old. It was a beautiful sunny summer day in Chicago. My grandpa had gotten tickets a few rows behind the Cubs dugout. Wrigley Field seemed so far away from home—I never dreamed I would be there. You can imagine my excitement. I wanted to see everything—the green grass, the ivy, the rooftops, the lake and, of course, Harry Caray. I remember being in awe of the whole experience; seeing the players warming up and my first glimpse of Harry waving hello to the fans as he entered the booth. With a touch of Wrigley magic, my greatest wish came true. Ryne hit one out. Great day! Wrigley Field is a very special place. I tell everyone it is the best place to watch a baseball game, even if you are not a Cub fan. I took my future wife to Wrigley in 1998 when she was a Cardinal fan. After that day, she was a Cub fan, so much so that she named our dog Wrigley.

—Craig Mitsdorffer, 33,
Evansville, Indiana

I recall going to a game with one of my neighbors in Park Forest when I was six. Walking in, the green grass, the ivy, the dirt, the sounds—yes—fantastic! I would say this—hopefully Wrigley fans won't be insulted to know that most kids experience this at any ballpark. In fact, I take my kids to minor-league parks here in Iowa, and they get that feeling, as well. It's professional baseball—you just get that feeling when you walk into the park. However, no way will I dispute that Wrigley is special.

What I recall most vividly is sitting in the middle of the row, watching the game, when all of a sudden, a cup of soda pop gets handed to me by the person on my right. I remember thinking, "Dang, I'm at a Cub game, and someone just gave me a Coca-Cola I didn't ask for! Can't get much better than this." I start to pull back the wrapping on the soda, to drink MY soda. Of course, someone says, "No. Pass it down." Turns out, it wasn't for me, but rather I was doing what all fans do—passing the soda, beverage, food down to someone else. I can't remember if I passed the money back the other way.

I start to pull back the wrapping on the soda, to drink MY soda. Of course, someone says, "No. Pass it down."

As a five-, six-, seven-year-old, with a short attention span, I watched a lot of the first two to three innings of a Cub game, and a lot of the 8th and 9th innings. It went like this. In the morning, two of my buddies and I, all around seven years old, would play baseball against these two eleven- to twelve-year-olds in the neighborhood. We would bat first, get a few runs, get out. Then, the older guys would bat . . . and bat . . . and bat. If we got them out, they cheated and said they were safe. After about twenty minutes of this abuse, I cried and went home. Mom comforted me with lunch, and then the Cubs were on. *Leadoff Man,* "Hey, hey, holy mackerel, no doubt about it—the Cubs are on their way. It's a beautiful day for a ball game, for a ball game, today." I'd watch a couple of innings then simulate baseball games on the dining room table with those little football guys that come from the old electric football games. By the time I got back to watching the game, it was the late innings. I watched on a 19-inch black-and-white set with rabbit ears. We would go to Grandma's apartment on the

South Side of Chicago, thirteenth floor, occasionally to visit. She was a Cub fan, too. Another 19-inch TV, black and white, rabbit ears, but since she and Grandpa lived among other ten- to fifteen-story apartment buildings, the picture was fuzzy. But, that was all right—we're Cub fans and Chicago fans, so the picture was fuzzy . . . the team was fuzzy . . . the fans were fuzzy . . . we were fuzzy—that's the way it was. When I later watched the games on a "big" television, in color, in the late '70s, I would keep score. I remember scoring about eight to nine games a year when I watched. Then I would combine them together to see how the Cubs, individually, were doing in the games I scored. Can you believe it? Mick Kelleher was about **a .350 hitter** one year when I scored him. . . .

I went golfing with Grandpa when I was about thirteen. We're around the first tee. I look over to a bench near the starter's shack and I'm certain it's him—Ernie Banks! I tell everyone, and Dad urges my brother Jim and me to go over. We do. We ask if he's Ernie Banks, and, of course, he is. Do you think he talks to us, gives us an autograph, asks about us? You bet your hindquarters he does! He's everything you can imagine when you hear about him. Even after asking Jim and me if we go to Cub games and our telling him, "No, we mostly go to Sox games," he still was great. No doubt about it—he's Mr. Cub based upon my one chance meeting with him. I still have Ernie Banks's autograph on the golf scorecard, September 1977.

> . . . . the crowd going "Ooop-oooo" when foul balls would go back to the screen and yelling "Swish" when Bill Nicholson came to bat.

—Mike Parker, 44,
attorney, Davenport, Iowa

I've been a Cubs fan since I was nine years old, living in the non-village of Cooksville in southern Wisconsin. I listened to games

---

a .350 hitter: The difference between a .250 hitter and a .300 hitter is one base hit per week.

on the radio and still remember Pat Piper on the **P.A.**—the crowd going "Ooop-oooo" when foul balls would go back to the screen and yelling "Swish" when Bill Nicholson came to bat.

The first time I saw the Cubs play was when they played an exhibition game against their Class-D farm team in Janesville, Wisconsin. Dizzy Dean pitched, hit a home run, and was called out for passing the lead runner between third and home. My first time at Wrigley Field was May 18, 1951. I was twenty years old, in the Air Force, between trains returning to Massachusetts from leave. I had the afternoon to take in a ball game. The Cubs played the Phillies and won 18–9. Two years later, I had the same opportunity. This time, my mother and Joanie, my wife-to-be, were with me. My mother claimed to be a White Sox fan, but I think she said that because I was a Cubs fan. She used to tease me by saying, "Those Cubs can't play marbles."

—Rollie Nesbit, 77,

Eau Claire, Wisconsin

The Cubs *need* luck. Here are some very sad stats: This is the sixty-first season for the Cubs since I was born, way back in April 1947. In that time the Cubs have a record of 4,444–5,097. That is a winning percentage of .465. In sixty-one full seasons, all at Wrigley, the Cubs have had winning records in only sixteen seasons. Only five times have they been to the postseason (1984, 1989, 1998, 2003, 2007). In the other fifty-six seasons, only four times have the Cubs been less than double figures in Games Back at the end of the year. How can anyone explain being a Cubs fan? A good argument can be made that the Cubs have the largest fan base of any Major League club.

I do remember my first Cubs game. The Cubs beat the Phillies 4–0. I was six at the time. I went with my dad and grandpa. I'll never forget seeing the green grass of Wrigley Field that first time. To this day it is

---

P.A.: The public address announcer for the Astros (Colt '45s) in 1962 was ex-CBS anchorman Dan Rather. John Forsythe, the actor, was the P.A. announcer for the Brooklyn Dodgers in 1937 and 1938.

my favorite thing to see when I go to a game. I've been hooked on the Cubs ever since, for better or worse (usually worse).

My grandpa was a huge Cubs fan. I remember going to his house and reading a book he had about the Cubs and their history during the '30s and '40s. He gave me the best advice about being a Cubs fan: "Never bet on the Cubs." I doubt that anyone could bet on the Cubs and remain a fan.

People might be surprised to know that I'm a big fan of another baseball team: whoever is playing the White Sox. If the Cubs can't win, well then maybe the Sox will lose. As a kid I remember going to the dentist, who was a big Sox fan, and going round and round with him about our teams. He would wait until my mouth was full of contraptions and then start in on me about the Sox. Not much I could do or say then.

The dentist would wait until my mouth was full of contraptions and then start in on me about the Sox.

My favorite Cub of all time was Ernie Banks, a great shortstop and hitter. I always admired his optimism even though the Cubs were so pathetic. The very first thing I ever bought with my own money was a Ernie Banks model glove from Sears. No one is more deserving of being Mr. Cub.

As a kid I would sit at home during the summer watching the Cubs and keeping score, just as if I were at the game. In those days the *Chicago Sun-Times* would write out what happened in the game, each play, inning by inning. I would love to read through these accounts because it made me feel more in touch with each game. It was much more informative than to read a box score. I remember many times going to bed with my transistor radio under my pillow listening to the Cubs game when they played on the West Coast. It seems as if **Don Drysdale** or Sandy Koufax versus Dick Ellsworth would always lock up into a 1–0 game, usually with the Cubs on the short end of the score.

Don Drysdale: Don Drysdale said his most important pitch was his second knockdown one because it told the hitter that the first knockdown pitch was not a mistake.

When I turned sixteen and could drive, I would take the South Shore train into Chicago then catch the subway to Wrigley. In those years, the Cubs always held 20,000 seats for the day of the game so you could wake up one morning and say, "this would be a great day for a game" and be able to get tickets. Bleacher seats went for one dollar the day of the game and I would be waiting in line to rush to the leftfield bleachers as soon as the gates opened.

It was always hard to sit through high school on days when the Cubs were playing. My senior year I cut the pages in my economics book (it wasn't good for anything else) so my transistor radio would fit into it. Then I would just lay my head down on the book and listen to the game.

There have been many memorable games and players throughout the years, but never a World Series for my Cubbies, almost twice, 1984 and 2003. In 1984 the Cubs won the first two games against the Padres and only needed one more win to go to the Series. I bought a bottle of champagne to celebrate what I've been waiting for so long. Needless to say, I did not pop the cork. In 2003, with just five outs to go, I had that same bottle of champagne that I had been saving all those years already dusted off and ready to open. Finally, after all these years, it was going to happen! Then the foul ball to Bartman and the bottle is back collecting dust.

It's not easy being a Cub fan. The frustrations keep mounting. I can honestly say for as long as I can remember I have never, ever failed to check to see how the Cubs did in their last games, even though the odds say they probably lost. BUT, one of these years it WILL happen, the Cubs will go to the World Series. I just hope it will be "Just Once in MY Lifetime."

—Rick Evans,
Valparaiso, Indiana

Having been a solid Cub fan for my fifty-plus years on this planet, I've exulted over the good times, but recall more than vividly the agonies—of 1969, 1984, 1989, 1998, and then the sheer tearing-the-wings-off-a-fly torture of October 2003.

Although in the end there was serious pain resulting from the 1977 Cub season I tend to remember it in nostalgic, almost wistful terms. A year that began forebodingly with a terrible Loop el train crash in February that killed eleven and injured 180, it was blossomed into spring and summer joy with both Chicago teams playing well above their heads. Bill Veeck's White Sox battled the Whitey Herzog–skippered **Kansas City Royals** throughout the year, bringing cheers to those south of Madison Street for their South Side Hit Men.

But the '77 Cubs—managed by the phlegmatic Herman Franks and featuring the likes of pure hitters Bill Buckner and Bobby Murcer and emerging great reliever in Bruce Sutter, but the rest a motley group of journeymen and role players, caught lightning in a bottle for most of a long, hot summer.

As it was for me, I was twenty, home for the summer from college, working from 4 a.m. till well into the afternoon on the decrepit old South Water Produce Market, unloading 80-pound crates of iceberg lettuce from refrigerated trucks, spending many afternoons on Oak Street Beach amid drinks and scenery. I worked hard and partied harder, seeing great bar bands like Pearl Handle every weekend night at haunts like Huey's, the Thirsty Whale, and B'Ginnings after roasting, shirtless, in the leftfield bleachers at Wrigley Field. We were invincible and we thought the Cubs were as well.

Although the Cubs lost three of four to Philadelphia going into the All-Star break on July 17, they were still 54–35 and well atop the National League East. Then in the All-Star Game, Jerry Morales, hitting .315 at the time and playing a stellar centerfield for the Cubs, was hit on the knee by a Sparky Lyle slider. While that temporarily sidelined Morales, at the time the Cubs cleanup batter, the injury in and of itself wasn't what submarined him and inevitably the Cub season.

Derrick, my neighbor and best friend from childhood, had never

Kansas City Royals: In the 1979 baseball draft, the Kansas City Royals selected Dan Marino in the fourth round and John Elway in the eighteenth round. That same year the Royals hired Rush Limbaugh for their group sales department. Limbaugh left in 1984 for a radio opportunity in California.

had much parental direction, especially for the cozy middle-class suburb in which we lived. I distinctly remember walking through his back door into the kitchen at ten years old, my Cadaco All-Star Baseball board game in hand, and being hit by the combination smell of stale air conditioning, gin, and vermouth. Derrick was attending a good Catholic high school when his father died of lung cancer, and soon after he befriended a group of young toughs from the North Side.

. . . . my Cadaco All-Star Baseball board game in hand, and being hit by the combination smell of stale air conditioning, gin, and vermouth.

It was early August of '77, a Friday night that Derrick and his friends were cruising the North Side, looking for trouble. They approached a stoplight, and in the next lane were (unknowingly to them) Jerry Morales and a friend, returning from a Hispanic restaurant.

Words and oaths were exchanged through the car windows and in short order they had parked along a main street (I think Irving Park Road) and came to blows. Morales, from what Derrick told me, got the worst of it and was trying to fend off the young hoods with a maraca that he had gotten from the restaurant.

Witnesses called police and the four youths, including Derrick, were arrested. The incident made the next day's *Tribune*, complete with quotes from Morales, who reportedly said, "What could I do? I tried to hit him with my maraca."

Soon after, Morales went on the disabled list and was relatively ineffective for the balance of the season, finishing at .290. I haven't seen Derrick in a long time, but I know that he has had many rough times with drug addiction in the ensuing years since the incident. But I remember him saying quite often that he was convinced that the fight messed up Morales's back and because he was the biggest Cub fan I knew, he would ruminate that it was somewhat ironic that he may have personally played a part in tanking his team's chances that year. The Cubs finished at .500, 81–81 in 1977.

—Jay Martini, 54,
Chicago

I was born and raised a Cubs fan. Will die one too. Although I've not lived in Chicago for about twenty years, I still have the cap I bought outside Wrigley when I was sixteen. I used to ride my bike to take a bus to the Skokie Swift and shoot into the games. I grew up in Deerfield. I live in Pittsburgh now, though I still wear my Cubs hat to games when they're in town.

When I was a kid, I was always trying to sneak into the box seats from the bleachers. I would tag along on my brother's endless trips to Wrigley. He was an original member of Ray's Leftfield Bleacher Bums—still has the tie to prove it. I remember thinking during the '03 National League Championships, when I happened to find myself overnight in Chicago on business the night of Game 1 and trying to buy a ticket. "I've never sat in the upper deck and I'm not about to start now," I said. I got a seat about twenty rows off of first, right behind the break, and near the outfield grass edge for $100 and I never missed a pitch. When the Cubs lost on a dinger by Lowell to the basket in center in the eleventh I thought, "I'm not that upset—it's to be expected of the Cubs." I was there at the 23–22 game against Philly on a school field trip when Larry Bittner pitched. I can remember nearly every position player from 1971 on. And of course the heartbreak of '69.

One day they were selling all the very old iron and wood folding-chair box seats that had been warehoused at Wrigley for years.

I would go down to Wrigley in high school on my bike or by bus or el train. One day they were selling all the very old iron and wood folding-chair box seats that had been warehoused at Wrigley for years. My buddy and I each bought two—they were one dollar each, two was all we figured we could carry back on the bikes—and dragged them home with the intention of sanding and painting them. The chairs are gone now, but when Three Rivers Stadium came down a few years back, they were selling sets of seats at $400 per set of four. The insult of not having the seats might affect others, but not for a Cubs fan—it's expected.

In 1984 I was a sophomore at Purdue University. We used to listen to WGN Radio on September and April evenings to catch the Cubs games. This was before cable and **Superstation WGN** was known around the country. When the playoffs came and we were in, we went nuts—I lived in a fraternity, so we all packed into the rooms with TVs to watch the playoffs. After the Cubs won the first two of a best of five in the National League Championship from San Diego, I bought a bottle of champagne. No team had ever lost three, when needing to win only one, to lose a series. The Cubs, of course, became the first and repeated in 2003. I still have that bottle—unopened until the Cubs win the National League pennant.

I have a friend with a license plate that says CUBS WEN. I'm thinking of getting one that says 5 OUTS.

—Mark Erickson, 43,

Pittsburgh

When Cabbage Patch Kids were big in the '80s I wanted one, but not just any one, I wanted the Cubs Cabbage Patch Kid. The Cubs one had the home uniform, a blue Cubs jacket, a batting helmet, and a Cubs pennant. I named him Rick Sutcliffe, then Ryne Sandberg, then Mark Grace, then Jody Davis, then Andre Dawson. This Cabbage Patch Kid had the name of just about every Cub from the '80s except **Don Zimmer**. I probably would have named the thing Zimmer if it didn't have so much hair.

A few days after my first Wrigley game I looked at my parents and told them that the next game I went to I wanted to try some of

Superstation WGN: WGN is an acronym for "World's Greatest Newspaper". . . WLS–Chicago is an acronym for "World's Largest Store"; it was owned by Sears.

Don Zimmer: Connie Mack, Jimmy Reese, and Wayne Terwilliger are the only baseball people to wear a major league uniform (Mack normally wore a suit) for fifty years.

the Budweiser stuff that they are always advertising on TV during games. I was six years old. My mom and dad found that funny and informed me that I would have to wait a few years to do that.

I went to plenty of Sox games growing up because they practically gave tickets away just to get people to come to games.

I have only been to one other Cubs game with my dad. After the game my dad and I waited by the players parking lot for autographs. I got Bob Scanlan, the pitcher who recorded that day's save, to sign my program. I was disappointed with a few of the Cubs players and how they treated the waiting fans, but I remember Andre Dawson spending about an hour signing autographs for as many fans as he could before his hand started to hurt. He was a class act.

I went to plenty of Sox games growing up because they practically gave tickets away. . . I would go to the police and firemen nights with my dad and his co-workers if they were off, and then there were other times with Boy Scouts, and just getting tickets from people who bought tickets but didn't want to go. I experienced the old Comiskey Park and the new. The old one was ugly, dingy, and uncomfortable, not even close to a Wrigley Field, but it was still better than the piece of * %@ they have now that has seen major renovations and it's not even twenty years old yet. For all the Sox games I have been to, I would still rather go to Wrigley Field and watch the Cubs lose than spend my time in either of the Comiskey Parks and have to sit by Sox fans.

I was much too young in '84 to feel the letdown, and I don't remember much of '89. The '98 playoffs run was short-lived, but I don't think that many Cubs fans truly felt it was "the year." I think most were just happy to be in the playoffs in '98. The 2003 season was truly my christening into Cub fandom and feeling what it really means to be a Cubs fan. To me being a Cubs fan means being optimistic. It means being able to find good in the bad. It means simply enjoying the moment.

—Joe Drennan, 27,
Forest Lake, Minnesota

L ogansport is a real Cubs town. Oh, there's one Cards fan and one Reds fan, but I'm maybe the No. 1 Cubs Fan—have been for sixty years, since my older brother Cliff and I pretended to be Phil Cavarretta, then Andy Pafko and Eddie Waitkus, then Banks and Gene Baker. My dad, the judge, took us to the Cubs dugout where I met Ernie and Warren Spahn. I still have Spahn and Burdette's autographs. I just sent a note to my brother saying we have to go to Wrigley again one more time. Some loves just never die. A World Series at Wrigley would be the greatest. Time's a-wasting!

> —Rich Wild,
> Logansport, Indiana, coached four
> state high school baseball champions

I was nine years old in 1938 and lived on a farm in western Ohio. My aunt and uncle lived in Chicago a few blocks from Wrigley Field, and they invited me to come see them. My parents put me on a train and sent me off. I had never been anywhere by myself so I was pretty excited. My aunt was a Cub fan and a couple of the Cub reserves lived in her apartment building, so she took me to the game every day and taught me how to keep score . . . well, the Cubs won the pennant that year, so I was hooked big-time. I went home and taught my mother how to keep score, and we would try to get the games on WGN, which sometimes came in pretty weak and with static, but we always listened. After I got married in 1949, my wife continued to keep score for me because I would be working and could not hear the games. We had a really big stack of scorecards. When we moved to Indiana, somehow, they were lost, which was a big blow to me.

A couple of years ago, I was trying to remember the players from 1938 and 1945 so I called the Cubs and a nice fellow sent me the roster from 1938 to '39 and 1944 to '45 so I could reminisce about those guys. It sure brought back some great memories.

I will be eternally grateful for my aunt getting me started as a Cub fan even though there has been an awful lot of pain. It is still worth it . . . and Wrigley Field is a real gem. I hope it stays that way.

> —Bill Springer, 78,
> Florida

When I was about five years old, my dad took me and my brothers to Wrigley Field. He was living in Aurora, a suburb of Chicago. My parents were separated, so he drove all the way back to Osceola, Iowa, where we lived to pick us up. It was my first Cubs game, and I've been a Cubs fan ever since. I owe that to my father. He died when I was a senior in high school.

He takes us to this Cubs game. We're going down Michigan Avenue, looking up at the tall buildings. We're from Osceola, where there's nothing, and now we're going down Michigan Avenue with these skyscrapers. At five years old, it was amazing to me. Then we come to the block where Wrigley is. There's this big gray-looking building, and we're like, "OK, and the game is in here?" That thought went away immediately when we stepped foot in the place. . . .

I got the job running the manual scoreboard for the Iowa Cubs.

Years later, we were in the leftfield bleachers at a Dodgers game in '94 when the Cubs are smoking the Dodgers 20–1. We're yelling at the few Dodger fans and at the Dodger outfielders, "Hey, What time is it? Twenty to one!" Even they were laughing.

I got the job running the manual scoreboard for the Iowa Cubs in Des Moines, the Triple-A club. In '06, I went back to school in Des Moines. I went into the stadium and applied for a job. I didn't know what kind of jobs they had, perhaps an usher or something. I ended up running the scoreboard all summer for them.

It was really cool. The very first game, they played the **Iowa Hawkeyes** in an exhibition game. So we have the Iowa Cubs against the Iowa Hawkeyes. The Iowa Cubs scored twenty-three runs. I'm running the manual scoreboard for the first time. I worked my butt off. That was the first game, and I was like, "OK, we have to change

Iowa Hawkeyes: In 1939 the Heisman Trophy winner was Nile Kinnick of Iowa. He is the only Heisman winner to have his university's football stadium named after him. In 1934 Nile Kinnick was Bob Feller's catcher on an American Legion baseball team.

some things." They had the numbers in stacks on a little card table–type thing back behind the scoreboard. So I built a rack to hold the numbers, like the back of Fenway's.

The bleachers are behind the scoreboard, and it sits on top of the fence. The crowd watches me run the scoreboard. It was all open back there. People were running up and trying to open the number slots. We roped it off so they couldn't mess with the scoreboard. The board was sponsored by Sports Clips, a barbershop chain. They would draw names out of a bucket and they'd have a guest scoreboard operator. The winner would come out to the scoreboard and I'd show them how to operate it. Nine times out of ten it was a kid . . . not just one kid but a kid and four of his buddies. They had the time of their life running that thing. The best days were when it was a beautiful afternoon and nobody was out on the party deck; it was just me, the scoreboard, the field, and the sound of the hits. Home runs going over my head. Those were the good days.

Felix Pie, I watched that kid. I've seen a lot of baseball, and I've seen a lot of outfielders. I've seen a couple of Hall of Fame outfielders. Felix Pie gets the best jump on a ball of anybody I've ever seen play the game. The kid is halfway to the spot to catch the ball seemingly before the ball has left the infield. He just gets a dynamite jump. He goes up to Chicago, he struggles, but the kid is going to be good.

—Rick Farlow,

Indianapolis, Indiana

I attended my first Major League Baseball game in the spring of 1946, when I was nine years old. The Chicago Boys' Club group I belonged to had scheduled field trips on successive weekends to Wrigley Field and Comiskey Park. Until that time, I had never heard of Wrigley Field, Comiskey Park, the Chicago Cubs, or the Chicago White Sox.

I did not know there were two leagues and that there was a championship tournament known as the World Series, or that the Cubs had been a participant the previous year.

The fact that my first game was at Wrigley was strictly a matter of chance and but for the grace of God, I might have become—*horror of horrors*—a White Sox fan.

After no more than two innings, I was hooked on the game of baseball in general, and the Cubs in particular. I still remember most of the Cub team that day, including Phil Cavarretta, Stan Hack, Don Johnson, Clyde McCullough, and my first baseball idol—**Andy Pafko**.

I knew instinctively that the Cubs would blow the lead in 1969 to an expansion team. That is so Cub-like! . . . In 1984 I had playoff and World Series tickets but I knew they would fold again, even with a two-games-to-none lead. . . . In 2003 I was sure the long wait was finally over, but when they again reverted to form, I was disappointed but not really surprised. These are, after all, the Cubs. . . . I am still the longest-suffering Cub fan. That's the real Cub curse.

—Matt Parypinski, 71,

Arlington Heights, Illinois

There's a win chill factor at Wrigley Field.

Andy Pafko: In the very first set of Topps baseball cards, the first card (#1) was Andy Pafko.

2
Sweet Home Wrigley

Ivy Man

Open the Gates and Open Them Wide . . . Cubbie Fans Are Coming Inside

Bleacher Creatures

Tony Brown

Tony Brown, 37, is another South Sider who fell in love with the Cubs. An actor, Brown lives in the Bucktown section of Chicago when he's not doing acting gigs in Los Angeles with the likes of George Clooney, Morgan Freeman, and Cicely Tyson.

I started watching the Cubs in 1979. I always joke about Chicago teams and your first player that you love, or your first coach, your first manager, et cetera. My favorite player was **Bill Buckner**. I loved the way he played. I was also a big Dave Kingman fan. I was eight years old and I didn't know the politics of the game. I didn't know he was a jerk most of the time. All I knew is that he could hit home runs from Chicago to Milwaukee. There's nothing more that I loved than my great-grandfather, who was affectionately called Dad, not just by my family, but the neighborhood. Everyday about 2:30, my "dad" would pick me up from school, we'd walk home, and by the time we got home there was still time to watch about an hour of the Cubs game. I lived for that. The best times in my life were sitting with my dad, eating a hot dog with a tall glass of Nestlé Quik and we would watch the Cubs games. We would just talk and watch. As each game would come on, there was always a new player from a new team, and he would always tell me little details about them. That was the last year my great-grandfather would be alive on earth. He passed away in January of 1980. For

The best times in my life were sitting with my dad, eating a hot dog with a tall glass of Nestlé Quik.

Bill Buckner: When Bill Buckner botched Mookie Wilson's weak ground ball in the 1986 World Series, he was wearing a Chicago Cubs batting glove for "good luck."

a long time, the Cubs filled that void for a father figure in my life. When Harry Caray joined in 1982, he became a de facto father figure. With that, in addition to school, I was also acting and doing commercials. I did a TV feature with Morgan Freeman. My life really revolved around the Cubs. I would talk about the Cubs at school with classmates and friends, none of them had the Cubs passion.

Whether you're a kid or an adult, you do different things. In my eyes when I was young, I always thought, "Hey, everybody watches the Cubs." Obviously, that's not very true. For me, the train ride to Wrigley as a kid is still a wonderful memory. To this day, I love taking the train. It's just exciting, especially when you're in the subway and you go from the el into the subway, and you come out onto the el and then the train is moving and moving, and I'm in a new neighborhood. I'm on the North Side. The train stops are going by. Slowly but surely in those old green el cars back in the day, you come to the ballpark. Here comes Wrigley and you're moving closer.

I'm looking at eight years old, and I've got an Afro bigger than my body back then, because I was really short. Even bigger than my Afro was my eyeballs—getting closer and closer, then the train comes to a stop and there it is clear as day. You see the green scoreboard and the wind is blowing the flags. I didn't even know what they meant but the flags were there. There were about twenty-something thousand there. I was taken by one of my neighbor friends. He takes me to the game, we go in through the Sheffield-Addison side, and we had great seats. Twenty-five rows up on the first base line. A cloudy day could never have been sunnier. I'm just looking all around, left to right, up to down, corner to corner, angle to angle, and side to side. I'm here. I'm inside my TV. Here's the green grass and the ivy. I'm looking at the bleachers and I'm smelling the smoke from the hot dogs and the smoky links back then. There's no other place I wanted to be. I always called Wrigley Field "heaven on earth." From that day on I knew that I was going to be a Cubs fan forever, I was going to go to as many games as I could, I would watch them whenever I could. In my eyes the Cubs were not losers. They might have lost games, but I didn't refer to them as "the losers." I would detest people calling them "losers."

I didn't have a lot of people that would want to go with me to a Cub game. It really wasn't until high school the following year that my mother let the leash go a little bit. She knew by listening to WGN when it was a day game; she knew I was going and what time I was expected back. If I wanted to go to a Cub game with a high school friend or sometimes my aunt or by myself, my mom would let me go. The irony was I never knew about anything around Wrigley Field. I never knew what was on the other side of the street until I became much older. From 1986 up till I moved to Los Angeles for my acting career in 2004, I went to every Opening Day. That was eighteen years.

As I was getting older, I was going to more Cubs games by myself. In 1989 when the Cubs won the division, I was right there. Actually I was watching the end of the game at Sluggers. We were all out at Clark and Addison and whooping it up. I had this jacket on and people had champagne that they were spraying. I was getting sprayed. I was eighteen and I'm getting champagne. It just amazed me how a sports team can really bring a city together. I'm getting hugged, picked up, the whole thing. I'm having this great time. I'm not even mentioning that all these times the playoffs were lost. Eighty-four was obviously worse than '89—the Game 5 in '84 where I'm watching the first seven innings from my Aunt Lee's house and the Cubs were winning. It was time for my two younger brothers and I to go home. We ran about five blocks home. By the time I got home my mother and other extended aunt were watching the game and it was bottom of the eighth and my aunt looked at me and said, "Tony," and shook her head because they were losing. I just yelled, "NOOOO" and watched the rest of the game on the TV. When that final out was made I locked myself in my bedroom. I just could not stop crying. I hadn't cried that hard since the day my great-grandfather passed away. The next day at school I was teased endlessly. I didn't get in any fights, but I was just thinking how can other Chicagoans hate the Cubs like that? This is your city. Isn't this your team? For that whole day I was just silent, because I couldn't believe what I had seen the day before. . . .

It hit me like a ton of bricks. Why was I not sitting in the bleachers prior to this time?

I started sitting in the bleachers in 1990. It hit me like a ton of bricks. Why was I not sitting in the bleachers prior to this time? This was like my second childhood. I'm showing up for batting practice—not voluntarily—but so I can protect my territory. So I can catch baseballs. Between 1990 and 1995 I never interacted with anybody. I just kept to myself. Even after I turned twenty-one in '92, I honestly don't remember drinking one beer in Wrigley Field until 1995, which was the year after the work stoppage, strike, whatever you want to call it. I was very reluctant to go back and offer my soul again to baseball. I had just moved into Wrigleyville. I slowly started going back to games in late June of '95. One day during a game a bleacherite approached me and said, "Hi, my name is Ron, I've noticed you've been coming to some games lately. After the game, why don't you come over and hang out with us over at Wrigleyville Tap?" When this stranger offered me this invitation, it was literally like Willy Wonka and the Chocolate Factory and I got the key. I'm like, "Oh, my God, I'm going to hang out and have beers with the Bleacher Bums." There are some of them that don't really like to be called Bleacher Bums. I went after the game ended. I looked around at the history of the bar, all the bats that they had, and the memorabilia and everything. That day it was just sweet victory; I'm meeting all these people. It was always very surgical—arriving at the ballpark, waiting for the gates to open, batting practice, ball game; after the game I would go home. That day changed everything—the way I wanted to go to the games, how I entertained myself, everything. From there, I have a friendship with a lot of Cub fans and that just builds. . . .

One day in the bleachers this drunk jumped onto the field. He broke both of his ankles on impact and the crowd-control guys carried him arm-in-arm, while his ankles were dangling unnaturally. There were always a bunch of fools that would challenge their friends to go on the field for a hundred bucks. That's about a 15-foot drop. Plus, the fact you've got to go over the basket, too. The basket is about 2½ feet. It's not a clean jump. You worry about the basket and you worry about who's seeing you. There's just no rhyme or reason. He wasn't the first one I'd seen do that, but that was the most graphic. It was just ugly.

It was always a great time when the announcers would come out to the bleachers and sit with us. It's a little more exciting because the TV is right next to you. The announcers are right next to you. To be honest, after a while you really forget about them. The one cool thing about Bob Brenly sitting in the bleachers was looking at his World Series ring. That thing is almost bigger than the sun. That rock is huge. That added its own excitement and electricity. There's always different things going on in the bleachers. You can meet a woman that may or may not be a baseball or a Cub fan, there's an elixir, an electricity, not just the alcohol, something happens around that ballpark where men and women can mingle unlike any other ballpark . . . . A woman would really have to mess herself up to not look hot in red. There's something about a woman in red that turns the heat up a little bit.

I met a fan in the bleachers in '97—who I later found out was also an actor—Dave Lewis. One day in 2003 a casting-director friend of mine called me up and tells me there's a commercial for MasterCard being filmed up on one of the rooftops near Wrigley. He gave me the number and said to call the producer. The producer said, "Can you come in?" I asked if I could bring my friend, he said, "Yes." So we both go there and we shoot this commercial for a couple of hours. We shot it the day after the Cubs won Game 2 of the 2003 Championship Series against Florida. In the commercial, one of the pieces we're talking about—you probably only see us for ten seconds—is the Sammy Sosa game-tying home run in the bottom of the ninth. Their plan was to show that commercial during the World Series in 2003 when the Cubs would go to the World Series . . . but it didn't happen. We get a call in April of 2004 that they were going to show the commercial.

The other thing that I notice is that there's this Cub-fan arrogance that goes around. It happens whenever there is any kind of Cubs and White Sox dialogue. All you hear from certain Cubs fans—these aren't even real Cubs fans—is about attendance being part of the mix. Unless you're a stockholder with the Tribune Company, you really should not care about over 40,000 people coming into the ballpark every day, especially when they lose. You just can't make an excuse for them anymore. A lot of these Cub fans aren't true fans. They're transplants and the reason why they're transplants is because their real team is still where they grew up. They move to Chicago because Chicago obviously has the better job base. They attach themselves to the Cubs. They party. I love having a cold drink, but sometimes it just takes away from the game itself. Obviously, with some of the

Shouldn't they offer a free brick to their loyal season-ticket holders?

women that are at the ballpark, a cold drink is not a bad distraction. . . . Three years ago the Cubs had this garage sale where they had a bunch of bricks and seats on sale. One of the problems I have with the Cubs organization is, shouldn't they offer a free brick to their loyal season-ticket holders? Especially the ones that have had tickets for five, ten, twenty years? That is what really repulses me because you really should take care of your season-ticket holders and I don't think the Cubs do. I got my season tickets in '99. Every now and then you get a calendar in the mail. Then a notice that they are raising their ticket prices.

We have friends of ours that have been priced-out. They can no longer afford to go to games. You might see some of the same friends and people at three or four games a year rather than twenty or thirty. There are friends of mine that I've been sitting with for years who don't even go to the games anymore because they charge $45 for a bleacher ticket. It's horrible. For a family of four at one game, you're going to spend over $300. For one game, I can drop $100 to $150 with the tickets, food, and beverages. In the mid-'90s I was going to forty or fifty games a year, and now I can probably go to a dozen games a year. Sometimes it's really hard to choose what games you want to go to because it's so much money. It's like being a kid, you want to get to the ballpark before the game for batting practice. Now, as an adult you go for three hours and then after go to an established watering hole with your friends, have a few cocktails, talk about the game, meet some ladies, and take it from there. It becomes really hard now. There are a lot of kids of all backgrounds, all neighborhoods that would love to get to a Cub game. Being a man of color, there are more African-American baseball fans than baseball wants to give credit for. I do not deny that it's gone down significantly, because of price, because of basketball or football and because of 1994. . . .

Nineteen ninety-eight was one of the most exciting years of my life. There was so much passion. There was so much going on. When Harry Caray passed away and the Cubs started winning games and Sammy was hitting all these home runs. There was an electric atmosphere every day. We didn't know which to reach for first, the alcohol or the Pepto Bismol.

What's the definition of Gross Sports Ignorance? 144 White Sox fans.

It's a Jungle Out There— Dress Accordingly

Ward Tannhauser

That's not the Wrigley Field outfield wall you see moving around—it's just Cub fan Ward Tannhauser. Originally from Hoffman Estates, Tannhauser now lives in Crystal Lake where he owns Cybrid Systems. Tannhauser is known as Ivy Man because he attends Cub games in an elaborate costume constructed of ivy.

I vy Man was initially a Halloween costume in the mid-'90s. I wore it a couple of years, and my brother and I always talked about if the Cubs ever made it to the playoffs, I would throw on that costume and go to the game like that. In 2003, two weeks before the playoffs started, I went over to *Field of Dreams*. ESPN was there, and I said, "You know, if you want to see something interesting, go to the first playoff game and look for the giant green guy." It took off from there. I was actually very nervous that first time.

The costume weighs about 45 pounds. It's basically green sweat pants and a green jacket wrapped in wire mesh. Then, the ivy is wound into the wire mesh. I'm standing on giant stilts, and I have crutches attached to my arms. It takes about twenty, twenty-five minutes to put it on.

I'm standing on giant stilts, and I have crutches attached to my arms.

I've been tackled in the middle of the street. People thought it was fun to tackle me. It's dangerous. I had a whole audience when I went into an outhouse once, all standing there, with

Field of Dreams: Matt Damon and Ben Affleck made their movie debuts in 1988 as extras in the Fenway Park scenes in *Field of Dreams.*

three photographers and a camera crew all not believing I could go into an outhouse. When I came out, I got a standing ovation.

People pluck away for souvenirs. I have to add thirty to forty dollars' worth of ivy every season, because I lose pieces every year. I've been questioned by some pretty interesting people.

I got my picture in the Hall of Fame. They more or less just found me. It was amazing. They called my house, and my wife thought it was a salesperson, so she almost hung up on them. One weekend, they opened an exhibit called Sacred Grounds, which is all about the mystique of ballparks and fans. It was Father's Day weekend at Cooperstown, and they asked me to come out and speak. I gave a half-hour speech on how Ivy Man evolved. Then, the next day, they opened up the new exhibit, and I was also there for that. My whole family was out there. That was in 2005. I got a check from the Baseball Hall of Fame! The most touching kind of the experience—I acknowledged my dad on Father's Day and had him stand up in the audience. Five weeks later, he passed away.

I've won over $10,000 in Halloween costume contests. . .

My wife doesn't mind. She was the creator of Ivy Man. I've won over $10,000 in Halloween costume contests, just at local bars and downtown. All with the Ivy Man costume.

The Cubs acknowledge me. I was one of the two "super fans" in last year's Cub calendar. They won't let me in the park yet. No one with a costume is allowed in the park.

My kids love it. My oldest son's dream is to someday wear the outfit. I've gotten knocked down a couple of times. It's hard to walk in. You can't walk on grass in the outfit—it has to be cement. I've never been seriously hurt. A lot of times people will help me back up.

I charge people a dollar to take a picture with me. Then I donate it to JDRF (Juvenile Diabetes Research Foundation). That was Jim McMahon's favorite deal.

The Tooth about the Cubs?
You Can't Handle the Tooth!

Joel Justis

Joel Justis has followed the Cubs since the '50s. He is an electronic subcontractor with the Morey Corporation. The Lane Tech and Eastern Illinois graduate lives in Downers Grove.

I have two crowns on my teeth. I got one about a year and a half ago. I was sitting there in the dentist's office and I asked him, "I'm getting this crown. Can you guys do anything with it, like cover it up with anything?" They said, "Yeah, sure, what do you want?" I told him I'd like a Cubs logo on it. They said they weren't sure but they thought they might be able to do that. They sent it to their lab, and it comes back and has this beautiful Cubs logo on it. It was for a third or fourth molar in the back and I said, "What's this going to cost?" They said, "Nothing. The lab just loved doing it!"

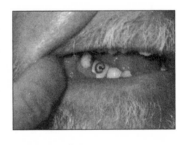

I had another one on the opposite side recently. I was sitting in the dentist chair, and they were doing a root canal. I design another Cubs logo and put a No. 10 in the middle of it for Ron Santo, so now I've got two of them.

We grew up on the North Side. My brother and I used to take the Addison bus to games in the '50s. At that time, you got two tokens for 25 cents. One token would take you to the ball game, and another token would take you home. I was about twelve years old, my brother was eight, and I would take him. We thought nothing of getting on the bus and traveling for thirty minutes to get to the game. We'd usually get grandstand seats. On Ladies Days, every Tuesday,

If you did that, they gave you a ticket for the next game as your pay.

kids got in free so we liked to go then. They don't even have Ladies Days anymore because they can sell all those seats for a lot of money—forty bucks and up—it's unbelievable. Bleachers are $43 right now. After the game, we'd go down underneath the stands where they would hire kids to go clean up the stands or go out onto the field to pick up debris out of the ivy and from down in the dugouts. It was great. If you did that, they gave you a ticket for the next game as your pay. You'd go back the next day for only your 25-cent bus tokens and see another ball game. Randy Jackson played third base—they used to call him "Handsome Ransom Jackson." Cavarretta was gone by then. Dee Fondy played first base. Hal Jeffcoat pitching. Sad Sam Jones pitching. Bob Rush. Hank Sauer was one of my favorites. He was unbelievable.

A sportswriter recently wrote a story about Hank Sauer. After the game, they'd tell the kids to go clean up something, so this guy and his buddy were cleaning up the dugout and saw a ball glove there . . . it was Hank Sauer's. His buddy grabbed it and stuck it in his shirt, and the two of them snuck out. Later on he became a sportswriter. What his friend had done always remained on his mind. He was at an All-Star Game in San Francisco and happened to bump into Hank Sauer. He said, "Hank, I've got to tell you this. About forty years ago, my buddy and I were cleaning out the dugout, and my buddy stole your glove." Sauer grabbed him around the neck like he was going to choke him and said, "I'm glad you told me this." The other guy kept the glove, and I don't know what happened to it . . .

Fairly recently, we were at a game and were out in the bleachers—we love the bleachers. Sosa is playing up to the crowd. The crowd would yell down, "Sammy, how many outs?" Sammy would turn around and signal. "What's the count?" And, he would turn around and signal. Suddenly there was a line drive hit to him. He's not paying attention, and the whole crowd yells, "Sammy, in!" He turns and sees the ball and goes flying in and makes a diving shoestring catch.

That night on TV, here he is making this spectacular catch. He would never have made the catch if the crowd hadn't yelled at him. . . .

A few years ago, we got tickets to go see the Cubs-Yankees game, the interleague series. We're out in the bleachers, and the Cubs are whomping on the **Yankees** at that time—just killing them. Robin Ventura, who is playing third base for the Yankees comes up to bat, and he hits a home run into the rightfield corner of the bleachers. You know how everybody yells, "Throw the ball back. Throw the ball back." The whole stands are yelling, "Throw the ball back. Throw the ball back," and nothing is happening. No one is throwing the ball back. Now, people are starting to panic . . . because you've got to throw a ball back.

People always bring an extra ball just to be able to do that. They'll catch an opponent's game ball but will throw back a fake ball. Everybody is yelling, "Throw *any* ball back." There was a little kid, ten to twelve years old, and his dad sitting up behind us, and he had brought in some baseballs. He pulls a ball out of the bag and looks at his dad, and his dad says, "Yeah, go ahead and do it." He throws the ball out onto the field. Everybody is screaming and yelling and cheering. The ushers don't know what is going on over here by us. They see the ball come out of the wrong part of the stands so now they're starting to come down, and they're going to grab this guy and throw him out of the game. *He's throwing debris on the field!* Everybody is pushing these ushers back and trying to keep them away from the kid. An usher near us saw what was going on. Finally, he waved the other guys away. So that ended it.

Meanwhile, Sosa and Corey Patterson, in right and centerfield, come out and were warming up, throwing the ball back and forth. Sosa took the ball and threw it up in the stands. The ball went right

Yankees: The Yankees once had a bullpen car (Toyota) that fans constantly threw trash at. The trash attracted rats that ate through the engine cables. The car was scrapped in favor of a golf cart. Both the Toyota and the golf cart were used to transport the relief pitcher to the mound.

over this kid's head, right to the guy behind him, and the guy caught the ball. Now everybody in the stands was chanting, "Give the ball to the kid. Give the ball to the kid. Give the ball to the kid." This guy was dying—here he has a **Sammy Sosa** ball, probably the first ball he ever got, and he's dying. Finally, he hands the ball to the kid. The whole stand erupted—all cheering. The dad pulled out a pen, and he took the ball and everybody in the stands was signing it now for the kid. His dad had tears running down his face. It was like a "magic moment.". . .

We took my two sons to a ball game, and we were in the bleachers. My youngest son was five or six at the time, so he was getting bored. He disappeared. We were looking around and he was up against the fence, staring out there. Then we see other people stopping and staring out into the street. We were wondering what the heck was going on out there. I sent my other son up to find out what Billy is doing up there. He goes up there . . . and he didn't come back . . . he was staring out into the street. So I said, "OK, I've got to go find out what's going on." I look out there—there are two drunks lying spread-eagled on the street. People are tossing quarters and 50-cent pieces at them. These guys are trying to catch them in their mouths while they're lying out in the street. Bizarre!

One time we bumped into one of those ball hawks who was in the stands. There's one who has like 3,000 baseballs. He's caught them coming off the walls or in batting practice. They have a network of friends who are up there with walkie-talkies, and they tell them who's at bat, right-handed batter or left-handed batter, so the ball hawks know where to station themselves. I always wondered how these guys could be in such perfect position to catch these fly balls when they came off the walls.

Sammy Sosa: Sammy Sosa had a corked bat, and Graig Nettles had Superballs. In 1974 the Yankee third baseman's bat broke and six Superballs fell out.

They interviewed the guy who had the 3,000 balls. He lives in a basement apartment. He's a postman, working as a supervisor at the post office. He works nights and then he comes during the days to ball games. He's got trunks full of the balls—they're all over his basement. People ask him what he's going to do with them, and he says someday he's going to donate them to the Cubs. I think he's already talked to them, and they're not real crazy about getting all of them. A lot of them are meaningless—batting-practice balls.

Today marks the 10th anniversary of the last time Sammy Sosa hit the cut-off man.

Raise the Roof or Lower Wrigley Field

George Loukas

George Loukas was born in Greece and emigrated to the South Side of Chicago when he was four. After seeing action as a quarterback at SIU–Carbondale, he became a Chicago schoolteacher. Then one year out of college, everything changed.

I n 1974 my brother and I bought the building in left-centerfield at 3700 Sheffield. Two years later we bought the Sports Corner at 956 Addison, then two years after that we bought the Cubby Bear building. That was in '78. There were probably 3 to 5,000 fans in the seats during those years. I never dreamed I'd see what's going on now. Basically, our experience was working at bars. I worked at Butch McGuire's when I got out of college. When I first met Butch, he was the owner of this great bar and he also owned the building. That was our motivator. My brother and I, our thing was to always buy the property we were in, not just waste money on the lease from a landlord.

"Can we come over and watch from your rooftop?" I said, "Sure, c'mon over."

We had a lot of Puerto Rican tenants in our building. The Puerto Rican guys were always into baseball, and they would go up to the rooftop. They'd have lawn chairs, and that was about the extent of the seating. We'd join them on the rooftops. During the course of the game a lot of my friends would see me from across the street, and they would yell at me, and we'd wave. They would say, "Can we come over and watch from your rooftop?" I said, "Sure, c'mon over." Guys would ask me if they could bring beer and burgers. One of the tenants had a grill, so they would grill their burgers and hot dogs. In '84, when the Cubs went into the playoffs, that was the start of the rooftops being noticed.

There was a book that was recently put out by former Reds pitcher Tom Browning on weird things that happened to ballplayers in **Cincinnati**. Tom Browning had asked one of the visiting clubhouse managers if he knew anybody that had access to a rooftop. He wanted to get up on the rooftop, so the guy called me up and I went the next day and fetched Browning. Browning had pitched the day before, and he wanted to make his friends laugh. He had his uniform on. He put on a jacket over the uniform so nobody would recognize him as we were walking out of Wrigley. I walked him up to the rooftop, and he took his jacket off. He had his uniform on and he's waving at his friends in the bullpen during a game (I have the picture that was in the paper.) He was fined by his manager at the time. It was national news what he had done. If I would have known it was going to be national news, I would have worn a Cubby Bear jersey or Cubby Bear T-shirt. He really enjoyed it.

In '88, the rooftops really took off. The Lakeview Baseball Club got their license to build out, and that was the first year a city-approved operation was in effect. It didn't affect me, I was already operating my rooftop. My neighbor and I would always hope we wouldn't get shut down. By that time I had three rooftops. The people looking out of the stadium seeing the people on the rooftops looking in, that added an extra dimension.

People would go up our back porch through our rooftop hatches. You would have to put a ladder up to go through a hatch. In the beginning, all our friends would go up through the ladder. We used a lot of rickety ladders up there. Picture a guy 6-feet-5, about 270 pounds, trying to carry a keg of beer up the ladder with his friend helping him. I had my young guys that were working for me carrying kegs of beer up on the rooftop. It started getting so profitable that I started making changes to the building. I extended the staircase up to the rooftop at

Cincinnati: In 1998 the Cincinnati Reds started an outfield trio of Chris Stynes, Dimitri Young, and Mike Frank. You might know them better as Young, Frank, and Stynes. (The author couldn't resist. He'll show himself to the principal's office now.)

that point. We started making improvements as we were increasing our revenues. A lot of my friends from college were salesmen. As five or ten years went by, these guys went from being salespeople to sales managers to corporate presidents, and they would bring in their customers. It created a continual growth in our business. These people were using it as a marketing tool for their business. It became a great thing for them and a great thing for me. My customers come from everywhere: Wisconsin, Iowa, Indiana, southern Illinois, St. Louis, Missouri. We get so many out-of-towners.

Seeing Spuds MacKenzie on a rooftop balloon was the start of the downfall of the balloons up on the rooftops. The building at 1032 Waveland had a balloon, then at 1010 Waveland was the Old Style balloon. Eventually one of the players said, "Hey, that's a real big distraction up there." The Cubs complained to the city, and the city made us take down our balloons.

When I was younger there was a lot of animosity between Cubs and **Sox fans**. Things have really calmed down. This one guy, he was a loud Cubs fan. This guy would go as close to the field as possible and pick out a player on the other team who had screwed up, and this guy would get on their case. He would yell and scream at them. It was nonstop. He had a buddy that would come into the bar and they would just be loud and obnoxious and they would carry their shtick over to the ballpark. He was a South Sider.

We get a lot of South Siders who are Cubs fans. Being in Chicago, you are not just a Cubs fan or just a Sox fan, you're a Chicago sports fan. You support both teams. People that say they are only a Cub fan or a Sox fan, that's not true. People get on the bandwagon to be just one or the other. Most people are very happy that the Cubs win and the Sox win.

I don't own the building with the Budweiser sign on it. That was grandfathered in there—the Budweiser building and the Miller building. The gentleman who owned the Budweiser building was a school principal; he passed away some time ago. He was a very nice man. Mr.

Sox fans: The 1983 White Sox were the first Chicago team to break the two million attendance mark for one season.

Kelly, his name was. His kids are now owners of the property, and they're nice folks too.

The players would make their rounds around the ballpark like all the customers do.

The most frequently asked question in the bar is, "When did the Cubby Bear open up at Wrigley Field?" At first, it was the Cubs Pub and the Cubs Grill. It became the Cubby Bear a few years after that. It's been the Cubby Bear for all these years.

We used to get a lot of players in there. They would make their rounds around the ballpark like all the customers do. Keith Moreland . . . they would all come by often.

When my lawyer was going to law school and he had finished, he came to Chicago with his friend. They came to me and asked if I had work for them while they studied for the bar exam. I said, "OK, you guys can work for me as coat check." I let them work coat check for a week, and then I put them behind the bar. When they finished with their law exam, I said, "What are you going to do now that you passed the exam?" They said, "We're going to work for some big law firm." I said, "You ought to start your own business." They said, "Well you need an office and a phone and electricity and you got to pay for all that stuff." I said, "Listen. I got an office. You can share a desk." They took me up on it. One kid got married and moved to Michigan and the other still works for me now. He works for himself and he's got his law office and me as his No. 1 client.

The Best Damn Band in the Land

Ted Butterman

Ted Butterman is the leader of the Chicago Cubs Dixieland Band. Butterman saw his first Cubs game in 1940 when he was five years old. Bill "Swish" Nicholson was his favorite player. After graduating from Hyde Park High School he attended the University of Illinois at Champaign and DePaul.

I always dreamed of having some association with the Cubs. I wasn't concerned about what capacity or anything. I figured maybe, just maybe, they would be interested in having a band. Actually, the idea came from the old Brooklyn Dodger Symphony. I saw pictures of them in sports history books and I thought, "This looks like fun." The seed was planted at that time. I just never called upon it until later years.

> I always dreamed of having some association with the Cubs.

The first game for the band was April 9, 1982. I called up the members of the band in February of 1982. I had written the Cubs letters over and over throughout the years suggesting that it would be a nice touch to have a Dixieland band at the ballpark, but I never got any response. So I almost gave up. I talked to Buck Peden, who was a marketing guy at the ballpark. The first time I called, I talked to the person in charge of entertainment. They said, "WHAT?" It took me a while to get to talk to Buck Peden. He said, "Call me sometime in the future, and we'll talk about it." I called him three weeks later. He said, "Why don't you call me back in a month?" So the next week I called. Actually, I just pestered him to death. Finally he said, "Why don't you come down for an audition and we'll see." So I went down there. Got my guys together. Made four phone calls and found five guys who weren't working that day. We went down there to Wrigley, and the whole marketing department was standing there. We played underneath the concourse. There was no game that day.

We played a few tunes. Finally, he said, "Yeah, that sounds pretty good. . . . Why don't you just plan on coming on Opening Day and play?" So we did. We had five seats right behind the screen, with microphones. We sat there and played between every inning over the loudspeakers. It was a foot in the door.

I had to get permission from the union to play there because according to the union rules, at a sporting event you had to have a band of at least fifteen people. So I had to go to the union hall downtown and present my case before the board of directors. I said, "Doesn't it make more sense to have five guys working fifty or sixty times a year than to have one fifteen-piece band play on Memorial Day or Fourth of July?" They changed the rules.

We have a song list of approximately 550 or 600 tunes. I determine where we play on a day-to-day basis. We devote a whole day to one section of the park. The best sound as far as the band is concerned is behind the Cubs bullpen. For some reason or other, it seems to be the best acoustics in the park.

Once the catcher throws the ball down to second base, that's our cue to stop playing. We're not supposed to play while the game is in progress. Once in a while we get a request, but mostly we just play what we want to play. It's a five-piece group, but by the end of the year about twenty or thirty musicians have played at various games.

The biggest hassle I have is sometimes it gets really crowded and people have a tendency to bump into you while you're playing. That could be a dangerous situation. So far, nobody has gotten hurt. We get compliments all the time, from everybody, including kids young enough that they don't even know what music we're playing. Fifteen- or sixteen-year-old kids love us. The old-timers, of course, love us because they like it when you play tunes from their era. I don't plan on retiring any time soon. I'm too young, I'm only seventy-three. I haven't worked a real job in thirty years, actually.

Normally crowds are 40, 41,000 people every day. All the seats are taken, so we stand on the stairwells till the inning is over. Sometimes we'll find a seat and sit down for ten or fifteen minutes. The ushers are great. I know all of them by name.

We start at noon in front of the Harry Caray statue. We play there for a half-hour.

I get guys fighting to NOT be in the band. It's hard work, and most of the guys are professional people. They have other jobs. One guy is a professor of French history. One guy teaches Spanish in high school. For a normal 1:20 game, we start at noon in front of the Harry Caray statue. We play there for a half-hour. Then we go to the main gate, Gate F, and we play there for another half-hour. Then, about a half-hour before the game starts, we start playing inside the park. In the middle of the eighth inning, we're out of there.

People do try and tip us occasionally. We don't take one- or two-dollar tips. If they're going to give you two dollars that means they're hard-pressed for themselves, but they want to express their appreciation. So we just say, "It's OK. Don't worry about it, we get paid." They appreciate that. The guy who owns Boston Market laid a fifty-dollar bill on us one time. A lot of twenties and a lot of tens. We put it in a coffee can, and at the end of the year we split it up.

We have played all over the place: The Chicago Cub Dixieland Band. We used to be called the Chicago Cub Quintet. I have had I don't know how many people want to pick a CD up of the band, but then the record companies won't go for it. They say it's controlled by Major League Baseball.

Wrigley Field is only of a few ballparks left that have horizontal aisles. If you've been to Comiskey Park (U.S. Cellular Field), you'll notice all the aisles are vertical. There's no way these fans can walk sideways. Therefore, there's little personal contact in the stands. Wrigley Field, there's fans going all over the place, in the aisles. It's more of a social event than a sporting event.

Beer Is the Reason He Gets Up Every Afternoon

Mark Carlson

Mark "The Beer Guy" Carlson puts his own distinctive flair on his work at Hohokam Park in Arizona—where the Cubs train—at Wrigley Field, and elsewhere. Although Carlson lives in Minneapolis he is a huge Cub fan and often is a beer vendor at Wrigley. Carlson has his own baseball card, "Mark the Beer Guy."

I started working at spring training in '96. It was a fluke, because I had been working at starting my own business with my older brother. That was my part-time job, selling beer at the ballpark. I had been doing that kind of work since 1980. I started working at Twins games when I was in ninth grade.

I tried to figure out how to tie a part-time job, beer vending, with a daytime job that would allow me to travel. I found a job that I didn't hate, and that was a window-cleaning business, which is what brought me to Arizona. So I'm down in Arizona three months every winter. I do residential window-cleaning in January and February, then I sell beer at spring training.

> *I tried to figure out how to tie a part-time job, beer vending, with a daytime job that would allow me to travel.*

In '94 I worked for the Brewers when they were in Chandler, then I worked at the Peoria Sports Complex, where the San Diego Padres and the **Mariners** play. I didn't work in '95 because of the baseball strike. Then, in '96, I decided to go back down there. I thought it'd be exciting to work at Cubs spring training.

Mariners: During the Seattle Mariners' first year in 1977, the distance to the fences was measured in fathoms. A fathom is 6 feet. For instance, where a park may have a sign that denotes 360 feet, the Kingdome's sign was 60.

One of the first things I did, because I'm a character, I said, "Hey, Harry Caray! Hey, you need a beer?" He ignored me the first few games, but I was persistent, and I finally said, "Hey, Harry, you need a cold one? I'm buying!" He finally cleared his throat and said, "If you get a haircut, I'll buy a beer from ya." It was hysterical. Everybody was laughing. I did go up and get my picture taken with him. There are two pictures. In one you can see him grabbing my ponytail, and he has a big grin on his face.

Now at spring training, it's a family reunion. I see the same dedicated Cubs fans year after year. Maybe they sit in different areas of the park, but a lot of people know each other. I feel a camaraderie that I don't get anywhere else. I've become friends with a lot of these fans. I call them up in February to see if they're going to be there that first week of March. I call people up and say, "Hey, are you going to be at St. Patrick's Day this year?"

My beer style that works well for me is to mix things up and do a bait-and-switch trick. I have fun with it, showing fans that my job is about having a good time and spring training is a fun, good time, all the time. If I can make people smile, they're more into buying something from someone who's having a good time versus a beer vendor who's walking around all grumpy. I do some things that are out of the ordinary, like my bait-and-switch trick. It's shouting something I don't have. My first experience doing that was at a spring-training game, and I yelled, "Frozen margaritas!" I was walking around yelling that, but I was working on the first base side, and there **Vendors** was another vendor on the third base side, so when I'd **are really** be walking past his section I would yell, "Frozen mar- **competitive.** garitas!" It was a really hot day. Then, when I'd get over to my own section, I'd just yell, "Beer!" I ran into that vendor and he was like, "Who in the hell keeps yelling frozen margaritas? All the fans are asking for them."

I learned that the vendors are really competitive. We're all friends, but at the same time everyone wants to know who sold the most at the end of the day. This vendor was so frustrated. I would routinely sell two or three cases of beer more than him; it would irritate him.

He was maybe five or six years older than me and had been working spring training longer than me and he could never figure out how I could sell more than him. So he's the guy walking around all grumpy, and I'm the guy walking around with a big grin on my face. Some of the other things I do is, I yell, "Chicken wings!" or "Jagermeister!" or "Cotton candy!" when I don't have cotton candy. I just start rattling things off—"Airplane parts!" Sometimes it doesn't matter what you say because the fans aren't there to pay attention to the beer vendors. They're paying attention to the game.

Some vendor from Arizona gave me this big, huge magnifying glass. He thought it would be a good prop for me. So the other vendor yells, "Cold beer!" and I'll yell, "Colder beer!" so they go, "I've got the coldest beer!" Then I hold up a bottle of beer and put the magnifying glass in front of it and yell, "I've got bigger beers!"

A beer vendor gets paid on commission at most parks. At the Metrodome it's really good, it's 18 percent. Wrigley Field is about 10 percent. The nice thing about working at Wrigley is that the games are almost always sold out. You're making less commission, but your sales are twice what they are at other places. For me it's not how much money I'm making, it's how much fun I'm having.

Wrigley fans are not shy. That's the main thing I like about them. It's an R-rated event. They stand up and yell when they're not happy. I noticed this at the Metrodome this year: There was a fan that was standing up cheering for the Twins, and the usher came up and said, "Sir, you must sit down. You need to be quiet." I was like, "Wait a minute, did I just hear this usher tell this fan to stop cheering?" At Wrigley Field that doesn't happen at all. Wrigley is a totally different atmosphere, I love it. At a Twins game I feel like I'm at a golf game.

If I stand up and go, "Let's go, Twins!" you don't hear anybody clap. You do that at a Cubs game, and you have ten people clapping instantly. You go, "Let's go, Cubbies!" Next thing you know, you have three sections clapping, almost instantly. The fans are a lot more hardcore.

Determining fans who are drunk and when I have to cut them off is a tricky deal right now.

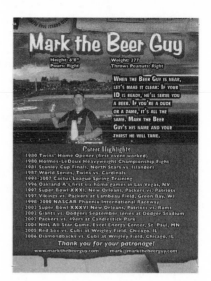

Determining fans who are drunk and when I have to cut them off is a tricky deal right now. The MADD mothers and all this alcohol training that we're taking, it's a big deal. I do cut people off, and you really have to. If I cut somebody off, it's because I'm watching out for their own safety. It's important for me to have a good time, but it's important that people don't die.

I started doing a baseball card in 2001. There's a vendor up here who has his own card, and for a lot of years people were like, "Wow, you're a fun vendor, why don't you have a card?" At that time, I didn't see any value in it. Then I got to thinking that it'd be fun.

The difference between working a game at Wrigley Field and the Super Bowl is that the Super Bowl is exciting, but I'm turned off by the six-hour pregame show and the one-hour halftime show, I'd rather work a baseball game than the **Super Bowl**.

I love working at Wrigley, because they don't have the constant pushing of entertainment on you like they do at a Twins game. There's a T-shirt toss between every inning. Wrigley Field is really about baseball. I love the old scoreboard. I really love the atmosphere.

The Cubs fans are the best I've seen.

Super Bowl: Before Super Bowl XI, no one sang the "National Anthem." Vikki Carr sang "America the Beautiful."

Sign of the Times

Marty Prather

Cardinal fan Marty Prather—aka "The Sign Man"—isn't afraid to venture into Wrigley Field. Prather, headquartered in Springfield, Missouri, owns two dozen Dominos Pizza stores in the "Show-Me" State. He's a fixture at every game in Busch Stadium with his collection of funny signs. A trivia expert, Prather has been a vital cog on a national championship–winning sports trivia team. He's been testing Cub fans for nineteen years with his anti-Cub signs at Wrigley.

C ub fans once had this sign, it was the Shawon-O-Meter for Shawon Dunston, and they always updated his batting average every at-bat. So I just played off that and put the Cubs Logo-O-Meter. Now it says, 99 YEARS AND COUNTING. It's how many years it's been since they won the World Series.

I used to sit in the grandstands, but one, I don't like it as much, and two, for security it's much better in the bleachers. If you sit down by the basket, which is the front row of the bleachers, and you hold up the sign every half-inning and you're facing the crowd, you only have to defend one front. People can throw stuff at you, but you can see it coming. You just block it with the sign.

I wore a Cubs jersey with the name "Bartman" on it. The number was 96 and it said, YEARS AND COUNTING.

There's been a lot of peanuts, a lot of wadded-up cups. I didn't have a beer thrown on me until the last two years. The last two years, there's been a little bit of beverage come at me. The scariest year was after the Bartman episode. I wore a Cubs jersey with the name "Bartman" on it. The number was 96 and it said, YEARS AND COUNTING.

Then, I had a sign that said, THE CURSE LIVES. Someone ripped it out of my hand, ran up the steps, and tossed it onto Waveland. I grabbed him and got him in a headlock. Then security came and arrested the guy and asked if I wanted to press charges.

In 2006 when Preston Wilson of the Cardinals hit a two-run homer, I held up my sign that said, THAT'S A WINNER! Somebody grabbed it out of my hands after the game and threw it onto the field. He tried to get away, and I grabbed him by his belt. Security grabbed him. People were throwing beer and trash on my sign. It was a great picture. The sign was down there on the warning track saying, "That's a winner!" with all the debris around it.

In 1998, when the home-run chase was going on, I formed a group called the Mac Attack Pack, and we all wore hard hats out to Wrigley. We walked in with about thirty guys wearing these helmets. This one guy says, "Who the hell are you? The Village People?" I looked over at him, the first time I saw Steve—a noted Cub fan—and said, "Who the hell are you? Meat Loaf?" He says, "Hey that's good, come here!" After that, we became best friends.

He is the best heckler I've ever seen. He gets on Cardinal centerfielder Jim Edmonds. Turns out we have kids the same age, both girls. When I come to Wrigley, he sets me up with bleacher tickets, and he'll be sitting with me at Busch for a four-game set. The Cubs-Cardinals rivalry definitely doesn't have the hatred of the Red Sox and Yankees. Then again, if the Cubs ever become competitive, and it looks like they're going to be, it could get snotty. . . .

The *St. Louis Post-Dispatch* has made replicas of the Cardinals' ten World Series rings, and I'm going to get them sized so they fit all my fingers. I get a lot of verbal abuse, and the middle finger goes up a lot at me. Now, I'll be able to just turn around and hold up all ten fingers right back at them. I've got about a dozen signs that are strictly anti-Cubs. If they win, about ten of them will be useless. The Cub-O-Meter will be gone. The curse will be gone. I have a sign that says, THIS IS YOUR BRAIN and it has a Cardinal logo, then, THIS IS YOUR BRAIN ON DRUGS, and it has a Cub logo. That seems to cause the most problem. Security came down and said, "Look, Marty, let me check that sign for you." I let him. So I go to get it after

Some guy claimed he was me, and they gave him my sign.

the game, and it wasn't there. Some guy claimed he was me, and they gave him my sign. I blew a gasket. Former Cardinal catcher Tom Pagnozzi happened to be walking by and asked what was going on. I told him and he said, "Just let it go." We were over at Sluggers after the game, and some guy came up to me and asked, "Aren't you the guy with those signs? Well, the guy that stole your sign is sitting at the bar bragging about it." There was a tussle. We got my sign back, but we were asked to leave the bar because they didn't just hand it over. We had to take it back. That sign is just beat up.

It was probably twenty years ago when I first walked into Wrigley with a sign. The first sign I had was WGN—WHO'S GOING NOWHERE with a Cub logo on it. Then one, CHOKER—SINCE 1908 with the Cub logo being the C. My wife used to go with me. We've learned to not go on Sunday-night games, because most Cardinal fans have left; they all go Friday and Saturday. If it's a Sunday day game, they'll hang around.

We stayed around for one Sunday-night game, and Omar Olivares hit one out onto the street. You can only hold up signs every half-inning, so you can't just do it right when it happens. I'm not exaggerating, there were probably sixteen to twenty policemen surrounding me every half-inning. Security said, "I know you're doing it by the rules, but . . . " I said, "Look I've been getting abused the last two games here. I'm going to rub this in." I went for it, and people were throwing stuff right and left.

My wife said she'd never come back again. Which is great, because now she goes with my daughter to the American Girl doll shop and I get to go to the game. I love Chicago, and I love the field. Cub fans are passionate. At times I'm envious of how passionate these fans have been, even though their team has been terrible. You have to admire them.

I've met friends. I've got about twenty Bleacher Bums that if anything gets rowdy, they'll come to my defense. The true fan is out there on a day-to-day basis, and they know me, and we have a blast. The ones who've never seen me before, they're the ones who get all riled up. We always eat at Harry Caray's. Sandberg was there signing autographs one night, and he knew me from my signs. Back in my earlier days we used to go out to Rush and Division. We went up to a place called The Lodge. There were a lot of Cardinal players who went there.

The business cards I have say, "I'd rather my sister be a prostitute than my brother be a Cub fan."

The Cardinals were playing bad, and he said, "You got a sign for that? You got a sign for that?"

I had a little bit of a run-in this year. There was a guy who just went nuts. The Cardinals were playing bad, and he said, "You got a sign for that? You got a sign for that?" I just ignore them, because you can't get into a shouting match with everybody. You're not going to win.

We were in the bleachers last year, and I had my signs. Ryan Dempster was out there spraying people down with the grounds crew hose. He saw me and turned it on me. It was bending my sign. I was getting drenched. He was laughing. The picture of that made some publications. When he came into Busch, I had a sign that said, HEY, DEMPSTER, YOU'RE ALL WET. He came over and shook my hand and introduced himself. That's good, spirited fun.

Why do Bleacher Bums drink chunky beer?

Bits and Bites—Begged, Borrowed, and Stolen

My father was a Cub fan, and he passed the torch to me at birth in 1948. White Sox fans inhabited the South Side and had a fierce hatred for the North Side "loveable losers." Win or lose, rain or shine, my dad and I were Cub fans. Hey! My dad worked at a factory in the inner city and proudly displayed his Cub pennant by his locker. When they would lose a game, he would come to work the following day to find it hanging upside down—this usually happened around eighty times per year—ugh!

I remember going to the park and buying cheap tickets in the grandstands on the third base side . . . and, as the game progressed, slowing inching my way down into the box seats when the Andy Frain ushers were looking the other way. I got caught a few times and tried to get out of it by saying that my father had the tickets and was getting me a hot dog or Santo's Pro Pizza and would be right back. After a few more minutes, I had to tell the usher that Dad was delayed because "I think he had to go to the restroom, too." This usually got me about an inning or two in the box seats or just enough time to try and catch a foul ball from my heroes—Moose Moryn, Ernie Banks, George Altman, Ron Santo, Aldolfo Phillips, or Billy Williams— which, in thirty years, I never got! . . .

As kids, my sister and I would make fun of the vendors who roamed the stands during the game selling their soft drinks, beer, peanuts, frosty malts, et cetera. Now I firmly believe a prerequisite to becoming a vendor at Wrigley Field was that you had to be "unusual" in appearance and also be able to sweat profusely! Throughout my thirty years of going to Cubs games, I saw a potpourri of vendors. One of my sister and my favorites was the "Coke Guy." He was an unkempt, portly individual who would sweat so much that the black-framed glasses he wore always slid down his nose. He would constantly keep pushing his spectacles up with his index finger, never spilling a drop of that precious elixir and all the time bellowing out,

Another one of our memorable vendors was the beer guy—he who would sell beer to a ten-year-old and never bat an eye.

"Cooooooooke, 50-cent Cooooooooke. Who wants an ice-cold Coke?" Another one of our memorable vendors was the beer guy—he who would sell beer to a ten-year-old and never bat an eye. This refreshment employee would be decked out in his classic gray uniform, which was usually drenched with sweat after the first inning. He wore a makeshift headband, which was a piece of foam rubber strapped across his forehead and tied with a shoestring. If he had only patented that makeshift invention, he would be a millionaire today. Ah, yes, give me a Hamm's or an Old Style beer and hold the perspiration!

Now, we never had the luck to get tickets on the end of an aisle, we were always in the middle seats. When my dad would order a brewski, the beer guy would pour it into a cup and have all the people in the row pass it down. By the time he actually got the refreshment, half of it was gone. But, hey, who cares? This was Wrigley Field. Once my dad bought four beers during the Don Cardwell no-hitter—two were actually drank and two were spilled over the bald-headed guy sitting in front of us!

—Bill Herod,
Las Vegas

Our family has always been Cubs fans, dating back to my grandfather who used to go to the games before they played in Wrigley Field. My mom played word games with me as a baby by teaching me the roster of the 1949 Cubs. I suffered through the '50s, cheering for some really bad teams. My first favorite player was Hank Sauer. Then, it was Ernie Banks because that was all they had back then. Our family always went to a few games a year, and I'll never forget the beauty of Wrigley Field the first time I saw it in person and in color—since I'd only seen the black-and-white TV broadcasts.

We were not allowed to watch or cheer for the White Sox in our house. In my vast collection of baseball cards—which I still have—you will not find one single White Sox card. When I got them in the gum packets, I'd trade them for the stick of gum . . . and I hated the gum!

I'd always follow the Cubs no matter where I was, as best I could. Then came 1969, Opening Day. I was in the hospital at Great Lakes Naval Station recovering from wounds received in Vietnam. My friends in Waukegan decided we should go to the game. I sneaked out of the hospital, and we sat in the leftfield bleachers. Ernie hit two that day, the second one bouncing off my fingertips. I remember the Phillie leftfielder, Ron Stone, got drilled in the head by a thrown Easter egg early in the game. He played the rest of the game with a purple eggshell hanging from his cap. More importantly, the Cubs won and the great summer pennant race was on—only to lead to the fall to the Mets. I thought Billy Williams was the best hitter in baseball.

Harry Caray was not the Cubs. Think about it. He came from the Cardinals and took a downward career move by going to the White Sox. Two times nothing is still nothing! Jack Brickhouse and Jack Quinlan were the best. Vince Lloyd had a great time on the radio with the original good kid, Lou Boudreau.

Before we were married, my wife surprised me with tickets to a Cubs game. When she asked me what time we had to leave Milwaukee to get there, I told her I'd pick her up at 8:00 a.m. so we could be there by 9:30. She looked at me like I was crazy since it was a 1:30 start, but I told her she had to experience Wrigleyville. She was totally impressed and amazed at the neighborhood, shagging batting-practice balls on Waveland, and, of course, Wrigley Field. Now my kids are feeling the same excitement. They are amazed at the beauty and excitement of Wrigley Field and Cubs baseball. We all cheer the Cubs on, watching as many games as possible on WGN in Anchorage.

—David Schwartz, 61,

Anchorage, Alaska, Waukegan Native

A fter all the games I'd been to, I never caught a foul ball, let alone a homer. It was always my dream to catch at least one ball, sometime in my life. I had them hit within inches of me, even so close that my son, who was six at the time got a ball and an inning later his brother, who was five, got one too. But none for me.

That was until about three years ago. It was April and the Cubs were playing a doubleheader against San Diego. It was Wood and Prior starting against Eaton and Peavy. Anyway, I went to the game with four of my buddies from work. We were drinking some beers and my pals were ripping me because I had never gotten a ball. Every time we ever went, I lamented that fact to them. About the fifth inning of the first game, a ball careens off the wall by the Cubs bullpen. We were about five rows back from the Bartman seats. The Cubs bullpen catcher picked the ball up, looked me dead in the face, and chucked it right to me. There was a bit of a scrum, but I came up with it. Soaked in beer, I looked down on it and was absolutely ecstatic with my prize. My buddies were celebrating like we had just won the World Series. All was right with the world . . . then suddenly from the rear I hear, "Give it to the kid . . . c'mon, it's her birthday!" I look back and I see this adorable little girl, she's smiling and holding up a big banner that says, GO CUBS, WIN FOR ME ON MY BIRTHDAY! Without hesitation, I walk back to her and I said, "How old are you?" She said, "Eleven today." She was the same age as my oldest son. I looked down at her and said, "Happy Birthday, sweetie," and I handed her the ball. The crowd around her all applauded and one of the guys even bought me a beer. Never had one that tasted better.

The Cubs bullpen catcher picked the ball up, looked me dead in the face, and chucked it right to me.

In the end, as great as I felt finally getting my mitts on a game ball, it was nothing compared to the feeling I got looking at the smile on that little girl's face on her birthday.

Just another day in The Friendly Confines!

—Sonny Dyon,
Las Vegas

A few years ago, I went back to Illinois for a class reunion. I didn't graduate there—I graduated out here in Phoenix, but they always considered me a part of the class because we grew up together. I was working for Best Western and had arranged for accommodations in

Chicago for a couple of nights. My niece had a contact who was supposed to get bleacher tickets. That contact failed, but the hotel was able to help me out at not too much over face value. We paid $50 each for a ticket. I had my brother, sister, niece, and her son with me so there was a group of us.

The bleachers are full of interesting people, but Carmella Hartigan was one of the more interesting ones I think there was out there. She died in 2002 at the age of 100. As the oldest Bleacher Bum, she threw out an honorary first pitch in 1998.

Carmella Hartigan was one of the more interesting ones I think there was out there. She died in 2002 at the age of 100.

With my entourage, I was trying to keep everybody together and going in the right direction. We had pretty decent seats on the back row on the aisle. I thought it was great that we would be able to lean back and relax. I was sitting on the aisle, and, lo and behold, some little lady came up and said, "You're sitting in my seat. The rain must have washed my name off. I had the seat." She hung her bag on the seat part and walked off to get something. I thought, "What the hell is this? I'm not going to put up with something like this." Here, I had struggled to get us all here and get organized. Fortunately some guy, about six rows down, came up and said, "I see you've met Carmella." I said, "Yeah, what's up with that? A bunch of us want to sit together so we got here first."

He told me a little bit about Carmella's story. I ended up talking with her and having a fun time. She even takes the seat in front of her so she can put her feet up. There's no bar there—just open seats. She said she won't give up either seat even to an old person, then she said, "Well, maybe to a pregnant woman, but that's about it." I don't know if she was teasing me or what. A lot of people came up to talk to her. Very interesting meeting her, but it was one of those situations where I'd struggled to keep us all together and then this strange lady comes and kicks me out of my seat. It turned out to be nice all the way around.

—Jim Anderson,
Phoenix, Arizona

This was one of our Opening Day trips, and one of the coaches from Philadelphia came out and played catch with us out in the leftfield bleachers. For some reason, every time he threw them the ball, the Bleacherites couldn't catch it. So he just shrugged his shoulders, took his mitt off, and threw the mitt up into the stands. I couldn't believe I was seeing it. You can't get away with that in New York—your mitt is gone. That impressed me. He started catching them barehanded, showing them how to do it. Pretty soon, somebody threw his mitt back to him.

> **He just shrugged his shoulders, took his mitt off, and threw the mitt up into the stands.**

He picked me out, threw me the ball, and I caught it. He was impressed that I caught the ball. Everyone was tuned into this; it was amazing. There were three Phillies standing around there. He threw me the ball and crouched down into the catching position. Everybody around me gave me some room. I put my right foot on that ledge, and I just let one rip, threw him a strike. The crowd just went wild. He said something to the other guys standing behind him.

So now he was catching, one of the guys was acting like an umpire and the other guy was a hitter. They threw the ball back to me. I wound up and zipped another strike in, and the crowd goes wild. Now the catcher is giving me a sign, like "Brush him back," so I did it. I threw right at the guy, damn near hit him. The guy behind me was real witty. He made his cell phone ring and handed it to me and said, "Hey dude, it's Riggleman. He wants you to suit up."

On another Opening Day, my friend Mookie was standing right beside me. He's my buddy from Colorado. I looked around the bleachers, and I saw a guy sitting there to our right about eight or ten people down. First of all, he had an **Oakland A's** hat on. You don't sit out in

Oakland A's: The Oakland A's copied their green and gold colors from Notre Dame. When LaPorte, Indiana, native Charles O. Finley bought the Kansas City A's in the late 60s, he changed the colors to honor his friend, former Irish coach Frank Leahy. . . . The Green Bay Packers took the Notre Dame colors because Curly Lambeau played at Notre Dame.

the leftfield bleachers with an Oakland A's hat on. The second thing was, he was filing his fingernails. If you know Mookie, all you have to do is point something like that out to him and he's all over it. We have a little saying about the American League; we call them Triple-A Losers. So Mookie stood up and walked over to him and said as loud as he could, "What do you think you're doing? Sitting there filing your fingernails with your Triple-A Loser Oakland A's hat on!" The guy was speechless. The crowd was applauding.

—Randy Farlow,
Ankeny, Iowa

The first time I ever went to a game was 1950. In the wintertime, as soon as the schedule came out my dad would tell my mom, "Find that schedule, find when they're playing a doubleheader with Pittsburgh—I want to see Kiner hit some homers—and then get some tickets." Back in the '50s, nobody went to the games. Ten thousand would be a big crowd. If they drew a million people a year, it would be a big deal. That was their goal every year, and they very, very seldom made it.

My dad loved the doubleheaders. He'd sit down there and have a few beers. He'd buy them two at a time in case the guy forgot to come back. My mom would keep score on a scorecard. We'd go to these games and stay to the bitter end.

We would go and watch the Cardinals and Musial. The Cubbies had Hank Sauer and Frankie Baumholtz in the outfield. One year Baumholtz and Musial had a race for the batting title. Near the end it was clear that Musial was going to win the batting title. The Cubs played the Cardinals the last game of the season. Musial pitched to Baumholtz and Baumholtz pitched to Musial during the game. Bob Ramazzotti would be playing second. Phil Cavarretta at first; he was one of the few guys to come right from high school to the big leagues and never go back to the minors. The catchers were Bob Scheffing and Clyde McCullough.

Musial pitched to Baumholtz and Baumholtz pitched to Musial during the game.

I went on to become a minor-league ballplayer, and McCullough was my manager three different years. Back then nobody cared, because almost all the ballplayers made the same amount of money. Today, these guys are making millions of dollars. I played in the '60s in the minors, and I was averaging a thousand a month. We got paid for four-and-a-half or five months, so I got paid 4,500 or 5,000 bucks. The big-league minimum back then was $6,500. When the season was over, guys would take a week off and then they'd go get a job. I'm talking big leaguers.

All of the games of the Cubs were day games. So when I was going to school I'd hurry home and catch the last few innings of Harry Creighton. I went to five games a year until I got to be about fifteen or sixteen. Then I could go on my own or with my buddies, so I went to about ten games a year. I very seldom went to a Sox game.

Even though my dad was from Sweden and knew nothing about baseball until he came to this country, he got into it. He was a Cub fan.

Thursday was always Ladies Day. You can't have Ladies Day anymore, because the men were complaining. Ladies got in for nothing. When Jackie Robinson came, that place would be packed on Ladies Day or any day. He's the guy who really brought in the fans. The bleacher tickets were 60 cents. Now bleacher tickets—No. 1, you can't even get them, and No. 2, they are $43.

When I was playing in the minors with the Mets in 1963, I hurt my leg in Raleigh, North Carolina. So the Mets said, "Get on a plane and come on up here to New York. We want to have our doctors look at it." I dressed in a Met uniform and walked on the field and took batting practice at the Polo Grounds. The Mets just so happened to be playing the Cubs. Ernie Banks and the Cubs were walking on the field and getting ready for batting practice. Billy Williams was there, and Lou Boudreau was the announcer. I walked up to these guys. I was in a Met uniform and they thought I was a player. I introduced myself and said, "Hey, I've been a Cub fan forever." Ernie was very nice, and Boudreau was nice. Two days later, I was back in the minors.

There was absolutely no weightlifting then. I had started lifting weights in '59 in college. My college coach said I was nuts. He said,

"You'll never be able to play golf when you get older." I was a walk-on at Illinois and I started lifting weights, and overnight my arm became much better and I got some hitting power. I kept lifting those weights in the off-season. Believe me, I probably only lifted half as much as these guys do now, but back then I didn't want to do anymore because I was the only guy doing it. I thought, "God, this might ruin me."

—Lloyd Flodin,
native of Glencoe, Illinois,
professional poker player
in California

F or those who think we need a new ballpark in Chicago, I suggest a trip to St. Louis to see what their new ballpark is like. Last summer, some friends of mine traveled from Cape Cod to Pittsburgh to Cleveland to Wrigley Field to St. Louis for ball games. Obviously, the Wrigley experience was wonderful. The St. Louis experience was horrible. The music was horrible, the concessions were horrible. In the first inning the ketchup bottles were so empty that they splattered all over my friend's brand-new white shirt. There were no wastebaskets to put the hot dog wrappers in. There were vending machines with no visible price. The lines for the ladies room were very lengthy, which is hard to believe in this day and age—to have a brand-new ballpark and not have adequate ladies' rooms. The signs for the men's rooms were nonexistent—you had to hunt and eventually just ask somebody to find out where the men's rooms were. The scoreboard is an abomination. The two auxiliary scoreboards down the foul lines were worthless because most of the time you looked up there, there was a text message up there from one fan to another. For $2.99 the fans could send a text message. The Cardinals were much more interested in making that money than they were having their fans have a nice experience. Now a fan is filing a lawsuit over a slanderous message. The problem with the scoreboard is that there are so many ads up there that they didn't have

The St. Louis experience was horrible. The music was horrible, the concessions were horrible.

vital information to make your time more enjoyable—unlike Wrigley where it announces that there is a night game for a game that hasn't started yet in the day time. The Cardinals don't even put the "N" up there. They have no pitchers' numbers so you don't know who is pitching for the other teams. The statistics for the batters are lacking. For instance, Cleveland and Pittsburgh had beautiful ballparks. In those ballparks if the batter was hitting .310, you knew how many at-bats he had and how many games he had played. In St. Louis if a guy was hitting .310, you don't know if he had a hundred at-bats or 500 at-bats. So enjoy Wrigley while you can.

—Craig Crotty,

Falmouth, Massachusetts

Some say that Tony LaRussa is the backbone of the Cardinals. I wouldn't put him quite that high.

3
Ah, a Female Cub Fan—One of Life's Most Misunderstood Creatures

A few of the Cubs' female fanatics

No Man is Worthy!

Runs 'n' Hoses

Karen Kruse

Karen Kruse is the author of *A Chicago Firehouse: Stories of Wrigleyville's Engine 78,* about her father's adventures at the firehouse across the street from Wrigley Field. Kruse, 49, is a member of MENSA and a lifelong Cubs fan.

On May 28, 1961, in the rightfield grandstand, a hot dog cart—the weenies were actually cooked on this thing—caught on fire. The whole incident was captured by WGN-TV as my dad, a fireman, put out the blaze—the gas supply in the cart fed the flames! Mom and I, three years old at the time, saw it on the tube. Imagine my mom doing her ironing—remember ironing?—in front of the TV when Brickhouse says something to the effect of "get a load of this." The camera pans over to catch dad with hose in hand—they had to lead out with a hose, a handpump wouldn't do it—putting out the fire. Mom just stared at the TV. The next day, the picture was carried in the local paper—*Tribune*, most likely—with dad in perfect silhouette with the caption, "Hot time at Wrigley Field . . . but it couldn't spark a Cubs win." I still have my very own copy of that yellowed newspaper clipping. Since my book came out, I get lots of people who tell me they were at that game!

We would always go to the firehouse before our annual visit to the ballpark. I ate more ballpark food in that firehouse than I ever ate at the ballpark. The vendors in those days—the '60s—would give leftover Frosty Malts—still my favorite—peanuts, popcorn to the firemen. I would sit on the engine and eat ice cream. If I was lucky, I would get to ring the bell and blow the siren. When it was game time, we would sit in leftfield foul territory against the wall. Why? Let's face it. They are the Cubs. I had no reason to watch the field. I watched that firehouse! When the firemen went out on a run, screaming down Waveland, the guys on the back step would look up and wave at me. They still rode the back step then. It's how one little girl falls in love with firemen and the CFD.

When the firemen went out on a run, screaming down Waveland, the guys on the back step would look up and wave at me.

When I was writing my book on firemen, the captain invited me to lunch. After lunch, we ended up walking over to Wrigley Field. The Cubs were out of town, but the grounds crew was there. I stood in the leftfield bleachers gazing at that pristine green field. The color was striking—green field, green seats, green scoreboard. Simply magic. Ferris Bueller had to share Wrigley Field with 39,000 fans on his day off. I got to share it with a sprinkler.

Several years ago, I wrote a piece for a writing program on *Sacred Places, Sacred Spaces*. The gist of it was to describe the place most special to you. I chose Wrigley Field. There is nothing like coming up the stairs out of the bowels of the park to see that majestic green field. It takes my breath away—every time! Where else are 39,000-plus fans all together on their purpose? They all root for a Cub victory, united as one. The piece is stored in the permanent collection of the Field Museum in Chicago.

I was born this way. Dad was at the firehouse in 1956, and being in that location right next to the ballpark, he's a Cubs fan. I was born in 1958, so it's literally in my blood; I don't have a choice. Going all the way back, even my mom, long before she met my father, used to watch Cub games. We've always been North Siders; it's been something that's been in the family. My mother used to go to Ladies Days years ago. Both my mother and I will turn on the TV and watch a Cubs game. We don't need the male of the household home to watch a Cubs game. In fact, when Dad went to the firehouse and she knew a Cubs game was on, that was the perfect time to do her ironing. She could set up in front of the TV, and she could watch the game and be entertained and do her mindless housework, and that's how we saw the hot-dog stand fire. All of a sudden she looks at the TV and gawks because there he is putting out the fire in the right grandstand. I tried to get the tape from WGN. I would have loved to have that tape and give it to Dad for Father's Day. They said, "We don't have anything documented, and it's all a mess."

When I was a kid, we would do the family outings once a year. It was fun to see Johnny Bench. I was eleven years old during the '69 Cubs, when they were a hot commodity. I was coming home from school to catch the last inning of the game and watch Ron Santo click his heels as they went to the clubhouse after a win. That was great. You always wanted to see that win at the end of that day. That's when they played day baseball. I didn't get to see as many games, either. It was a big deal to come home and be able to see the last inning.

Many, many years ago, probably about that same time, my mom surprised my brother and I one day. She said she was taking us someplace, but we had no idea. We were at a car dealer, and all of a sudden Don Kessinger pulled up and we stood there in line. I look like a dork in the picture. We have little pieces of paper that he signed. He had a glossy picture he signed for us, too. He said to my mother, "Do you want the kids to come behind the desk with me?" So my brother and I stood behind him at the desk. So we thought this was the greatest thing in the world. Don Kessinger was huge for us.

I see Cub numbers, and my brain thinks of who had that number before.

I see Cub numbers, and my brain thinks of who had that number before. One of our guys has "2" on, and I'm thinking, "That's Leo Durocher's number. How could you possibly wear that as a player?" If I see anybody with "11," I think of Kessinger. Beckert is "18" and Rick Monday was "7." Of course, he's later.

Ryne Sandberg Was Just a Regular Guy Who Some Days Wore a Cape

Jo Ann Williams-Krumwiede

In her late fifties, Jo Ann Williams-Krumwiede has been a Die-Hard Cubs fan for over twenty-five years. She grew up in the western suburbs of Chicago and is the certifications manager for a local steel and aluminum distribution company.

I remember vaguely when I was nine years old, my parents would get into friendly arguments over baseball games on the television. My mom was a Cubs fan and my dad was a Dodgers fan. I never paid much attention at the time. My dad would sit in his big easy chair, watching a baseball game and I would come into the room and look over at him, and he'd be sleeping. I would go over to the TV and turn the knob to change the station to my favorite afterschool program, *Garfield Good*, and Dad would yell, "Don't touch that dial!!" I'd say, "But daddy, you're sleeping!" and he'd say, "No I'm not, I'm just resting my eyes." My dad, John Richard Williams, was a cool guy. He once told me we were related to Ted Williams, the famous Boston Red Sox player, but at the same time that didn't mean anything to me. After all I was only a little girl then.

"But daddy, you're sleeping!" and he'd say, "No I'm not, I'm just resting my eyes."

In 1966, after I got married, my parents and brothers moved out west to Reno, Nevada. I didn't get interested in baseball until 1982, the year my father passed away. It was because my mom had a really rough time watching her Cubs after my dad was gone—especially when they played the Dodgers. She no longer had Dad to engage in friendly rivalry with, so she would occasionally call me during a game, just to have someone to talk to. This was the beginning of my becoming a Cubs fan.

I started watching the Cubs games whenever I could, just so I'd have something to share with Mom, and before I knew it, I was

91

hooked. In 1984, I knew every player, his position, and his jersey number. I will never forget the afternoon of my birthday, June 23. I was sitting on the couch folding laundry, watching a Cubs game. They were playing a home game at Wrigley. They were down by two runs in the bottom of the ninth with one man on, when my all-time favorite Cub, Ryne Sandberg, steps to the plate. I said out loud to the TV, "Come on, Ryno—hit me a two-run homer for my birthday!" He promptly cracked the next pitch out of the ballpark! I jumped off the couch, dumping the laundry basket on the floor as I squealed with delight. He tied the game! Then in the bottom of the eleventh, game still tied, Ryno come up to bat again. I yelled at the TV, "Make my day, Ryno—hit another one and win this thing for me!" while thinking another home run would be against all odds. Ryno didn't let me down. Next pitch he hit the game-winning walk-off homer! On my birthday! I'll never forget it! I was pretty much alone in my worship of the Cubs, except my mom. No sooner was that game over when the phone rang. Her excited voice said, "How was THAT for a birthday present?" We had a good laugh over it. But it was a long-distance phone call. I really had no family or friends who lived near me that shared my love of the Cubs. My husband was not a Cubs fan; in fact he wasn't even a sports fan—he was into rebuilding cars. But he loved me and enjoyed making me happy, so one Saturday afternoon he took me by the hand and said, "Come on, we're going for a drive." He wouldn't tell me where we were going, just that I would like it. We pulled into the parking lot of the Edward Hines Lumber Company in St. Charles. When we got inside, it was very crowded, and I was a bit puzzled as to what was going on. Then I realized why my husband brought me here . . . all these people were standing in line waiting to get Jody Davis's autograph! Oh my God, I almost fainted! I was so embarrassed at meeting a celebrity that I couldn't speak to him when I got up to the table. He signed my picture and handed it to me, and I finally managed to squeak out a "thank you." When we got back to the car, I said to my husband, "I can't believe you did that for me!" I was so touched that he would stand in line for over an hour with me just so I could meet Jody Davis in person and get his autograph.

Then, the following year on my next birthday, he decided to surprise me with two tickets to a Cub game at Wrigley Field. I will never forget the moment we walked up those steps into the ballpark! The view of the field was so breathtaking it overwhelmed me and brought tears to my eyes! My husband thought I was crazy to get so emotional. He just didn't understand but he suffered through it for my sake.

The view of the field was so breathtaking it overwhelmed me and brought tears to my eyes!

Over the years, I began collecting Cubs stuff, everything from a coffee cup and beer mug to the usual hats and T-shirts. On my 35th birthday, my husband gave me a Cubs home white jersey with the pinstripes. He had the No. 35 put on the back so I would always remember what birthday I got it for. I don't think any Cubs player had the No. 35 at the time so it was every more special . . . meant just for me. I still have the jersey.

My mom passed away in 1994, and I miss her still. In August 2004, on what would have been my mom's eighty-seventh birthday, I took my daughter, Kim, to her first Cubs game. She is all grown now and has four boys of her own, but had never been to Wrigley Field. I would love to go more often, but it's hard to get tickets and way more expensive than it used to be. But I decided to honor my mom's memory by making her birthday a mother-daughter day at the ballpark. I wish she could have shared it with us.

I let Kim borrow one of my Cubs hats and a Cubs shirt. We drove down to Wrigley Field and got there around 10:30 for a 1:20 game. We parked about ten blocks away, but already there were droves of people, all decked out in their Cubs gear, heading for the ballpark. I hadn't been to Wrigley in many years, and as we walked up those steps, I remembered how I'd cried the first time I'd been there. The feelings came flooding back. Kim saw the emotion in my face, and understood. I think the awesomeness of it struck her like it did everyone who enters The Friendly Confines. We got there early enough to stand down by the wall on the third base side and watch batting practice. I pointed out some of the players, Nomar Garciaparra, Mark

Prior. She didn't know who they were, she's still new at this, but she could sense my excitement. Unfortunately, the Cubs lost that day. But the Cubs could lose all 162 games every year, and I will forever be a Die-Hard. It's unconditional love. Maybe next year . . .

What's the difference between B*rry B*nds and Government Bonds? Government Bonds mature.

A Cubbie Fan through the Grace of God and the Grace of the Cubs

Jennifer Glick

Jennifer Kay (Barrett) Glick, 34, was born in Chicago, raised in the western burbs, and now lives in Savannah, Georgia. Her dad grew up on the North Side on Addison Street. He and her Mom met at Butch McGuire's on Division Street. Her only sister Elizabeth, who was two years younger, died suddenly when she was fifteen, in 1992.

I n 1988 Mark Grace was a rookie. This was where my love of the Cubs got serious . . . watching every game throughout the summer with my sister Elizabeth and our neighbor and best friend, Cindy. Every game. Those were great summers at that age. We knew every player. We made up cheers for different players and for different points in the game. They came mostly from softball cheers from Cindy and Elizabeth's Hustler softball teams. Here are some that I remember:

"We need a hit to run, a run to score, and a score to win, so let's hit!"

"Show me where you live!"

And a personal favorite: "Ya know, Grace, you got a hot face."

Of course, I had a crush on Mark Grace. When other girls my age had posters of movie stars on their walls, I had posters of Mark Grace. When he was a rookie in 1988, we were at Harry Caray's restaurant and Dad said something to the waitress about who our favorite player was. Mark Grace was there with his family. We got to go to his table and get his autograph on a Harry Caray's menu. I got his autograph again in 1991 when my boyfriend, Steve, took me to M. Hyman and Sons in Oak Brook where Mark was signing autographs. I got my picture taken with him too, and that picture made my high school yearbook. I remember screaming and jumping up and down when the Diamondbacks won the World Series

When other girls my age had posters of movie stars on their walls, I had posters of Mark Grace.

in 2001. I was probably the only person in America rooting for the Diamondbacks after September 11, but I wanted Mark to get a ring.

I remember . . . Cubs spring training in 1989 and 1990 seasons. Those were the best family vacations. Hohokam Park, the sun, baseball in an intimate setting, that was that best . . . I remember . . . going to a game in September of 1989 with a group of girlfriends and the Cubs went ahead of the Cards for good that season. After the game we all bought ST. LOUIS SUCKS T-shirts . . . I remember . . . the day before senior prom, "Senior Ditch Day," and Steve and I went to a Cubs game. I wore a T-shirt that said BASEBALL FOREVER. Steve didn't stick around forever, but my love for baseball has.

> I wore a T-shirt that said BASEBALL FOREVER. Steve didn't stick around forever, but my love for baseball has.

My husband, Chris, got me to love M*A*S*H and college football. I got him to like baseball and love the Cubs. We try to get to a Cubs game at least once a year. Now that we're far away, it's tough, but whenever I go home to Chicago in the summer, a Cubs game always gets fit into the schedule. And I've learned to tolerate Braves-Cubs games in Atlanta. If that is my only chance to see the Cubs that year that I got, it's worth it. But there is way too much besides baseball going on at Turner Field. Wrigley is way more pure.

My most vivid memory of the Wrigley bleachers is when bleacher tickets were still sold day-of-game only. They were four dollars then. Mom would take Elizabeth and I downtown and we'd get in line early, standing up against the outside brick wall. One time we were really early in line and we didn't stop for food or pop on our way up to our seats, we just went straight up there. I ran up the ramp, I was the first one up there, the first one in the bleachers. It was so green, so big, so peaceful. Really, it was like heaven.

I remember . . . Game 5 of the NLDS in Atlanta, 2003. I saw the Cubs win a playoff game in person! Central Division champs. Kerry Wood. I was just speechless when they won. I was almost crying, almost screaming, but just speechless, jumping up and down with my mouth wide open, like was I really witnessing this?! I couldn't believe it. My first-ever live playoff game and they win and it had to be their year. And then the NLCS happens. It's almost like it wasn't even the same season. It's still hard for me to believe that unbelievable high and unbelievable low really happened right next to each other like that. I just said to Chris the other day, "Was that really the same year?" It just doesn't seem real.

There were little funny things about that playoff game I remember. The computer printout ticket we had, the awesome seats, the ball Chris caught from Gary Sheffield, all the Cubs fans around us with the same computer printout tickets, people that had driven all day from Chicago and people from Richmond, Nashville, Tampa, all over, all Cubs fans. It was awesome it was like Wrigley South. We drove home that night, got home at 4 a.m. and went to work the next day.

I remember . . . two times I got to step on Wrigley's outfield grass. One time was one of the Photo Days back in 1989. I was wearing my Mark Grace T-shirt and the players came out of the clubhouse and walked along this red rope to pose for pictures with fans and Mark said, "nice shirt" to me and I thought that was the coolest. We didn't get our picture taken with him, we took a picture with Shawon Dunston though. I picked some outfield grass then that I still have in a Ziploc bag in a scrapbook. I made a whole scrapbook about the 1989 season. The second time I was on the outfield grass, I laid flat on my back in the grass and it was so soft. That was the best feeling.

I love the way the game is played. Strategy. The pitcher against the hitter. Every moment counts. It's a thinking-man's game. I may have begun my love of the Cubs with a schoolgirl crush, but I know the game now. I know other players and understand the strategy and keep up with the stats, watch other games, watch every World Series. I even go to the games of the minor-league team here, the Savannah Sand Gnats. Have gone by myself to the college tournament, the Memorial Health Diamond Classic. When it's a beautiful day here on a weekend and I don't have anything planned, I go out to Grayson Stadium and just relax and wish I was at Wrigley.

I remember . . . the Cubs Convention and taking a picture of Cindy, Elizabeth, and I on a couch with Harry Caray. . . . Now, in Savannah,

I love listening to the radio broadcasts, Ron Santo and Pat Hughes. I love those guys. I listen to them through the Internet radio. I feel like I'm home again. It sounds just like home . . . "This Old Cub." I just don't understand why Ron Santo is not in the Hall of Fame. I just don't get that.

Following the Cubs keeps me closer to Elizabeth now that she's gone. Keeps me connected to Mom and Dad. No matter what was going on as a family, the Cubs were the one constant, the one thing we could talk about when there was nothing else, when I was being a typical teenager. I feel closest to Elizabeth when I'm listening to the Cubs, watching one of their games or at Wrigley. Time just stops at Wrigley. All your worries, your problems, they go away. For those three-plus hours, time just stops. I always feel close to heaven when I'm at Wrigley Field.

Time just stops at Wrigley. All your worries, your problems, they go away.

Wrigley Field—baseball fans' cottage by the lake.

It's Hard to Cheer with a Broken Heart

Sharon Boudreau McLain

Sharon Boudreau McLain has been around baseball players her entire life . . . first as a daughter of Hall-of-Fame player, manager, and announcer **Lou Boudreau** and as wife of Denny McLain, baseball's last thirty-game winner. Before McLain, her husband of forty-five years, she was the steady girlfriend of Kenny Hubbs, the young Cubs star who was killed at age twenty-two when the plane he was piloting crashed in the Utah mountains. For several years, Mrs. McLain spelled her first name "Sharyn."

I t was funny because my family was not White Sox fans, we were Cub fans. It was difficult back then because where we lived it was White Sox territory in Harvey, Illinois. That was dad's hometown on the Chicago South Side. We had the rivalry with the Sox kids we hung around with.

Kenny Hubbs was a special guy. I really fell head over heels for him. I met him at the airport when I'd go to pick up my dad. I graduated high school in '61. That was when he first came up. He only played a few games,

> Kenny Hubbs was a special guy. I really fell head over heels for him.

and in 1962 he was the National League Rookie of the Year. We dated that season and it continued until the next season. We had a few problems due to him being a Mormon. The distance was also a problem. He would go back home to California when the season was over and that didn't help.

Lou Boudreau: In 1942 the Cleveland Indians paid player-manager Lou Boudreau $25,000—$5,000 for playing and $20,000 for managing. That ruse allowed the Indians to adequately compensate their best everyday player without upsetting the other players or increasing their payroll.

99

After high school, I was a bank teller. It was awful when I heard about his plane going down. I had the radio on. I was sitting in my living room and the news of the crash came on. I was breathless and in shock. I couldn't believe it. I called our mutual friend that lived in my area to see if she had heard anything about it. I was the one that told her. She was going to try and get a hold of Mr. and Mrs. Hubbs. They were terrific people. Kenny was flying a friend of his back home after a golf outing. They flew into a snowstorm and it blinded him or he lost his direction somehow. He just loved to fly. In spring training in 1962 he showed me what he was going to fly. It was parked up in the Arizona mountains somewhere. I thought he was nuts. I told him, "You've got to be crazy." It was just a one-engine, tiny plane.

My friends, maybe they thought I was crazy. I just loved going to the ball games. I loved baseball and I always wanted to marry a ballplayer. I always went to the ball games with my dad. I can remember games more in Kansas City when my dad was managing Kansas City his first year. It was awesome. People always treated you a little special. You got the great seats. You got to see the ballplayers afterwards. You got autographs. It was a great childhood.

We always lived in Harvey. We would go wherever Daddy was when school was out in the summer. As soon as school was going to start again, we'd go back home. It was unusual to my friends. Dad passed in 2001.

Kenny's mom and dad came and visited our mutual friend in town and I would go over there. After Kenny's crash, I had a special relationship with Mr. Hubbs. He was a very sweet man. I would drop them a line every once in awhile. I would get little notes from them. Eventually, it stopped.

I used to love to watch Kenny play. I thought any ball hit to him was an out. He was a good ballplayer. It's really a shame because he loved playing and loved the game. He would have stayed in it as long as he could have, probably would have been the greatest Cub second baseman of modern times and would have made the Hall of Fame. He was terrific on and off the field.

Denny McLain and I got married in '63.

Denny McLain and I got married in '63. When he pitched the first no-hitter, that's when I met him. That was in Harlan, Kentucky. He had called me after the White Sox had protected Dave DeBusschere and Bruce Howard instead of him. He was going to quit. He really wanted to play with the Chicago team. But the Detroit Tigers picked him up. When Denny was pitching for the White Sox farm team in Clinton, Iowa, he would drive back to Chicago to see me after the games. The Clinton general manager arranged a deal with the toll takers on the Mississippi Bridge. When Denny paid his toll, they called the GM who then called the Highway Patrol.

There's an ironic sidebar to the Kenny Hubbs tragedy. His friend growing up in Colton, California, was Jay Dahl. Jay was an excellent pitcher and started the final game of the 1962 season for the Houston Colt-45s, now called the Houston Astros. Dan Rather was the P.A. announcer for Houston that year. Houston decided to start nine rookies that last day of that first-ever Colts/Astros season. In doing so, Jay Dahl became the first person born after WWII ended to make the Major Leagues. The year after Kenny Hubbs died, Jay Dahl was killed in a car accident after a Carolina League game. Two great guys, two excellent Major League ballplayers from the same little town, and neither one saw their twenty-third birthday.

Hey! Hey! I've got a ball _not_ signed by Pete Rose.

The Cubs: The Promise of a Lover, the Performance of a Husband

Deb Kolze

Deb Kolze, a self-professed Cub nut from Wood Dale, Illinois, found the perfect mate when she was introduced to Doug Kolze of Bensenville. Deb is a professional organizer who celebrated her fiftieth birthday on 03/03/03.

My mom was really into it; she loved to go to Wrigley. I was about ten when I went to my first game. I'd see it on TV and I wasn't too interested. Then I walked up the stairs to heaven right behind the plate. My father would drive around and drive around looking for a place to park because he was too cheap to pay to park. We'd finally park and we'd have to walk a mile. My father was a slow-moving man until it came to either golf or baseball. He worked nights; he was a printer. To get him up before noon was unbelievable unless it was for golf or baseball. He just about raced to the ballpark from wherever we parked. I watched him with his baggy pants with the cuffs and his long-sleeve shirt that was rolled up a little bit, and he was wearing a fedora. He always wore a hat, usually a fedora. He was fifty-two, maybe fifty-three. He was in all of this hot clothing in August almost racing two at a time up these stairs behind the plate. He was standing at the top of the stairs and I'm holding onto my mother's hand going up the stairs, Dad stood there, put his hands on his hips and just looked. I was like, "What the heck is he looking at?" At ten, I didn't say it in those words, but when I got to the top of the stairs I saw it all myself. It was love at first sight. Then I started watching the games on TV. I was aware of the Cubs. At that time we had already traded Lou Brock and everybody was all upset about that. There were all kinds of fear that we were going to trade

Billy Williams. Of course, there were the '69 Cubs that excited everybody. I had a boyfriend who was a Cubs fan and we were crazy about the Cubs in '69 and even through the '70s I was one of those two people sitting with an open umbrella. There were 3,000 people in the whole ballpark. I would go. I just didn't care, I

There were all kinds of fear that we were going to trade Billy Williams.

would go. I went to lots of openers. All of a sudden it was "the thing" to do and it was too crowded. If others didn't want to go, sometimes I'd go by myself. My husband, Doug, is a big Cubs fan. When we met he asked me what my favorite team was. I put my head down, real embarrassed and ashamed to have to admit that I was a big Cubs fan. He said, "Oh, I've got season tickets." About that time is when I jumped up on his lap and asked him to marry me. Not exactly true, but that probably went through my head.

Mark Grace, like Billy Williams, was always like the second fiddle. The last game in 1999, WGN had me on camera in the bottom of the eleventh inning crying for about fifteen or twenty seconds. I had phone calls from all over the country. The game meant nothing. This was really a bad game. It went into the eleventh inning and Mark Grace was up. He was tied for the most doubles of the decade. He hit a ball into the corner. He could have stopped at second and nobody would have said a thing, but he went all the way to third. The game meant crap, but he's still the baseball guy. During rain delays Mark Grace would be out on the field playing bucket ball like Bozo's Circus with fans. Then he'd run to the dugout and sign a glove or a bat and give it away. He'd be on top of Murphy's and be playing catch with somebody down on the ground. You could catch him at Sluggo's in Mesa, then called Harry's and Steve's, in the middle of a bit and you could say, "Can I have your autograph?" and he'd sign. His mother sat in front of me at a playoff game, and I heard her say that Mark would play at Wrigley for free. He's a baseball man. On top of that, I find him attractive. It's a whole other thing.

We used to have these seats, eighteen rows behind first base at Wrigley. I always knew when Grace was going to hold somebody on first base. So right before he would put his right foot up against the bag and lean over and put his hands on his knees. I would call out "Hold 'em, Mark!" He would take his stance and bend over and I would say, "Thank you!" I would do this at spring training, I would do it at Wrigley. My poor husband would sit there and roll his eyes. When they're in uniform they're mine, I'm paying to see them, I can yell at them, I can boo them, I can cheer them, they're mine. Once they're out of their uniforms and in street clothes I leave them alone, I'm not going to bother anybody. Unless they're in a group of people and they're talking and you feel comfortable approaching them. Grace was standing in a bar one time and a friend pushed me right up to him and said, "Mark this is one of your biggest fans, could I take a picture with you two?" There he is with his arm on my shoulder, "Ah, he's touching me!" and my hand is next to his hand, but it's also touching his leg! It was a very wonderful experience. . . .

I would accidentally walk into the men's room and there would be Mark Grace in Speedos, cowboy boots, and a cowboy hat and nothing else. It's my fantasy.

I've been going to spring training for sixteen years; 2000 was his last year at spring training. The very last inning he looked right at me and threw a ball to me. I was so excited. At any event, I like to sit by the restrooms. That's not probably the most desirable place in the restaurant to sit, but I like to sit there because then maybe I could see him going in and out of the men's room. Then maybe I would have too many cocktails and I would accidentally walk into the men's room and there would be Mark Grace and he would just happen to be in Speedos, cowboy boots, and a cowboy hat and nothing else. It's my fantasy. Play along, okay?

Several years ago there was that Got Milk? thing going on with the milk mustache and my friend got me a full-length Mark Grace Got Milk poster. She also got me into the Cubs Convention. She brought me this Mark Grace Got Milk poster and we decided to tuck "him" into my bed at the Hilton Towers. I didn't realize they had turndown service. That was a little bit embarrassing having a poster of Mark Grace tucked in. Later on my friend said to me, "How do you like your Mark Grace poster?" I said, "You know what, Judy? I really need to get another one. Last night I was drinking too many margaritas, got naked and rolled all over it and it's wrinkled." I made that up, it wasn't true. But she did get me another poster.

They say if you mail Mark Grace anything he will sign it and mail it back to you. He's just a baseball guy who gets the whole picture. He was not a fast runner, he was a good fielder, and he was good for a clutch hit and an occasional home run. He just has the whole depth, the whole package for being a baseball guy compared to a lot of these players today who are just in it for the money or the fame. Oh my God, I cried when Mark Grace left. I was just so excited he got a World Series ring with Arizona in 2001. . . .

My husband and I, from the time we met were taking vacations. We went to Jamaica, Mexico, and every year he said, "Where would you like to go on vacation?" One year I said, "Well you know, I've never been to spring training." Finally, the year before we were getting married I said, "We really can't afford a big vacation, how about if we go for just five days to spring training?" We did, and we haven't really gone anywhere else since. Now we do little trips to see the Cubs on the road. We were in **Denver** last week. Last year we went to Cleveland. We've been to Milwaukee a lot, Cincinnati, San Francisco, and Pittsburgh. I love PNC Park in Pittsburgh; it's such a big surprise. Jacobs Field in Cleveland and Coors Field in Denver are like twins. They look exactly alike. They're supposed to be modeled after Wrigley and I don't really see it. But PNC is a big surprise. You can take a boat to get there. Where they drop you off there are all these bars and restaurants and fun stuff. Pittsburgh was a big surprise, we didn't expect what we got. It's a beautiful city. . . .

We make away-game plans way early. For Denver we were drinking margaritas in the basement at the end of January. Don't let me drink margaritas and put me on a computer. Do you know how many bricks I have from Wrigley? I got a bill for over 400 bucks. I'm still hiding the

Denver: At Coors Field in Denver—in the upper desk—there is one row of purple seats that encircle the stadium designating the "mile-high" level.

bricks around the house because I forgot I ordered them. I might be sitting there drinking a margarita and get on the darn computer and order more. I gave one to Doug for Christmas. I've got two more wedged in with some of my work stuff. So I was on the computer and we were drinking margaritas, and I don't really drink that much. One or two drinks and I'm blasted. Just don't let me get on the computer. So we made our Denver arrangements the end of January . . . Every time I go to a game with Carol Ann Bliss, a really big Cubs fan that I met at spring training, something weird happens. We met at a bar in Mesa where there used to be a radio program that was called *Dobson Ranch Fun Party*. They had a live radio show. My husband and I were sitting at the bar and started talking to her. Sometimes Doug wouldn't want to go to a game or couldn't go and I'd say to Carol Ann, "Hey, do you want to go with me?" About once a year we'd go to a game. Almost every time we would go to a game, something weird happened. About six years ago there was the "no rain rain-out game." It was a Tuesday night game, and they had a rain delay, but it wasn't raining. We sat there for about an hour and they called the game on account of rain and it never rained. It was a **no-rain rain delay**. We got there at 6 . . . 7:05, 8:05, 8:30, they still didn't start the game. I went downstairs at Wrigley to my friend John and said, "John, why isn't the game going on?" He went into his office and said, "Look," and he showed me the Doppler. There was a storm but it stopped at Western Avenue. They were waiting for it to come but it never went any further. They decided to call the game anyway, the game never happened. That was one of the weirdest things.

The other time I was with her, it was a Friday afternoon. The Cubs music people play the YMCA song when the other team needs to change a pitcher. We were sitting in Section 130 about eighteen rows behind the Cubs dugout. We looked over and somewhere between the plate and first base there was a guy doing "YMCA" but appar-

no-rain rain delay: On June 15, 1976, the Pirates were "rained in" at the Houston Astrodome. Ten inches of rain flooded the Astrodome parking lots and access roads. The teams made it to the park, but the umpires, fans, and stadium personnel did not.

ently he was standing on his hands because he was doing it with his legs. He was splitting his legs for the Y, making an M, he was doing it with his legs. It was really cute. Everybody was cheering and getting all excited about it. That was the same game that a guy managed to run onto the field and right up to the pitcher. The guy took off his T-shirt, pulled off his shorts, and stood there naked looking at the Cubs pitcher and nothing happened. Carol Ann and I are cracking up, we're laughing. Where is security? What's going on here? The guy is standing there naked, then he decides to turn around and flashed a double bird at the broadcasting booth.

The guy is standing there naked, then he decides to turn around and flashed a double bird at the broadcasting booth.

The pitcher is still standing there dumbfounded. Here's this naked man. Finally, security gets out there. They don't make him put his shorts or T-shirt back on. They just scoop him up and drag him up the aisle however they could get him out. I'm thinking, "At least they could have covered him up." There might be some little kids in there or grandmas that could be upset. They dragged him off! It's not a visual that you would want to dwell on. My dad always said, "You don't need a fence if you don't have a dog." That might explain why the guy wasn't wearing pants. . . .

Cubs games are my top favorite thing for as long as I could remember. Summertime would be a lot less exciting without the Cubbies. I love the roller coaster ride. I made a poster in 1998. I'm going to pull it out for the next game we go to. Just cross off '98 and 2003 and put big bold numbers "2008" It's a poster I made, it looks like an old wooden type of roller coaster. I've got people in the cars. One has a green face, like he's going to get sick. I really do like the roller coaster of the whole thing. I just love it right now we're up . . . 2006 was the worst, stinking, lousiest, crappiest, worst baseball I had ever experienced in my life. I was absolutely embarrassed and ashamed of them. This year they're up again. In 2006, instead of singing during "Take Me Out to the Ball Game" "If they don't win it's a shame," I sang "Since they don't win it's a shame." I changed the words. This year I'll sing it right, they're doing good.

If You Want Breakfast in Bed, Sleep in the Kitchen

My mom has been a fan since she was four years old. She used to go to Ladies Day with my grandmother, and they'd sit out in the bleachers. My mom says, "We'd sit in the bleachers before it became yuppie." My grandma would drink beer. My mom was a little entrepreneur. She'd go and get towels from the bathroom and get them wet because it'd be hot out there. She'd sell them to people for a nickel. . . . When she moved out here to California, my dad's friends had season tickets for the Padres. Every time the Cubs would come, she'd go to the games. This one game, we were in the dugout seats. A lot of corporate people own them. There was this pretty little blonde in the front row. A Cubbie hit a home run, and my mom went, "Yeah! Yeah!" The little blonde turned around and looked at her and said, "Are you rooting for the Cubs?" My mom said, "I have to, Billy Williams is my son." The girl went, "Cool!" This blonde didn't even know who Billy Williams was, certainly didn't know he was black. Airhead.

My mom got a picture taken with Billy Williams. She brought it back the next time the Cubs were in town—this was when Billy was a coach—and he signed it, "To my Mom, Billy Williams. Hall of Fame '87." He was a nice guy. She'd give him sunflower seeds all the time or whatever he wanted because at the dugout seats you get snacks. My mom would call it "eating for the cycle." Because you could sit there from the beginning and get whatever you wanted. Those were the greatest seats.

—Lisa Gallagher, 44,
Park Ridge native

I t's all my mom's fault—she had to move to Wrigleyville after the divorce. She had an apartment on Newport Street, right between Clark Street and the el tracks. See, up until then, I did not watch baseball . . . I always saw my papa "watching" the game (really, the back of his eyelids!) so I figured why did I want to take a nap? All of that changed when we went to see our first game at Wrigley Field. We sat in the leftfield bleachers. My instructions were to cheer for both teams since they were playing the Pirates, my grandpa's favorite team. She also said it would drive the fans nuts, cheering for both teams—sounded good to me! I also remember everybody teasing Jose Cardenal a lot. I don't know what happened that day—the whole scene just captivated me. I was hooked. So, on weekends, we were visiting Mom, and, if the Cubs were in town, we went to the games. We would eat at Chester's before the game. I would get my usual fried hot dog, French fries with gravy, and Bosco chocolate milk—what a combo! But I loved it because they brought the whole bottle of Bosco to the table so I could make the milk as chocolaty as I wanted to. That was cool to a seven-year-old. The unusual thing about all of this is that I turned out to be the baseball fan and my brother did not. So, in our family, it was a mom-daughter thing, and the dad-son couldn't care less about baseball. In 1976, my mom moved to Texas and left me in Indiana suburbia hell with no way to get to the games. I still followed the Cubs . . . I would take my dad's transistor radio outside in the summer so I could listen to the games while playing outside. I didn't make it back to a Cubs game until 1985. I took my then boy-friend, now husband, who is not a baseball fan—go figure. It was in September, and they were playing the Reds. **Pete Rose** was one hit away from tying Ty Cobb's record. The Cubs did not allow him a hit that day. The excitement in the stands—the Cubs fans cheering when he flied out, and the Reds fans booing the Cubs fans. My husband did admit that baseball is much more fun at the ballpark than on TV. The

Pete Rose: Pete Rose is enshrined in the Summit County (Ohio) Boxing Hall of Fame.

people behind us were trying to start the wave, and the people next to us turned around and said, "We DON'T do the wave in Wrigley Field!" Classic Cub fans! My mom moved back in 1994, and we went to the games a lot just like old times. We went to Opening Day one year and only lasted into the seventh inning—my feet were numb. We went to McDonald's to warm up, have some coffee and listen to the rest of the game. I swore I would never go to another Opening Day because it was so cold. Never say never! The next year, I went with some friends from work, and, wouldn't you know, it was even colder! I said to my friends, "You know, to freeze to death watching them lose is insane!" So, we left in the sixth inning!

We went to the Cubs Convention several times—even said hello to Harry Caray! Mom got sick and passed in 2000, and I'd like to think that perhaps she is helping the Cubs from above; if she could do it, she would! But, next year is here! GO CUBS!

—Sheerin Moss

When my dad took me to my first Cubs game, I did not have any idea the effect that Wrigley Field would have on me as a Cub fan. I did not put the two together, really. Somehow I was watching the Cubs play in this ballpark that absolutely was/is the greatest park there is! The feeling of the team itself sprang from that . . . it was like "Wow!" . . . the Cubs should be happy and grateful, playing in a park so wonderful as Wrigley Field. And then, you just started to love watching the Cubs play there—they became THE team to watch! My dad who was a fan way back in the day of the '45 World Series, which he was able to go to, shared the Cubs with me and my niece. That was back in the early '70s, and we have been fans ever since! As a young girl, I would come home from school and watch the Cubs on TV when they played at Wrigley because it was like a "fix" to see Wrigley Field on TV and remember how great it felt to go to a Cubs game there. I was born in the Chicago Heights area and grew up and moved out of state. But wherever I lived, the Cubs were the team I would root for! I will always be grateful to my dad for caring enough to share the Cubs and Wrigley Field with me.

The strength of that feeling made me want to pass that on to my own kids. We took all five of our kids to Wrigley Field throughout the years. My son became a big Cubs fan. I was so proud. In his art class, he made a clay/ceramic Cubs hat that he gave to me as a present for Mother's Day one year. I treasure it! He loved Ryne Sandberg—had his No. 23 shaved in his head with the haircut he had one year when we went to Chicago to a game. I was happy because he was able to take his best friend with us and share Wrigley Field with his best friend two weeks before my son was killed. It was hard to go back to Wrigley Field after that, but I will tell you this—when I do go, my son is with me because every game I go back to, somehow, the Cubs always win. It does not matter what team the Cubs are playing at the time, the Cubs end up winners! It is always a great feeling to go there. I know my dad felt that too, for the last game he saw both Sammy and Moises hit back-to-back home runs. The Cubs won on that day when he left to join my son, watching the Cubs play with the rest of the baseball greats, watching the magic that is truly Wrigley Field and the Cubs. That is what takes hold of every Cubs fan—through the heartbreaks, through the moments of great joy, true Cubs fans understand that feeling and that is what keeps them Cubs fans . . . always!

> He was able to take his best friend with us and share Wrigley Field with his best friend two weeks before my son was killed.

—Carol Kibler, 45,
St. Paul, Minnesota

Our dad was an avid Cubs fan. Many Sunday afternoons during the Depression days of the '30s he sat huddled in front of the Crosley console listening to play-by-play broadcasts from WGN radio.

During better times in the '40s, Dad occasionally drove to Chicago—my brother, David, in the front seat beside him—to watch their beloved Cubs. He liked to drive and was good at

> Without Mom to act as navigator though, he often got lost.

111

it. Without Mom to act as navigator though, he often got lost. He had no trouble getting there. Coming back was the problem. Sometimes he wandered around in the dark for hours, arriving home close to dawn the next morning. Dad joked that one time the attendant at the toll booth greeted him with the words, "YOU again?"

His enthusiasm was catching. After husband Harold, son Michael, and I returned to live in Iowa in 1963, we established a family tradition of going into Chicago once or twice each summer. On those trips, we parked on a street midway between Wrigley Field and a small shopping center.

Harold, Dad, David, and Michael headed directly to the ballpark while Mom and I went the other direction, browsed the bookstore, checked out a Ladies Ready-to-Wear Shop, and enjoyed lunch at a charming outdoor café. After eating, we returned to the car where we stashed our packages, then walked over to the ballpark to join our menfolk for the final innings of the game. We like the Cubs too—only in small doses.

Through losses, wins, and wars, David's devotion to the Cubs has never faltered. From the time he was six, he played make-believe baseball using toy metal soldiers. His arena was in the small sandbox next to our house on Kirkwood Street. In it, he carefully laid out a miniature replica of Wrigley Field complete with the buildings across the street.

He "played" a full nine innings, moving the minute figures around the field and calling the game with a pretend microphone. Being realistic, he occasionally let the Cubs lose. But not often. Once in a while they went so far as to win the World Series. His imagination took wings. At the age of twelve, he was another Harry Caray.

His dream was to become a sports announcer, but that was not to be. Most of his working days were spent as a laundry worker at Xavier and Mercy Hospital. That was a loss for listeners. David would have been an excel-

> The Cubs give all of us the opportunity to relax, to let off steam, to laugh at their foibles and at ourselves for getting so involved, to dream of a better tomorrow.

lent "voice." He knew the strategy, the players, and the managers. Still does. Today, sitting in his wheelchair, brought down by crippling Parkinson's disease, he accurately predicts the point in the game when Lou Piniella will change pitchers and reposition the outfield.

The Cubs give David and all of us the opportunity to relax, to let off steam, to laugh at their foibles and at ourselves for getting so involved, to dream of a better tomorrow. I understand there's a mythical church in Chicago, established exclusively for Cub fans. It is known as "The Church of Perpetual Hope." A more apt name could not be found.

—Lois Farley,

Dubuque, Iowa, retired

I was about seven or eight years old when dad sat me down in front of the radio, drew a sketch of a ball field and started me on my love affair with the Cubs. He indicated where each player stood and when the ball was hit, where it went on the field. Dad was the only Cub fan in his "Back of the (Stock) Yards" family. Those were the days of Big Bill Lee, Gabby Hartnett, **Augie Galan,** and my favorites Phil Cavarretta and Stan Hack. Then during the war years we had Bill Nicholson. I was listening that Sunday when he hit four consecutive home runs in two games. Imagine what he would have hit with today's lively ball.

When I was fifteen, the Cubs held Ladies Days on Friday and we got in the park for a very small sum. But we were supposed to be at least sixteen years old, so I would put my hair in an upsweep and try to make myself look older. . . . Taking the streetcars to Wrigley Field was a ride of an about an hour and a half from the South Side, but it didn't matter to me. I was going to see the Cubs play. . . .

Augie Galan: After grounding into a double play in his last at-bat to end the Tigers' pennant run in 1967, Dick McAuliffe went the entire 1968 season without hitting into a double play. Only two others in the history of baseball, with 500+ at-bats, have ever accomplished that feat: Augie Galan (1935) and Craig Biggio (1997).

When I was in high school there was some sort of an award where Cubs tickets were given to students. I received one of the tickets and took off for the ballpark. That day the Cubs were playing the Cardinals and Claude Passeau, No. 13, pitched them to a 13–1 victory. I was with some girls from the North Side and we hung around trying to get autographs, unsuccessfully. When we left the ballpark it was completely empty. We came out a different gate from where I had gone in and my girlfriends went their way and I tried to figure out where I was. It wasn't Clark and Addison where I would catch my ride. Wandering around, I finally saw a man way over to my left and I ran to ask how to get to my corner. It was Claude Passeau! I got his autograph, but I don't think I ever asked him directions. Who needed streetcars? I think I floated home that day.

Years later my husband and I were buying a new car and I thought the salesman looked familiar.

Years later my husband and I were buying a new car and I thought the salesman looked familiar. I asked if he came from the South Side, but he said no. I continued trying to figure out where I might have known him from but was unable to. When we arrived home I asked for the sales slip so that maybe his name would ring a bell. It was Vern Olsen who pitched for the Cubs from 1933 to '42. My husband, a Sox fan, hadn't recognized the name when he was introduced and I never heard it when at the auto dealer. A lost opportunity to declare myself a Cubs fan.

Oh, and one more thing, I remember listening to Bert Wilson announcing. I had the impression that he was the one that started that "Wooop" when the ball came down the net.

—Dolores Kozack, 81,
Chicago

*G*rowing up in Chicago, the Cubs and Wrigley Field played a dominant role in my life. Grade-school field trips took me to Wrigley for an afternoon in the upper deck, munching on french fries and hot dogs. As a teenager, the Addison bus drove me and my best friend to the corner of Clark and Addison, where we would get off and journey into Wrigley for an afternoon of baseball. As an adult, I walked over to Wrigley from my apartment blocks away from The Friendly Confines and enjoyed more of what Wrigleyville had to offer me as a person of legal age—the bars! There are so many to choose from and, at any time of day, before, during, and after a game, you will find crowds of faithful fans toasting one, or ten, to our beloved Cubbies!

I moved from Chicago, after twenty-nine years of living in the best sports city in the world, to our nation's capital. The move took place on July 31, 2003, a sad day for me and the team I love so much. They were losing, what my friends call their "No. 1 fan." What a time to move out of Chicago. If you recall, they began to pick up momentum after the All-Star break, rather than slowly plummet to the bottom of their division, as in years past. "How could this happen to me?" I asked myself. The one and, I know in my heart, not only time, in my adulthood the Cubs were going places, and I was not even there to witness it! September and October were painful months living outside of Chicago, not being able to witness history in the making. I was stuck in D.C., frantically searching for a sports bar that televised WGN—a place where I could cheer on my team with other devoted fans. No—the bar was not a Murphy's or a Wrigleyville sports bar, but I did get to see the Cubs squeeze out win after win. I also converted or at least made many of my fellow co-workers Cubs fans, or fans in the making.

I could not make it back home in October for the games since most were played on weekdays, but I did make it down to Miami for the playoffs against the Marlins. It was not the "magic of Wrigley Field," rather the magic was in the gathering of so many Cubs fans outside of Chicago. It was like having hundreds of your closest friends there to support you as you expectantly, yet nervously, watched as the Cubs inched closer to the World Series.

We all know the outcome of the 2003 season—no need to revisit it—but we also all know, as true Chicagoans do, there is always next year! I may live in D.C., but my true home is Chicago where my heart belongs to the Chicago Cubs.

—Rebecca A. Vesconte, 30,
Washington, D.C.

Flush twice. It's a long way to Comiskey Park.

4
Fandemonium

Starting young . . .

Cubs Fever? No Cure!

Aging Comes at a Bad Time

Dave Stowell

Cub fan Dave Stowell never thought he'd be on the field with Ryne Sandberg and Joe Pepitone, but he found out late in life that some dreams can come true. Still an active farmer in Burlington, Wisconsin, Stowell never had electricity in his house until he was thirteen. He never went to high school but did attend the University of Wisconsin. Even with his hip replaced twice, he was a hit at Randy Hundley's Fantasy Camp.

I 'll be eighty-three in September, and I was loading bales today at the farm. I've been a Cub fan all my life. I always wanted to play baseball, but my dad wouldn't let me. I had to come home and do chores. I never went to high school for that reason after I got out of grade school. I did play fast-pitch softball. When I was thirteen, my dad told me if I wanted to play baseball, I could leave home. You can't leave home when you're thirteen. When I was sixteen, I started playing fast-pitch. I didn't care then if he did kick me out. I was old enough that I could take care of myself.

My first trip to Wrigley Field—or the one I remember the most—was 1950. Some friends went to Chicago to see them play the Cardinals. My friend liked the Cardinals, and I like the Cubs. While going through Chicago, we came up to a stop sign and the police hollered out the window, "When you get through the stop sign, pull over." I pulled over, and he said, "Where are you going?" I said, "I'm going to the ball game." He said, "You know you're speeding." I said, "Well, I was keeping up with traffic." He said, "The traffic you're keeping up with is up in the air somewhere." He said, "You'll have to come down to the station." I said, "I'll miss the ball game." He said, "Well, then, you'll have to come tomorrow." This was on a Sunday. I said, "I can't because I run the threshing machine and they depend on me Monday." "Well," he said, "take it easy the rest of the way down." So,

I guess I talked my way out of it. At the game, the guy who was with me got a ball. I'm not sure who hit the ball, but on the way home we stopped at Gabby Hartnett's restaurant right around Wrigley Field. Gabby signed the ball for my friend. . . .

When I got older, Ernie Banks was my hero. Now, today, Ken Griffey is. I've got I don't know how many of his rookie cards. I hope some day they will be worth something. I could kick myself because I could have had Mickey Mantle rookie cards way back then, but I never collected cards. I didn't start collecting cards until my grandchildren were starting to collect.

I've been farming in Burlington all my life. I try to get down to see the Cubs once a year, but I don't all the time. I get a lot of ribbing from the Brewer fans. I went to the fantasy camp and got my own Cub uniform. Ron Santo told me if I ever came to Chicago, I could get up in the booth with him and Pat Hughes. I asked them about it, and I did get up there.

I went to the Cub fantasy camp in 2002. It was unreal how it all happened. It seems the Lord is in it all the way. I joined a Wellness Center to try to stay active. I met a guy there who had gone to the Phillies fantasy camp. We talked about the Cubs **Randy Hundley called me. I said, "But, I'm an old man."** having one also. I don't have a computer. He said, "Tell your grandson to get on chicagocubs.com and see what they can find out for you." He did.

Randy Hundley called me. I said, "But, I'm an old man." Randy told me that doesn't make any difference. It cost $3,500 and was held in Mesa, Arizona. It was unbelievable. It gives me chills to think about it. They were filming that *This Old Cub* movie about Ron Santo when we were there. I'm in the movie, but you can't see me—I'm in the audience there.

During the week, we played two games a day—one in the morning and one in the afternoon. I couldn't run very well because I've got an artificial hip . . . but they put in a pinch runner for me. I ran the pitching machine during the week. I had to field my position, pitcher. They let me do that; otherwise, I was going to play rightfield. We lost the first game. The second game I had torn my fingernail and was chewing on the fingernail trying to bite it off. The guy on the opposing team said, "Hey, ump, he's doctoring the ball."

My locker was right next to Ryne Sandberg's. He was a terrific guy. I got my picture taken with him. They had videos of every game. I got the videos of the games I got my hits in. I got videos of the meetings in the mornings. I got the videos of the banquet. They gave me such a hard time because I was the "old man." They used these four-letter words so fluently, and I complained about it. They said, "Welcome to the Major Leagues."

Joe Pepitone is a character. He called me the "old goat."

Joe Pepitone is a character. He called me the "old goat," because that's a four-letter word. I told him one day, in front of everybody, "Joe, I knew a guy just like you when I was a kid, and he only went to fourth grade, and he could only spell four-letter words." Everybody just roared. One of the guys on my team was a doctor. He said to me when I left that day, "I got front-row tickets for games in Chicago. You better come look me up. You don't know how many lives you've touched this week." I just couldn't believe it. Joe Pepitone, after all the razzing he did to me, when we left the hotel that day, he said, "Dave, you and I made the camp this year." I didn't even think he liked me because he was always giving me such a hard time. Then, at the banquet, Jody Davis got up because our team won the championship, and he said, "You know, I don't really know what to say. It's pretty hard to get up and make a speech with a Cub championship."

Rooting for the Cubs gives me excitement and peace of mind. The only reason I got DIRECTV is so I can see the Cub games. I have it turned off the first of November, and they turn it back on the first of April. The Cubs have brought a lot of joy to my life. I hope the Cubs can win a World Series in my lifetime.

Mick Kelleher's Home Runs Were Just Extra-Base Triples

Jason Myers

Jason Myers is a lawyer in Arlington, Texas, with the Dallas office of Vinson Elkins. He recently wrote a book on the economic structure of Major League Baseball. The Skokie native is a graduate of Illinois State and SMU Law School.

In the sweltering summer heat, even the top athletes in Major League Baseball need to take an occasional day off to escape the blazing sun for the cool shade of the dugout. On a hot August day in 1979, Mick Kelleher, a reserve utility infielder, took full advantage of an infrequent starting assignment given him so that the regular shortstop could rest. Kelleher, a lifetime .216 hitter entering the 1979 season, was not a household name. Perhaps his greatest claim to fame was that at 5-foot-9 and 176 pounds he instigated a fight with Dave Kingman, 6-foot-6 and 210 pounds, in 1977 when "Kong" came in a bit too hard at Mick to break up a double play. The bench-clearing brawl that ensued between the Cubs and Padres was so intense, many people wondered if the animosity between the two players would continue in the clubhouse when the Cubs signed Kingman as a free agent in the following off-season. Alas, cooler heads prevailed and the two professionals coexisted without incident.

On this day in August 1979, the weather was much the same as it had been for the past several weeks: bright sun that burns through one's skin and humidity so high that even the lightest piece of clothing seems too heavy. The fans in the bleachers were taking advantage of their quick escape from the office by soaking in the rays and a few brews. The crowd ventured to the ballpark to have some fun and watch the game. What they got was the baseball surprise of their lives.

Kelleher's first at-bat was in the bottom of the third. With no one out and a man on first, Kelleher dug into the batter's box against Bert Blyleven. Blyleven, a well-traveled veteran even at that point in his career, was an excellent pitcher and consistent winner although the teams he played on did not always reciprocate. Blyleven worked the count to 1 and 2. He received the signal from the catcher, who set up for a curve ball on the outside part of the plate. Perhaps a bit overconfident in facing Kelleher, Blyleven did not get the movement against the heavy air; Kelleher strode into the hanging curve. With a swing that resembled Mighty Mick from the Bronx rather than the Wee Willie Kelleher, the reserve infielder stroked the ball over the wall in left-center and into the waiting hands of the fans in the bleachers.

As Kelleher rounded the bases, he savored the moment of his first Major League home run. Most of the fans were aware of what they had witnessed. When the stadium announcer told the fans of the significance of the event, Kelleher was summoned out of the dugout for a courtesy tip of the hat.

Blyleven, who was well known for giving up the long-ball, was slightly embarrassed that he gave up the dinger that ended Kelleher's round-tripper drought. But he took a small measure of revenge when he struck out the diminutive infielder in the fifth. When the heat took its toll on Blyleven, he gave way to a pinch hitter in the top of the seventh. The Holland-born redhead joined his teammates on the bench to watch an even more shocking moment.

A middle reliever who has long since faded into obscurity replaced Blyleven in the bottom frame of the inning. After just one out, the heat and sun were starting to weaken the new pitcher as Kelleher strode toward the plate. Mick got ahead in the count 3 and 1. Not wanting to walk the generally weak-hitting Kelleher to put the go-ahead run on first, the pitcher heaved the ball with as much velocity as he could put on it to handcuff Kelleher with an inside pitch. Kelleher pivoted and got the bat around the ball. The ball benefited from a slight breeze blowing toward left. Kelleher glanced up as he rounded first to see the ball clear the wall just inside of the foul pole.

For the first home run, the crowd had jumped for joy. For this home run, they were stunned silent. Suddenly a laughter stemming from their collective disbelief started to erupt. Mick Kelleher, a journeyman middle infielder who made the best use of his glove to stay in the Majors, provided the winning margin with his bat. Mick Kelleher, for at least one game, was a home run king.

Mick Kelleher, for at least one game, was a home run king.

Now before all you aficionados of 1970s baseball go running to your *Baseball Encyclopedia*, you are right. Mick Kelleher never hit a home run in his Major League career. I remember a brief story in the *Sporting News* in the early 1980s about Kelleher hitting a home run in the minor leagues. But as far as Kelleher's Major League career goes he went 1,081 at-bats without a single four-bagger.

The game that was just described did happen, however. It is as real as any other played that day. It occurred not in The Friendly Confines of Wrigley Field but in the back bedroom of a house in Ashville, North Carolina. It was not played on natural grass or **Astroturf** with bats and balls but on cardboard with dice and a fielding chart. The game that took place was played by a twelve-year-old baseball fanatic who spent his summer days and nights watching the games that unfolded in the "Strat-O-Matic All-Star League."

Strat-O-Matic uses dice and probabilities based on real players' actual statistics to recreate a Major League Baseball game. Each player has his own card designed to reflect his real-life performance. When a batter comes up, three dice (one small and two larger dice) are rolled at once. The combined total of the two large dice determines which cell in one of six columns will be used to determine the batter's result. The small die dictates which column is considered. If it

Astroturf: An announcer once asked Tug McGraw about the difference between Astroturf and grass. Tug replied, "I don't know. I have never smoked Astroturf."

turns up as a 1, 2, or 3, the batter's card—based on his abilities as a hitter—will determine the outcome of the at-bat; with a 4, 5, or 6 on the small die, the pitcher's card is utilized. This is how Mick Kelleher could club two long balls in one game. Although Kelleher's card was void of any home runs, Blyleven's proclivity for giving up the gopher ball (430 in his career, ranking him seventh among the all-time Home Runs Allowed leaders) created the possibility that led to the first of Kelleher's clouts.

Strat-O-Matic mirrors the magic of baseball.

Strat-O-Matic does more than mirror the statistical probabilities of the game; it also mirrors the magic of baseball—of being at the game, of playing the game, of following the game, of loving the game. The excitement of seeing something improbable happen at a game flows through to the excitement of having the statistical improbabilities come up at the right time, just as they are most needed. From this, heroes are born, even if they take the shape of a 3-by-5-inch card.

I first played Strat-O-Matic in the early 1970s as a youngster learning the joys of baseball. Like many rookies, I struggled through the first part of my Strat-O-Matic career and built a losing streak that caused me great anguish. I finally reveled in victory in 1972 and it still holds a valued spot in my childhood memories.

By 1979 I took baseball on as my own, relishing every aspect of the game, from poring over box scores to listening to Lou Brock's 3,000th hit over heavy static from KMOX out of St. Louis. I created my Strat-O-Matic All-Star League and spent my time rolling the dice and experiencing the magic. But no moment was more magical than when Mick Kelleher beat the odds to hit these home runs. The Strat-O-Matic gods were smiling on Mick that day—and on me. After Kelleher hit his second home run, I smiled, I jumped for joy, I ran around the house celebrating, having been given a special gift and a new hero.

The game reemerged in my life nearly twenty years later. My wife surprised me at Christmas by reuniting me with the joys of Strat-O-Matic: a complete set of all the teams. Knowing the pleasure the game gave me as a child (I guess I might have rambled on a little bit over the years); she wanted me to have something enjoyable to do when my insomnia keeps me awake. The "new" 1998 Strat-O-Matic All-Star League saw many exciting moments, with perhaps the most dramatic being Rex Hudler coming off the bench to replace an injured Robby Alomar and hitting three home runs in one game.

As the saying goes, everything that goes around comes around and the same is true for my Strat-O-Matic experience. After a recent move into our first house, I finally had the space to break out a long-ago packed box of baseball cards and memorabilia. Buried in the midst of my Topps cards, *Baseball Digests*, and the program from the 1983 Chicago All-Star Game (I attended the practices and **Old Timers game** the day before) were my old Strat-O-Matic cards. As I thumbed through the pile of cards that I thought I had lost many years ago, I found Bert Blyleven's card and smiled. Finally, near the bottom of the pile, I saw Mick's card and I returned to that bedroom in North Carolina.

Naturally I incorporated Bench, **Rod Carew,** Blyleven, and other top 1970s players available into my current "Strat-O-Matic All-Star League" to see how they would fare against the likes of Sosa, Maddux, and Pudge Rodriguez. Of course I had no choice but to save a roster spot for Mick Kelleher.

In Mick's first at-bat, the most ironic thing happened: The roll of the dice turned up a chance for Mick to hit another home run. Whether he would homer was left to the roll of a twenty-sided die that has replaced the numbered split cards that were used in the 1970s. I paused before rolling the die to think about what I wanted the result to be. Did I want Mick, after a two-decade retirement from Strat-O-Matic play, to once again do the impossible? Or did I want to keep Mick's special accomplishments in the past? Still ambivalent, I released the die.

Old Timers game: In July 2007 Yankee starting pitcher Roger Clemens was older than five of the retired Yankees who played in that day's Old Timers game.

Rod Carew: Rod Carew was born on a train in Panama. He was delivered by an American doctor riding the train, Rodney Cline. Carew's full name is Rodney Cline Carew.

I am reminded of that part of me that blindly believes in the purity of the game; that has simple faith in things that are good; that always believes each spring that this year the Cubs will not only make it to the World Series but actually win the whole darn shootin' match.

Mick's shot sailed toward the fence. In my mind, Harry Caray was doing the play-by-play: "It might be . . . it could be . . . it's off the wall and Kelleher goes into second with a stand-up double." The odds and the gods were not with Mick that day, but he still managed to drive in what turned out to be the game-winning RBI. For my part, I decided that I was glad that Mick's only home runs remained a treasured part of my childhood.

Thanks to Strat-O-Matic I have been reconnected with those childhood memories and with the beauty of the game of baseball. I am reminded of that part of me that blindly believes in the purity of the game; that has simple faith in things that are good; that always believes each spring that this year the Cubs will not only make it to the World Series but actually win the whole darn shootin' match. As the twelve-year-old child in my memories reminds this thirty-something man, all in all, it is not a bad way to view the world. All this because a few rolls of the dice two decades ago beat the odds and gave me a new hero. Thank you, Mick. Wherever you are, I hope you keep slugging! Go Cubbies!

Free Agents Aren't Free: Pay Ball!

Alan Hartwick

Alan Hartwick is a lifelong Cub fan, except for a little twenty-one-year break. He found out that fan loyalty isn't something you can buy—or sell. In 1977, he declared himself a free agent fan. Now 57, Hartwick is a freelance videographer in Grand Rapids, Michigan.

I grew up a Cubs fan in South Bend. Had some wonderful older children next door, the Bare family. Jim Bare was the oldest kid in the neighborhood and loved the Cubs. He would invite us to come over. His dad would be there in his T-shirt with a beer, sitting backwards on his dining-room chair, watching WGN in black and white. I began to fall in love with Ernie Banks. Ernie would come up, and Jim loved Ernie. My brother and I would watch and pretend we were Ernie, holding a bat and wiggling our fingers, hoping we'd hit a home run. So that's when the love started, probably when I was three or four years old.

You were really the minority, because the White Sox were hot in the '50s, especially '59. You were always mocked being a Cub fan. It was easy to get into the games. Back in '64, a headline in the *South Bend Tribune* in early September was, "940 Watch Jackson Win 20th." Nine hundred and forty fans were at Wrigley Field when Larry Jackson won his 20th game. Back then, they weren't America's Team. I loved them, even though they were usually losers. I was a real strong fan, just like any other kid would be a fan of a team.

Years later, in 1977, I started thinking about free agency, about being a Cub fan and how I put up with a lot of losing seasons and never a pennant. I thought, "What's making me be a Cub fan? Why can't a fan be a free agent like

> Why can't a fan be a free agent like the players are free agents?

the players are free agents?" I tossed the idea around and shared it with a couple of friends who thought it was a great idea.

Initially I did it as a fun thing. After a while it became serious. I said, "Hey, I'm actually talking about giving up my favorite team here." I decided to write to the teams. I wrote to all twenty-six teams there were at the time. I sent them a picture of myself and told them I had been a loyal Cub fan all my life but I wasn't happy with their losing ways and was willing to offer my services to their team for the highest bid.

I heard from ten Major League teams. Most of the offers were ridiculous little things. Probably the worst, the most hilarious, was from the Minnesota Twins PR department. They were owned by Calvin Griffith, who was notorious for hating free agency. I got this one paragraph from PR saying they weren't interested in any nonresident fan. I couldn't tell if it was sarcastic or it was serious.

I got some nice comments from other teams, like the Dodgers saying, "Sure, we welcome you as a fan." Ted Turner didn't say anything, but he sent me a clip from the Atlanta Constitution saying, "Nice idea." I got bumper stickers, schedules.

The most fascinating letter I got was from Bill Veeck.

I got two intriguing letters from teams—one from the Toronto Blue Jays, who were a first-year team. I got a really fun letter from **Peter Bavasi**, the GM, offering me an opportunity to start with the new team. I actually called him and had a nice conversation. I thought maybe I could get some season tickets out of him or something else of value. He just thanked me for calling.

The most fascinating letter I got was from Bill Veeck. A few days after I got it, his secretary sent me a letter saying, "I'm sorry, I mistak-

Peter Bavasi: Peter Bavasi's father, Buzzy, was general manager of the Los Angeles Dodgers in the 1960s. Bavasi offered Dodger pitchers $25 for every mile they ran during spring training. Don Drysdale said, "I'm going to run a mile the same day that Jesse Owens wins his twentieth game."

enly sent you Mr. Veeck's first draft of the letter. Enclosed is the final draft." I thought, "This guy sat there for an hour or two." At the time he owned the White Sox.

Dear Alan,

It's with some sadness that we received your letter. Maybe I've maintained a certain naiveté. I continue to hope that unlike most other things in our materialistic world, fan support was and is not for barter or sale. Our position, very simply, is that White Sox fans are historically, and today, of a most unusual, loyal breed. Long-suffering, patient, yes, maybe even masochistic, but they have supported the White Sox through thick and thin, win or lose. Of course, there has been more of the latter in their careers.

Therefore, as much as we would like to have a new fan and as desperately as we need new fans, we must refuse your offer. We must even refuse to negotiate with any agent that you might employ. On the other hand, if you find us lovable and worthy of your support, not for an old jacket, a new contract, or a well-worn cap, we would be delighted to have you join the ranks of Sox supporters. Of course, your letter might stir thoughts of insincerity should you enroll in our group, but nevertheless, in your case, because of your ingenuity, unusual approach, and obvious sense of humor, we'd be willing to waive the probation period for people who have been suffering, ever-loyal Sox fans to welcome you into our midst.

If you find this a reasonable approach, we would be delighted to forward a multiyear fan contract for your signature. Thank you for contacting us, and we'll hope for your favorable considerations.

Sincerely,
Bill Veeck

Of all the Major League teams, that's the one I would choose, and I thought perhaps this was the way to go. Switching from the North Side to the South Side—what a great ending to the story. Then I received an offer from a minor-league team, which came through a radio station in New Orleans. I had done about twenty radio interviews around the country. On air, the DJ in New Orleans said, "We have some exciting news here, we have a new Triple-A team. We're hoping in the near future to have a Major League Baseball team in New Orleans. We're going to be playing in the Superdome, and this Triple-A team is owned by Mr. A. Ray Smith. He's on the phone with us today, and he'd like to make you an offer." Smith was an oil magnate from Oklahoma.

He said, "We'd love to have you come down here to New Orleans to support us. In fact, we'll fly you down here, and we'll let you throw out the first ball. We'd like to know if you'll accept that offer."

I told him I wanted to think about it, to which the DJ said, "Think about it? What are you talking about? You've received bumper stickers and pennants and you want to think about it?" He set it up for his own program that he'd call me back the same time next week and I'd make my decision.

They did. A guy from the Marriott French Quarter was listening to the show and offered to put us up free for a week in a beautiful suite. The team paid for the plane tickets and flew us down there. I threw out the **first ball**.

This old PR guy down in New Orleans said, "Alan, the good news is that you're going to throw out the first ball. A little bad news— Mr. Smith has promised four people that they can throw out the first ball. He just got carried away." He said, "The other three people are politicians, so I've decided you are going to throw out the first of the first balls." One of the politicians was Lindy Boggs, then a U.S. congresswoman from Louisiana. I threw out the first ball and had a good time.

first ball: Mike Ditka once threw out the first pitch at a Cubs game with Joe Girardi as his catcher. Girardi had a football cupped behind his back. After catching Ditka's pitch one-handed, Girardi stood up and fired the football at Ditka, who caught it with one hand.

I was a small part of a promoter's extravaganza. Mr. A. Ray Smith was really quite the promoter of everything. They had a parade; they had former Major League ballplayers down there. I got an invitation to go to a reception with all these old Major Leaguers. I missed the invitation in my mailbox! Ernie Banks was there, and Stan Musial. I did meet Stan at the first game, got his autograph. I met Mel Parnell.

Tony LaRussa was a third baseman for the Pelicans.

I never heard from the Cubs, major disappointment.

Tony LaRussa was a third baseman for the Pelicans. It was his last year playing, and he was also a coach, not the manager of the team. They had a few ballplayers who actually made it to the Majors. Ken Oberkfell, Eddie Solomon, he pitched for the Cardinals and the Cubs. It was a Cardinals farm team, which led to the question, "OK, now am I a Cardinal fan?" I never really embraced that. Some of the media thought I was. Like Jack Buck. He interviewed me on the radio before I made my decision.

It was like three days of fame. I was probably in one hundred newspapers. My wife was ecstatic, she just loved it.

After we got to New Orleans, I was in a parade with all those antique cars and the players. After that and throwing out the first ball, I could see them pull back, getting a little chintzy. I was asking for tickets to the remainder of the games, and the PR guy said, "We'll see what we can do." Then I realized I was just a small part of this whole big thing that was going on.

Here's the deal. I seriously, honestly, stayed away from the Cubs for twenty-one years. For the first three to five years, I opened the sports page and my mind would immediately dart to the National League East, which was where they were at the time. I would tell myself, "No, that's not where we're going. You're not a Cub fan."

What happened after a few years was, I didn't really have a team. I began to really enjoy baseball in a purer sense, because I was not rooting for a particular team and being @%#^* off that my team wasn't winning. It was more the beauty of the game. We would go to games at Wrigley Field, we would go other places, but I would cheer the good plays.

I happened to have an epiphany at Wrigley Field one day, when Willie Wilson hit a double between left and center to the wall and held up at second. Next time up, he hit to the same spot, line drive, left-center. This time, you could just see he was going for three. We were on the third base side, so he was coming at us with that speed. He was tagged out, and it was like, "Oh my God, I love this game." Because you just knew he was going for it, and you knew he was a veteran and he had lost that half step, and he was out. There was this epiphany that I did just love this game, it didn't matter who was winning here.

In 1998 I got sucked back in. The year with Kerry Wood, the 20 strikeouts. Sosa with his home runs and the wild card. Some might say I was a phony, but I thought twenty-one years was good. I didn't come back rabid like I was before. I didn't come back with the angst. I don't get overly disturbed with the failures. I take great pleasure in the victories, I always have. I came back with a fresher perspective on the game. I've retained that new, fresh love of the game.

There's more to life. We didn't think it was worth 100 bucks.

We have seen two Cub games this year in Cincinnati. But we made a trip to Wrigley Field in July, and we went without tickets, thinking that we might buy them if they're reasonable. Standing room only was $80. For $100, we could be on one of the rooftops across the street. We said, "No, we'll go to the art museum." Then we went and watched part of the game on TV. There's more to life. We didn't think it was worth 100 bucks.

Tell Ray Floyd That I Just Got My Ball Retriever Regripped

Ray Floyd

Ray Floyd chose golf over baseball at a young age. He was inducted into the World Golf Hall of Fame in 1989. He won four Majors including the 1976 Masters and the 1986 U.S. Open.

I grew up in Fayetteville, North Carolina. I was a St. Louis Cardinal fan as a kid, because I could get KMOX on my radio when I would go to bed. My parents thought I was sleeping, and I'd be listening to the Cardinal game. I was a big Harry Caray fan.

I almost played baseball instead of golf. Fortunately, I did make the right decision. When I went on the PGA Tour, any time we went to a city where there was a Major League ballpark, I would go to a game. In 1965, the World Series was the Dodgers and Minnesota. Bob Rosburg was a buddy of Drysdale, Koufax, and some of those guys on the Dodgers. We went to a couple of games in Dodger Stadium. I met Mr. Kawano, who was the clubhouse manager for the Dodgers. He said, "When you go to Chicago, you have to meet my brother, he's your biggest fan." Leo Durocher was coaching at the time for the Dodgers, then he became manager of the Cubs and, of course, I meet Yosh Kawano, who today is one of my closest, dearest friends.

I went to the Cubs spring training three years in a row; **1966**, '67, and '68 we were there. I even traveled some with the team. I'd shag balls at batting practice, I had a uniform and Yosh had a locker for

1966: According to *Sports Illustrated,* the worst time and place to be a sports fan was New York City in 1966. The Yankees, Knicks, and Rangers finished in last place, the Mets barely climbed out of the cellar for the first time, and the football Giants were 1–12–1.

133

me. This was out in Scottsdale, but I moved to Chicago in '69. When I was in town there, I went to the ball games and I would shag balls, be around batting practice, and do all that stuff.

I was traveling with the Cubs in '69 when they blew it to the Mets. I was with them in Philadelphia those last two series. I was in the press box at Shea Stadium when the umpire made such a horrible call: Cleon Jones was out of the base path, plus he got tagged, and the ump called him safe, which tied the game in the ninth inning.

I was traveling with the Cubs in '69 when they blew it to the Mets.

It was some ridiculous call. The Cubs ended up losing that game, then they lost the series and then went to Philly and lost. The Mets kept winning. That was it. It was the doldrums. We went to Philly in buses, and there wasn't very much activity on the buses, and it was gloom around the ballpark the next two or three days. I couldn't wait to get away from it.

When I was young, the Cubs wanted to sign me as a pitcher, but I also played third and first. I thought I was a good hitter, but when you kept going up a notch at the next level I probably was not a good hitter. But I was a very good pitcher. The best athlete has to become a pitcher early, because most kids can't get the ball across the plate early. I used to love to catch, but my dad wouldn't let me. He said, "If I ever catch you catching, you won't be able to play again." He wanted me to be a golfer, so he was always afraid I'd hurt my hands.

What happens when they do sign you as a pitcher, later on, you don't hit anymore. Most pitchers are the best hitters on their high school team. You don't take batting practice. Your psyche changes, you don't practice hitting anymore. They're teaching you to bunt and move runners. Some guys maintain it, though. There's still guys like Zambrano that hit the crap out of the ball. I never did hit a ball out of Wrigley. I hit one out in Shea Stadium.

It was pretty neat stepping on Wrigley Field for the first time. I was on the Tour, so it was that courtesy, knowing somebody. It was pretty special being twenty-one years old and being able to go out on a Major League ballfield. I threw some batting practice. My ball moved; I had a very live ball. Guys like the ball straight to get timing when they're in batting practice, so I was not a good batting-practice pitcher. I couldn't throw a ball straight if I tried today. The difference between pitching batting practice at Fayetteville and pitching batting practice at Wrigley is you go up in class. It was just like in golf, you played against other players but there was very rarely anybody that was at your level. Then you go into Wrigley Field, where the best of the best of the best come to the Major Leagues. Then you're overwhelmed. I thought I was a pretty good player until I got around those guys.

I had buddies throughout the years. Especially on those teams with Santo and Beckert and Kessinger and Randy Hundley and Fergie Jenkins, that '69 team. A nucleus through there, Ernie Banks, Billy Williams, they were all really good buddies of mine.

The great mistakes of all time? Well, if you forget, Lou Brock for Ernie Broglio. They let **Greg Maddux** go, and he wanted to stay.

I don't get to Wrigley much these days. I stay in touch with Yosh. My kids are all Cub fans; my two sons are huge Cub fans. They go to the ball games more than I do. In fact, my son was in the U.S. Amateur in San Francisco, and he went to two Cub games on a Tuesday and Wednesday night when they played the Giants.

There were a lot of guys out on tour that were Cub fans. Ken Still and I were the biggest baseball fans. He's from Seattle. He's an American League fan. . . .

Greg Maddux: Greg Maddux made his Cubs debut in September 1986 as a pinch runner in the seventeenth inning.

It Just Goes to Show You That Truly Great Comedy Is Not Funny

Brad Zibung

Brad Zibung is editor-in-chief of *The Heckler,* a newspaper and Web site for Cub fans with a sense of humor. If you're a Cub fan, you must see *The Heckler.* It's absolutely outrageously funny.

$\mathcal{S}$ ome friends and I had been going to a lot of games in the bleachers. We had started our Web site previously, and it started gaining popularity and business from all over. I had been writing for my college paper at the **University of Wisconsin**–Oshkosh. In fact, I've always loved the camaraderie that went along with being in a newsroom. In the back of my head, I always wanted to start something up like that again. My friends and I who had some editorial background started kicking around some ideas, and before I knew it I was getting quotes from printers. Our first issue rolled out in time for the Cubs opener in 2003.

We used to sit in the bleachers all the time; I still have bleacher season tickets. We'd sit in the bleachers in leftfield, and there's the "Leftfield sucks/Rightfield sucks" rivalry. We made our site, rightfieldsucks.com. It was a blog. We'd have pictures of ourselves. We let that expire. We decided to devote all our attention to *The Heckler.*

We put together a list of fifteen potential names. One of the guys who helped start it has an advertising background. He's had jobs where it was his responsibility to pull together potential names and brands for companies. He probably had a couple hundred, and the

University of Wisconsin: Arnold Schwarzenegger graduated from the University of Wisconsin in 1979.

people who were helping with the paper at the time put together a vote, and *The Heckler* was first.

I moved to Chicago in '99. I used to work at Leo Burnett, a Chicago-based marketing and communications company. That was my first job out of college. I had developed a pretty good network at Burnett at that time. I had some friends who worked outside of Burnett who had an editorial background. We started kicking around some ideas and let it fly.

The first issue was pretty rough. I did almost everything. I did a lot of the layout, a fair amount of writing. We didn't really do a whole lot of copyediting. I did a lot of the images myself, too. I'm OK at that stuff, but *Our first headline was about the Cubs conceding the National League pennant.* none of it is my strong suit. Our first headline was about the Cubs conceding the National League pennant. From Opening Day, they already knew they weren't going to make a go of it. We turned out to almost be wrong. They came pretty close that year.

We added color. We've tweaked our frequency; we now come out once a month. When we started, we came out every other week. That wound up being quite a bit of work for our small, largely volunteer staff. We also started doing other sports. Baseball is still certainly our bread and butter.

We generally strive to be the poke-you-in-the-ribs humor, not something that's going to upset you. We try to keep it pretty above the belt. Certain organizations' PR people get a little uptight when they see what we're doing. The Cubs had the Kerry Wood bowling fundraiser earlier this year, and we scored a couple of free passes to that. I went and checked it out and rubbed elbows with some players, and when I said I was from *The Heckler* they almost all started laughing, from Kerry Wood on down.

I had become exposed to *The Onion*, a satirical newspaper, in college, which at that time was based in Madison. They're definitely the godfathers at this. When we started the paper, I didn't want to go too much down their path. I wanted to carve our own little niche. I'm sure it was an influence.

It's not all that sexy of a process, that's for sure. Over the years we've built pretty good relationships with some pretty talented and funny writers. We have a team of six or seven guys who, two weeks before the issue, will start brainstorming headlines. A lot of the people who write for the paper, I've never even met, or I've met a few times. The majority of our exchanges are over the Internet. In a lot of ways it's allowed us to do a lot of what we do relatively cheap. One day I'd certainly love to have an office. We now have a full-time sales rep, and I'm hoping in the next couple of years we can have a few more and the need for an office will be warranted from the sales standpoint. For now, everyone just works out of his own apartment. With the amount of time that I spend on it, it is a full-time job.

In '04 a company that had been sponsoring our paper called stubhub.com was looking for people to help them with some of their on-the-ground operations in their bigger cities. I was looking for a job that would allow me a little more time to spend on *The Heckler* but would also pay the bills. So when this whole thing came about, they asked me if I'd be interested in helping them set up their office in Chicago. The paper has evolved into more hours than when I signed on, but it's not at the point where I would be able to sustain living on it. It works out really well, we do have an office for Stubhub, and it's in Wrigleyville. I'm right in Wrigleyville all the time, no matter what I'm doing, if it's *The Heckler* or for Stubhub. I don't have much of a commute, it saves me a lot of time.

> We do have an office for Stubhub, and it's in Wrigleyville.

I was afraid I'd get a cease-and-desist letter from the Cubs about three issues into it. I was also afraid my boxes around town at bars, restaurants, and coffee shops would get stolen or damaged. I was afraid no one would like what we were publishing. I would get phone calls with people asking questions about it and e-mails. I have a pretty strong base of friends in the bleachers, and they seem to be pretty big fans. If the lifers can appreciate it, that's a pretty good sign of acceptance.

The one that put us on the map was the Cubs-Sox series at Wrigley in '03, our first issue. We did an article called the "Million Mullet March." We had Cubs fans on the front with mullets walking down the street. They talked about how Sox fans were overtaking Wrigleyville. I love anything we do that plays off the Cubs-Sox rivalry. It can be so heated.

We've had articles that depicted Mark Prior walking on water, because people always treated him like he was going to be the savior of the franchise. We have a lot of recurring themes as well. Any time we quote Ozzie Guillen, we include "expletive deleted" at some point in his quote.

I never thought we were creating something that would wind up on people's resumes. In a lot of ways, it's been more. Once I started getting the feeling people were digging it, I didn't want to let up. I still feel like there's a lot that we could be doing in terms of overall development of our product and what's behind it.

On the Web site, we publish some content that is Web-only, so we'll do lighthearted game recaps, both the Cubs and the Sox. We also do breaking news that might be a little too timely to run in the hard copy. I've met a handful of players and coaches. I've met Dusty Baker two or three times, and the first time I met him, he was hilarious. He wanted to tell me the story about how the first time he saw the paper, he thought it was real. We had an article about Kyle Farnsworth, and Dusty was going to discipline Kyle Farnsworth for the antics we were describing. When the Cubs played the Expos in Puerto Rico, we said Farnsworth was hitting on Miss Puerto Rico. Dusty believed it.

The Milwaukee Brewers: Come smell our Dairy Air.

Quick Hits and Interesting Bits

H arry Caray was a great baseball fan and he would come to every game here, whether it was being televised or not. His last year here, the first year at the new stadium, he would come to every game.

After the seventh inning or eighth inning, he would be a little tired and want to go. So I would go into his box and take him down the elevator and escort him either to his car or to the Hohokam Room, where he would sit and relax.

The last time he was ever here, my daughter, who was seven at the time, went into the booth with me and the three of us rode down the elevator by ourselves. He was telling her what a beautiful little girl she was, talked baseball to her, and went on about the weather in Palm Springs. She's got flaming red hair. Her name is Shannon. He patted her on the head and said, "Shannon, you are the prettiest redhead I've ever seen." And he told me, "Dave you're going to have your hands full." When he passed away, she said, "I'll never forget that ride with Harry." That's a fun story for me.

He never let these people know he was tired. He never crabbed about anything.

Once after Harry had worked a game, he had to shoot a commercial. We got him in the elevator and we're going down to get him to the golf cart to take him where the shoot is going on out in the outfield. He looked at me and said, "Dave, I'm tired today. I've got to do this commercial. I don't know if I feel like signing any autographs." I said OK. As soon as that elevator opened, there were hundreds of people waiting there. And his whole countenance changed. I mean he went from being tired and kind of dragging to having a big, beaming smile on his face. He walked out into them and he was like the mayor.

He walked out into these people, they were shaking his hand, he was pressing the flesh, signing autographs for everybody. He never let these people know he was tired. He never let them know he had to get to this commercial. He never crabbed about anything.

So finally, he signed for just about everybody. He got in the cart, we went to the shoot. Then the commercial shoot ran a little long, got over, he got back in the cart and said, "Now, I'm going to be a little late for dinner with Dutchie." She was waiting for him in the Hohokam Room. He said, "I've got to get to the Hohokam Room really quick. I can't stop and sign autographs." I said, "OK. Here we go."

Same thing happened. We don't get 2 feet, and the people just mob him right outside where the commercial was being taped. They were all over. He stayed. He signed for everybody. Shook everybody's hand. Told stories. Just did the whole same thing, because he was a fan at heart and he wanted these people to go away feeling good about their day at the ballpark.

> —Dave Dunne,
> general manager, Hohokam Park,
> Mesa, Arizona

I went to a game in 1947, I was too young at the age of ten. I was out in the bleachers and it bored me. The next year, in August of 1948, I went to a doubleheader with my dad and saw Boston play the Cubs. It was the first time I'd seen a ball hit the ivy. Cavarretta hit the ball and Jeff Heath pretended he couldn't find it. Everybody knew Heath was faking it. It was an inside-the-park home run with the bases loaded, but the umpires bought it and called Cavarretta back to second and all hell broke loose. It was a near riot. It's late in August and they finished last, but once you get hooked on something like that, you just can't spit it out, I guess.

The Cubs were pathetic. They just didn't have any talent—from the front office on down. (Phil) Wrigley didn't care. He was a good man, but he should have run the gum company and given the team to somebody else. When he went to sell the company, he sold it to another major corporation, the *Tribune*. I think Wrigley bought it in 1920, so from '20 to recently, you've had nearly 90 years and two owners. These are people that own corporations in Chicago. They had other fish to fry. They didn't spend the time or energy on the teams. They had a civic responsibility to make the Cubs a winner. People come in year after year. They buy their products—they buy the gum, they buy the newspaper. . . . These people didn't give a damn because people didn't say, "We've had enough." That's part of the Chicago personality.

I took my grandson in two years ago. He'd never been to Wrigley, so we went up the steps that are right in back of the screen. I'll never forget, we got there, and he said, "Wrigley Field." He's a boy seven years of age. We were lucky to be able to get down on the field. We met **Dusty Baker** and went into the dugout and the locker room with him. It was a thrill for my grandson and for me to be a part of the whole thing. I had a Cub book out in the early '90s and was interviewed by Harry Caray. It was about three in the afternoon, and Harry asked, "What are the Cubs about?" I said, "Right now, you've got great weather, you've got this beautiful ballpark, there's no trouble, you get lost in yesterday." That's what happens. You get in that ballpark and you forget your problems.

I was watching a two-hour show on HBO on the old Brooklyn Dodgers, and they show that ballpark. It was a dump, and they should have gotten out of the place. I don't think people would say, "I went to Ebbets Field and the beauty of the thing just blew me away." It's the quality of the team, not the ballpark—but I think the ballpark has a lot to do with it, and that's why these new ballparks they build are not like those cookie cutters they were building in the '60s and '70s. They have character and style now, and people enjoy going, and it builds the fan base.

I always wanted to write a book but I could never come up with an idea. Then, one day, it dawned on me, "Why do people like the Cubs?" They shouldn't. They haven't done anything to earn it since 1945, for the most part. Why not talk to the actual participants and

---

Dusty Baker: Only six rookies have ever had a higher first-year batting average than Dusty Baker. Baker batted .321 for the 1972 Braves.

others who have broadcast the game, who've written about the game, who've played the game? I spoke with a lot of people and got their opinions from different periods, starting with the '30s. Claude Passeau was one of the guys I talked with. He was a very good pitcher, really a tough guy. He passed away a couple of years ago. He pitched in the '45 Series and played during the war. I talked to a number of these guys. Cavarretta played during the war, and they're all defensive about that—at least Cavarretta was. I guess there were a lot of questions, "Why aren't you in the service?" He said they were performing this great service by keeping the home front happy. I would ask guys about the Depression, and they couldn't talk about it. They didn't focus on it. All they could talk about was baseball—it was like the Depression didn't happen to these guys. The title of the book was *Our Chicago Cubs*.

I found that the older the ballplayer, the nicer the guy.

I found that the older the ballplayer, the nicer the guy. Some of these guys today who are thought of highly by Cub fans are a pain in the $*&. It was good to talk to these older guys—they were gentlemen. They'd answer your questions. They had no politics involved one way or the other. These older ballplayers had to go find a job when they were thirty-five or so because they didn't stay around that long. For most of the older guys, it was a tough life. They didn't have the opportunity these guys have now. It was a tough deal. . . .

The Cubs radio announcers over the years—the first one I remember was a fellow on WIND, Bert Wilson. He was a "homer," and it was all Cubs. It was almost laughable at times. At that time WGN was not doing well as a radio station. They had a general manager come in who did a wonderful job and turned it around. He got the Cubs. That helped. They brought in the next announcer, Jack Quinlan, who was probably the best announcer I heard in my life, with the exception of Vin Scully.

—Rick Phalen,
Santa Barbara, California,
retired radio honcho

I t was Thanksgiving Day, 1995, and I had just sat down for din-ner at my brother's house when the phone rang. My sister-in-law answered the phone and informed me that the call was for me. I thought this was strange. Who would be calling me at my brother's house on Thanksgiving? It turned out to be Randy Hundley on the other end of the line. He informed me that my wife was giving me a Christmas present—a January trip to Randy's Cubs Fantasy Camp in Mesa, Arizona. He said that he was telling me now, rather than Christmas, so I would have ample time to get my forty-seven-year-old body in playing shape. I was almost speechless! I came back to the dinner table and gave my wife the biggest hug and kiss I've ever given her.

My favorite Cubs team has always been the 1969 club. So, when I went to the camp, it was great to see people like Randy Hundley, Fergie Jenkins, and Gene Oliver. On top of that, my two coaches were Ron Santo and Glen Beckert. These two guys were fantas-tic, especially Ronnie. It was great to hear their baseball stories. On the last day of camp, we played the former players—Cubs, **White Sox,** and Cardinals. I had a chance to bat against Hall of Famer, Bob Gibson.

> I had a chance to bat against Hall of Famer, Bob Gibson. Luck of luck . . . I hit a line drive to centerfield for a base hit.

Luck of luck . . . I hit a line drive to centerfield for a base hit. I was on cloud nine! I have a videotape of that moment to show to any doubt-ers. What a great week—I couldn't divorce my wife, even if I wanted to . . . I love that woman!!!!

As a teenager in the early '60s, I would spend a whole two-week homestand at my grandmother's apartment. She lived about three miles from Wrigley Field. I would walk to and from the ballpark

White Sox: In 1944 the Chicago White Sox played forty-three double-headers. Last year, they played one. . . . In March 1954 the Lakers and the Hawks played a regulation, regular season NBA game using bas-kets that were 12 feet high rather than the usual 10 feet . . . the next night they played each other in a doubleheader. True facts, believe them or not!

every day and watch my not-so-good Cubs in a really empty ballpark. Ernie Banks was my favorite. I finished classes early at Loyola University and took the el train to Wrigley on the day Ernie hit his 500th home run. Yes, I was in the leftfield bleachers that day. There weren't too many of us out there that day as the ball bounced back out onto the field. Two years later, Mr. Cub signed my scorecard from that day.

—Bill McMahon,
Geneva, Illinois

I was eight years old the first time I went to Wrigley Field, back in the summer of '84. Little did I know that was going to be a special year and yet another heartache. Mom, Dad, sister, uncles, aunts, cousins, and grandmas went on the trip. We were playing the Dodgers when Tommy Lasorda was the manager. The boys went to the game and the women went shopping. I stepped foot into that stadium like it was a church. I never before saw something that special and unique. While we were there, my dad bought me a Cubs jersey, baseball, and a Jody Davis pin. I remember that famous chant and clap they used to do for Jody who was my favorite Cub. My dad, uncles, and even my teenage cousin drank beers bought by the Wrigley Field regulars. I couldn't even tell you who won that day, but I will never forget such an emotional moment. Probably one of the best moments of my childhood was that day. It felt great to be a kid!

In my day and age growing up, the Cubs and Cardinals rivalry has always been there. Where we live, the majority of people are Cardinal fans. That has even gotten worse the past couple of years with the Cards' acquisition of Scott Rolen, who is a local hero and fabulous guy. Now, Scott is a really great player and an even better individual. The one thing I didn't like about him is the fact that he played for the Cardinals. He has really killed the Cubs over the years, too, with his play. Now he's no longer a Cardinal.

In 2003 we had all eight of us Cub fans in town watching the playoffs together. We would rotate houses to take turns hosting the party. Throughout the year, we watched some games together and

Our chances were great to go to the World Series. We headed to the liquor store that night and bought some champagne.

came up with a system to host games. We kept records of wins and losses with who pitched that day and whether it was home or away. When the playoffs came, we became superstitious to whose stats were the best, and that was who hosted the party. Even though we lost Game 5 of the NLCS, we thought, for sure, with Mark Prior and Kerry Wood on the mound the next two games our chances were great to go to the World Series. We headed to the liquor store that night and bought some champagne. One of the guys said it might not be a good idea to jump the gun. We bought it anyway and iced it down for Game 6 of the NLCS. It was that eighth inning, with five outs to go, and Steve Bartman touched that ball. All of us knew bad things were going to happen. We tried to be optimistic for Game 7, but, in our hearts, we knew it was over. We looked at our champagne that night and shook our heads. One guy even took his bottle and threw it off a bridge into a river—he was so mad. All we thought about was maybe next year. Then, 2004 did come, and it was even more brutal than 2003.

—Brad Schmidt,
Jasper, Indiana

We live in the Quad Cities and have Cub season tickets even though it's 400 miles round-trip to Wrigley. I probably wouldn't have season tickets if I hadn't converted my wife, Jane, from being a Cardinal to a Cub fan. She was a die-hard Cardinal fan till she saw the light. I told her she could stay a Cardinal fan—it'd just be 162 days a year I wouldn't talk to her. She didn't want that, so she thought she'd become a Cub fan.

It's not a bad little ride to Chicago. It's a three-hour drive. We stay up there about forty-five nights. We've got a nice little motel where we stay. It's old, but it's clean. The Clark Street bus runs right by there. Free parking, can you believe that in Chicago? We barhop our way down Clark Street. They all wait for us to come in, and boy, if we're late they let us know! We don't like night games, so we sell those tickets. Sometimes we have more fun after the game than during the game. One friend of ours, Phil, is a big White Sox fan. He's of Japanese descent. Some Chicago bar he knew of closed down, and he had all these pictures of celebrities. He gave them to me. I've got pictures of Billy Conn, Joe Louis, and Jack Dempsey. . . . All different Cubs teams from the thirties. . . .

Free parking, can you believe that in Chicago?

At Wrigley one day, all of a sudden we notice there's a weird-looking guy. He just sauntered out onto the field. He didn't run, and he was waving to everyone. People thought he was going to throw out the first pitch. He got out on the mound and he started undressing. Bare naked. Bare naked on the mound. Completely nude. The security guards were just standing there. I'm sure someone got fired over it. He was there for close to a minute before they went out and ushered him off. He waved to everybody as they were taking him off. It really happened. It was 2002 or so. It was Randy Myers Poster Day. Myers gave up all those runs, and there were about 10,000 posters thrown out onto the field.

I always wanted to go to spring training. I finally went when the strike season was on in '94. We weren't sure if there was going to be any baseball out there or not because of that. **Jimmy Piersall** was still working with the Cubs at that time. This guy walks by in a nice warm-up suit. He started talking to the fans, and no one knew who he was. Finally, one guy asked him, "Are you Jimmy Piersall?" and he said,

Jimmy Piersall: Jimmy Piersall hit his one hundredth Major League home run off Dallas Green. To celebrate, Piersall ran the bases backward.

"Yes, I am." He was asked, "What do you do for the Cubs?" He said, "I'm in charge of the young ballplayers' sex life." Boy, that broke the crowd up.

We enjoy spring training baseball. We like baseball, and you have to love the Arizona weather. The thing I like about it is that you're really up close. You really get to see the players. Jane brings her camera, and we get a lot of pictures of ballplayers coming in. One of the worst ones was Ryne Sandberg. He would never look up to have his picture taken while he was playing. Sammy Sosa was the same way after he became THE Sammy Sosa.

—Dickie Walters, 59,

Rock Island, Illinois

I n 1988 I was consulting for a CBA basketball team in the Quad Cities. For each game, we would have a celebrity athlete put on the team's uniform and introduce that person last when we'd introduce the team. We had stars like Henry Aaron, Bob Cousy, John Havlicek, Rick Barry, Walt Frazier, and Roger Craig. One game it was "Sweet Swingin'" Billy Williams. The problem was that the team had been detained by a blizzard in Wyoming the night before, and the game started two hours late. Billy and his wife drove down from Chicago, which was a three-hour trip. Midway through the first half, Billy came to me and said, "Would you mind very much if my wife and I left at the end of the third quarter?" Well, since the game didn't start until 9:30 p.m. I was amazed that he was going to stay that long. He not only stayed, but he was just great about it, even though he could have been in a bad mood because that day Don Zimmer was named as manager of the Cubs, a job Billy Williams wanted.

Before I left that job, I told the general manager to schedule a game the following year around the time the Cubs Caravan came to the Quad Cities, which is what he did. So the next year when the Cub Caravan came it had Curtis Wilkerson and Mitch Williams, two guys the Cubs just received in a trade with Texas, and also Mark Grace. The players showed up late, due to no fault of their own, and there were hundreds and hundreds of fans lined up for their autographs. A few minutes into the autograph session, a Cub executive came and told the guys they had to stop signing. He said that it was a long trip back to Chicago, and they had to leave right away. Grace sized up what was going on, went over to the general manager, and said, "I understand the whole situation here. If you get the name and address of everybody in line, I'll personally send them a signed picture." Which is what he did. It had to cost him hundreds of dollars. He was just going into his second year. . . .

I'm certainly not a White Sox fan. In 1990 we had a deal with the White Sox that we would run buses from hotels all over Chicagoland, as well as various apartment complexes, to Comiskey Park. It was the last year of Comiskey Park, and because they were building the new park next door there was limited parking. The buses were a great way for people to go to a ball game without worrying about traffic jams or parking or drinking and driving. However, the White Sox, for no reason except for the fact we were too successful, pulled the plug early in the season. As much as I don't like lawyers or lawsuits, it was one of the few times we ever sued anybody, and obviously we won. . . .

In 1997 I was at a Cubs game with a friend of mine, Horn Chen, from the North Shore. Horn owned thirteen minor-league baseball and hockey teams at the time. Halfway through the seventh, Horn was leaving to make a phone call. I said, "Horn, you can't leave now. You have to stand and look at the booth when Harry sings, because you know this isn't going to last forever." That was the last time I saw Harry sing.

In 1987 in November, Harry Caray's restaurant was opened in downtown Chicago by three Notre Dame classmates of mine. I was invited to the pre-grand opening, and I was able to take a friend, Dennis Wagner from Arlington Heights, with me. As we walked into the vestibule, they had pictures of all these famous sports people signed to Harry, and there was a picture of Mike Madigan, who lived next door to me in college. So I said to Wags, "Why would Mike Madigan's picture be on this wall?" I was living in Arizona. I didn't know he was the speaker of the Illinois

"Why would Mike Madigan's picture be on this wall?"

House at that time. He said, "Madigan's the most powerful politician in Illinois. He's the guy who kept the White Sox in Chicago."

We were in a line stretching from the bar into the restaurant area. I saw this guy across the hallway from me, only a few feet away, and I said to Wags, "I think I went to Notre Dame with that guy." He said, "Why don't you go ask him?" So I went over and introduced myself and he introduced himself and his wife as Rich and Maggie Taylor.

I asked, "Did you go to Notre Dame?" He said, "No, I went to Providence." I said, "Well, you look just like a guy I went to Notre Dame with." We're talking along, he's a very nice man, and finally his wife said, in a huffy way, "Well, I don't believe you heard my husband's last name." I said, "Well, it's Taylor isn't it?" She said, "No, it's Daley." I said, "I'm sorry." We kept on chatting. I didn't realize at the time who Rich Daley was. He wasn't a household name in Arizona in those days. Wags knew all along and loved it. . . .

In 1969 I was living in New York City. I actually went to seventy-one Mets home games that year. A lot of the Mets players were the same age as I was, and I knew a lot of them. That truly was the year of the Miracle Mets. They did things that year that defied explanation.

On July 8 of that year, an employee of mine was visiting from Elkhart, Indiana. We were sitting in the upper deck. It was the game where Don Young lost two fly balls because of the white shirts in the upper deck at Shea. My friend took out a plain white matchbook and wrote on both sides of it. On one side he wrote, in real thick letters, "July 8, 1969." On the flip side, "The day the Cubs lost the pennant." It was hard to believe. I said, "What are you talking about?" He said, "The Cubs won't win this thing. They're going to blow the whole deal." Nobody dreamed the Mets could win it at the time.

We were at Shea the night Jimmy Qualls broke up Tom Seaver's perfect game in the ninth inning. We were sitting right behind home plate, about five rows up. It was just perfect, how you could see Qualls hit that ball to left-center. What was unusual about that, another one of my employees was there, a guy named Jim Smith. He later became president of a huge company in the western Chicago suburbs called Healthcare Compare, later called First Health. Smith was not a sports fan at all, had no time for it, didn't understand it, didn't care for it. He couldn't understand why everybody was getting so excited when the Mets pitcher kept getting guys out. He said, "Well, isn't that his job to get guys out?" Then when Qualls got the hit to left-center, he couldn't understand the disappointment. . . .

In May of '59, after the last day of school, a friend of mine named Jack Marlowe and three other guys picked me up outside of my high school and we went to Chicago to watch the Cubs play. It was my first big trip away from home as a young man. Who could ever forget a trip like that? We stayed at the Leyden Motel in Maywood, Illinois. We went to Wrigley, waiting for the gates to open every day and staying until they threw us out. One day, we were staying real late after a game and the Giants came back out and took batting practice, and we ended up with a gaggle of foul balls. There were very few fans left.

In Maywood there was this drive-in restaurant called Skip's Fiesta. What a popular place that was, mainly because their carhops were gorgeous. One night at Skip's Fiesta was when I first realized that women were intrigued by men's butts. I heard this one carhop say, "Those guys from Iowa, what asses."

—Dick Fox, 66,

native of Lost Nation, Iowa

When I was real young we listened to Cubs radio on WIND in Chicago. My dad was weird and listened to either the Cub or White Sox games. I really didn't know the difference.

In 1982, right after Dallas Green came to Chicago from Philadelphia, the Cubs started the Diehard Cub Fan Club. I got real lucky. They announced it on a day I happened to be at Wrigley Field and I got a low number. They said that they had a deal for Cubs fans and to pick up your application. It cost five or six dollars at that time. You got some discounts coming into the game, a membership card, and a newsletter.

Eventually, the Diehard Cub Fan Club died. You could tell it was dying. They weren't promoting it, and they finally just let it die. They had their first Diehard Cub Fan Club convention in Chicago, but now it's called the Cubs Convention. The first one was

In 1982, right after Dallas Green came to Chicago from Philadelphia, the Cubs started the Diehard Cub Fan Club.

in 1985, maybe '86. It was great fun. We met a lot of the players and ex-players, of course. The '69 Cubs were a part of it, and everybody knows that that the '69 Cubs are legendary.

Nick Sellon recruited me to be a director of the fan club. We had maybe ten people, but two of us were from the Quad Cities. We had a chapter out here in Rock Island. We were quite serious and involved. Nick signed up six hundred people, and I signed up four hundred people, so we were about a thousand members. That's how you became a director, you had to sign up at least one hundred memberships. You got some perks, and we started our Quad Cities Day at Wrigley because of that. Someone from the area got to throw out the first pitch or sing the National Anthem, have a flag ceremony. It was quite a lot of fun. That's why our fan club did so well, because we did have that privilege for fifteen or sixteen years.

Our fan club died in the year 2000. That's about the time the caravan stopped coming to the Quad Cities. They said weather was a problem, in general, in the Midwest. The distance they said was too much, although they still come to Peoria. Peoria and the Quad Cities are about the same distance from Chicago. I still have friends in the ticket office. Frank Maloney and Brian Garza are two good friends, and they're the main two guys in the ticket office. That's a good place to have friendships.

Throwing out the first pitch is a nervous thing. You feel that you can't do it. I threw it to Jody Davis. He said it was a great pitch, except it was a bit high. I did that in 1986, so I would have been fifty-three years old then. They showed it on WGN.

—John Raap, 75,
Quad Cities

5
Cubbiepalooza

Cubs fans in Iraq

Day-Dream Believers

Hear Me Now, Listen to Me Later

Spike O'Dell

 William O'Dell was nicknamed Spike by his mother one month before he was born in East Moline, Illinois. O'Dell went from being a night watchman at a **farm implement** plant to the most successful radio personality in the history of his home area in the Quad Cities. His low-key, friendly delivery has led him to the top of the Chicago radio market as he enters his twenty-first year with WGN.

When I go to a Cubs game I'm very quiet because I love baseball. I study it. I am guessing every pitch. I'm trying to figure out if he's going to steal over there from first base. I'm no fun to go to the game with. I'm a student. I just sit there and study it.

I've had season tickets at Wrigley as part of my deal twenty-one years ago. When my agent was putting together the contract he said, "Anything else you want?" I said, "Yeah, season tickets" as a passing remark. Lo and behold, I got season tickets. Last time I cried big crocodile tears was when the Cubs blew it in '84.

I did one of the last interviews with Harry Caray. I was listening to it not too long ago. I hadn't listened to it since the day I did it. I very rarely enjoy listening to myself talk. I found myself fascinated with it because of all the questions I asked. He was fascinating. I had been after him to come in for so long. Of course, Harry's schedule—this and that—he was always out and about. After the season was over, in late October of 1997, he came in. The subject matter was "Anything but sports." You can't talk baseball. You can't talk sports. None of that stuff. I laid down those ground rules. He said, "All right, fire away." I just asked him everything from politics to his family life to

farm implement: In its early days, Deere and Company had an advertisement that stated: "John Deere stands behind all of its farm implements except the manure spreader."

his marriages. Everything was fair game and he was a sport about it. He laughed and got choked up one time when we were talking about his wives. He just said all of his wives were good people and when he was young he played too hard and too fast. He said they raised his children and wishes he would have been a better husband at the time but those were the days you ran hard and played hard. That's where he got a little choked up. He was very candid about everything I asked him. He kept coming back to the family aspect. Harry was so proud that there were three Carays in the baseball business—the broadcasting business. He was so proud of that—he loves those boys. The fact that there were three Carays doing baseball play-by-play, you could just see the twinkle in his eye. He loved his family, he really did.

Harry was bigger than life. The glasses were the first thing you noticed. He was the idol that everybody looked up to and respected—they loved to listen to him and see him on TV. When I first got to WGN they made sure that I'd met him and he knew who I was for promotional purposes. There was a party out at Gainey Ranch in Scottsdale. They had a big

"Harry Caray has the softest lips I've ever kissed!"

client party, and Harry was there. We talked; I was the new kid. I introduced him to my wife, Karen, and he gave her a big kiss on the lips. Driving home that night, Karen said, "Harry Caray has the softest lips I've ever kissed!" A year later—almost to the date—we're at the same place doing another party and he walks up and remembered my wife's name. We were wondering how he did that with all the thousands of people he meets all the time.

On 8/8/88—the first-ever Wrigley night game—I did part of the rain delay in the booth with Harry that night. It was a lot of fun because they were just killing time. They were doing anything with anybody who had a set of kneecaps or could breathe that could go in there and give an interview. They were trying to get that game in and they couldn't get it in. That was cool. I was thinking, "What am I doing?" I'm a kid from East Moline, Illinois, doing a rain delay with Harry Caray at the Cubs game on one of the most historic nights in Cubs history. . . .

My dad was the chief of police in East Moline, and he always had his little blue transistor radio up to his ear turning it this way or that way trying to bring the Cubs game in. He loved Ron Santo and Ernie Banks. He loved those guys. My dad died way too early—he died when he was fifty-two years old—long before I got into the radio business. So I missed being able to take him to watch a game with Ron Santo.

I always had a fascination with the radio. I was always tinkering around with them. Growing up, I was always the guy that took the radio apart. I had a big floor-model radio with incredible reception. I had strewn copper wire outside all through the trees and made this big long antenna. I was pulling in stations from all over. The AM band pulled in WGN or KMOX—wherever the Cubs were playing. Just radio in general—I would just listen to different people up and down the dial. Wolfman Jack I would hear out of a Mexican radio station with 100,000 watts. It was always bigger than life for me. I thought, "How cool would that be?" I really had no idea I'd ever end up on the radio. I was sitting at the guard shack one day at International Harvester in East Moline flipping through the newspaper, and there was an advertisement for the Academy of Radio and Television—owned by Chuck Hamilton. It said, "Be a radio star in six weeks!" I thought I should try this, go over there and see what it's like. So I did. Chuck took a liking to me. He could tell I had something going for me. He pushed me harder than he pushed most other people. Through him and his connections with the radio business in the Quad Cities—at KSTT in particular—I got on the air. Everybody knows everybody and he helped out. I went on the air for the first time in 1976. By the mid-'80s they were giving me a six-figure salary to be in the Quad Cities, which was unheard of at that time. I won an award from *Billboard* magazine—Jock of the Year Award. When that happened the phones started ringing off the hook and everybody just wanted to hire me. I was grateful but I was making more money in Davenport than they could pay me in San Diego. Little did I know, WGN was looking for someone to come in—they were going to take Wally Phillips out of the equation more and more. They were looking for somebody young. Somebody that was good on the phones. That was my forte. They spent a week down at the Holiday Inn in Moline listening to me. They took a box of tapes back up to Chicago and one day I get a call from the boss up at WGN saying he wanted to talk to me. I said, "About what?" He said, "About a job." I said, "Me?" I was rock 'n' rolling. That was talk radio. He said, "Yeah, I'd just like to pick your brain. I'll send you a plane ticket and you'll come up tomorrow." So I went up there thinking, "Wow, at least I'll get to see the inside of WGN radio." I talked to him. They put me on the air. They set me up—I had to do a fake radio show. They wanted to see how I'd react to certain things. I landed back in Moline that night about 7:30, got in the house a little after 8, and at 8:30 the phone rings and they offered me a job. I couldn't believe it. It scared me to death. When I was going to the radio school they would always say, "I wonder if that's how they do it at WGN?" So it was always the standard everything was set by. I had to take the job. Even if I didn't last I could always say I have WGN on my resume.

"Wow, at least I'll get to see the inside of WGN radio."

In my Harry Caray interview, he talks about his politics. Harry was a registered Democrat and the only Republican he's ever voted for was Ronald Reagan because Reagan called baseball games. I talked to him for about an hour—counting commercials. People tell me that was the last time he ever sat down for a bona fide interview like that. I thought the subject matter was cool—let's not talk baseball, though he'd keep going back there from time to time. It was very interesting.

I'd put that experience up there as a top three. The favorite interview I ever did was Alan Shepard—the first United States astronaut. He was only scheduled to be in the studio for ten minutes. He could tell I loved the space program and I had an idea what I was talking about so he stayed for a whole hour. He's a little guy. He's not very tall but he has a big, deep, booming voice—it's a great radio voice. Here's the guy that was the first American to strap his butt onto a rocket and light the fuse and years later he lands on the moon on Apollo 14 and plays **golf** on the moon. He busted every rule in the book to get on the moon because all the alarms were going off that he shouldn't land, he should abort, and forget the moon and go back. Here he is, 100 feet above the surface of the moon, and he said, "No, I've worked too hard for this. I'm taking over manually and going to the moon." NASA wasn't going to punish a hero like Alan Shepard so nothing was really said about it. He used a makeshift six-iron and dropped a couple golf balls on the moon. He missed one because you couldn't put both hands on it because of the space suit, but he connected into the second one. Of course he said that ball is still going. That was probably my favorite interview. I walked out of there knowing I was talking to a true American hero.

My favorite Cub player is Ron Santo, no question—hands down. I wore No. 10 everywhere I went. I played third base, even in college. I went to the fantasy camp and wore No. 10½ because he was my coach at third base. I played at Wrigley Field. I come from that '69 era. All those '69 Cubs are favorites.

The fantasy camp was great. That was another thing the station did for me. I was relatively new in town. They put me in the Randy Hundley Fantasy Camp at Wrigley Field. You got to hang out with the Cubs themselves. It was a four-day thing and the fourth day you got to play the game. I play baseball pretty well—I had a good glove and I could hit for power but I couldn't hit for average. During practice at Wrigley Field, I jacked one out of Wrigley Field. I hit it into the bleachers, right at the well there in the leftfield bleachers. Santo saw that too and he never forgot that.

Jim Hickman hit a rocket right at me. I've never seen a ball go past me that fast and hard in my life. I backed up. I was not going to get hit with that. I'm being cocky and playing in on the infield on third, over to the line and I'm thinking, "No, you idiot, you're going to get killed."

---

golf: While playing golf in 1567, Mary, Queen of Scots, was informed that her husband, Lord Darnley, had been murdered. She finished the round.

There were no disappointments when I met Santo. We've become good buds. Before his medical problems, he'd pick me up out in Arizona and we'd go golfing. He's one of those great guys. He's nicer than you can imagine. A guy that wears his heart on his sleeve. You know right where he is at every moment. If you want to hear some Cubs stories, have a couple of beers and sit across from Ron Santo—he will have you roaring, laughing your tail off; he's hilarious.

Wrigley Field—One-Stop Fun Center

A Matter of Grave Importance to Cubs Fans

Dave D'Antonio

Dave D'Antonio has always had an interest in cemeteries. His uncle and aunt lived across the street from a large cemetery in his hometown of Santa Clara, California. In June of 1991, D'Antonio was at a used-book store in Berkeley looking at the *Whole Baseball Catalogue,* a book of baseball trivia. When he saw a photo of Satchel Paige's grave, with a question mark where his birth date was, it was the beginning of a lengthy adventure for the grade-school teacher.

That photo got me thinking, "Wouldn't it be neat to travel the country looking at the graves of baseball's greatest players?" At that time, there was so much emphasis on how much the players could make and how much money the teams could get from the fans with no regard at all for the history of modern baseball that I decided that's what I would do. I was able to get a sabbatical from the school district, so I took off at the start of the 1995 season. I was driving a 1993 Geo Metro that I called Nellie after Nellie Bly and Nellie Fox.

I left Denver on May 4 to head to St. Paul, Nebraska, where former Cubbie Grover Cleveland Alexander is buried. I got off to a lousy start; I headed east on the wrong interstate. I went two hours east on Interstate 70 instead of Interstate 76. Grover Cleveland Alexander was an awful alcoholic, as were his father and grandfather before him. In St. Paul, I ran into his nephew, also named Alex, and also his niece, who was eighty-one years old and named Elma. The great Alexander is buried a half-mile from the Grover Cleveland Alexander Ballpark, in Elmwood Cemetery. They had a plastic ball and two red plastic bats and some synthetic flowers next to his headstone. There was a plaque about his making the Hall of Fame in 1938. They had the wrong date for his death on the tombstone.

Next was Rogers Hornsby, who had a .358 lifetime batting average. Hornsby not only holds the highest single-season batting average in Cubs history, amazingly he holds the same record for the Cardinals and Braves! Hornsby was known as an irascible SOB as a manager and as a player. He's buried in Hornsby Bend, Texas, which isn't on any real maps of any consequence. To get to his grave site, I had to go down a dirt lane past a "No Trespassing" sign. There was a barbed-wire fence along each side of the lane. After walking for a little while there was a historic marker

> Hornsby not only holds the highest single-season batting average in Cubs history, amazingly he holds the same record for the Cardinals and Braves!

there talking about Ruben and Sarah Hornsby, who had built a home at that spot in 1832. It said that "the house was known for its Christian hospitality," but it was also the place where Josiah Wilbarger recovered after being scalped in 1833. Finally, I got to the burial area, which was full of tombstones for the Hornsbys. Rogers's grave was way over in the back corner, covered by plants and underbrush and grass. There was no one else buried near him. He died in 1963 at the age of sixty-seven. . . .

Joe Tinker of "Tinker to Evers to Chance" fame is buried in Greenwood Cemetery in Orlando. His grave is in awful shape. It's below a big tree. The entire grave site is covered by weeds and grass and ferns. He has a very small headstone, and on the headstone it says FATHER, but you can barely read the letters because the marker has sunk into the ground at an odd angle.

Babe Ruth's grave is in Hawthorne, New York, at the Gate of Heaven cemetery. Also buried at the same cemetery are Jimmy Cagney, **Billy Martin**, Westbrook Pegler, and Sal Mineo. Ruth's grave was considerably more gaudy than Lou Gehrig's—which is only 5 miles

---

Billy Martin: When the George Brett "Pine Tar" game was concluded, Ron Guidry was the center fielder, Don Mattingly was the second baseman, and Billy Martin read the comic pages in his office.

I also went to the grave of Hack Wilson, the legendary Cub slugger and drinker, who has a huge tombstone even though he died broke.

away. Ruth's had American flags planted nearby. It had a big picture of Jesus with a little boy, a little **Babe Ruth,** and it had inscriptions on each side of that picture of Jesus. More than ten people a day visit the grave, and most of them leave different things. When I was there, there were four baseballs, a Louisville Slugger bat with a crack in it, a Baby Ruth candy bar, four American flags, fifty-one cents in change, and notes from about a half-dozen different people.

I also went to the grave of Hack Wilson, the legendary Cub slugger and drinker, who has a huge tombstone even though he died broke. It's in Martinsburg, West Virginia . . . one of the larger ones in the cemetery with crisscrossed bats with a baseball in the middle. It was well cared for by the local organization that raised the funds for it. . . .

We're all going to die sometime . . . the only question is when.

Babe Ruth: Yankee Stadium is known as "the House that Ruth Built." The school that Babe Ruth attended in his youth, St. Mary's Industrial School for Boys in Baltimore—now called Cardinal Gibbons High School—was known as "the House that Built Ruth." . . . The cement used to build Yankee Stadium was purchased from Thomas Edison, who owned the huge Portland Cement Company.

Ron Santo Is God's Way of Being Nice to Cubs Fans

Frank Mastro

Frank Mastro of Bartlett, Illinois, is in sales with the IBM Software Group. He grew up on Chicago's Northwest Side where he graduated Holy Cross High School in '75.

Back in '69, the Mets and Orioles were in the World Series, which should have been the Cubs and **Orioles**. Brooks Robinson would make a great play. Granted, he made some good plays that Series. My dad looked at me and said, "Nice play, but what's the big deal? Santo will make that play a hundred times. Santo makes that play every day." He was right. He should be in the Hall of Fame. He didn't get the national exposure at the time. Without national exposure, he lost a good opportunity. . . .

I remember it like it was yesterday. My dad had a heart attack in '69, so he was off work. I would run home from school. I'd get home around four o'clock, run up the stairs to see what the score was or if it was already over, if they won or lost. I'd run up, and my dad would be standing there with his thumbs *"Kid, they're blowin' it." I said, "Dad, c'mon, you can't say that!"* down. "Aw, c'mon!" Next day, thumbs down. He said, "Kid, they're blowin' it." I said, "Dad, c'mon, you can't say that!" He said, "I'm tellin' you right now, they're blowin' it." This is the thing I'll never, ever forget. He said, "This team has not been in a World Series for twenty-four years. What makes you think they're gonna do it now?"

Orioles: Since 1977 John Denver's "Thank God, I'm a Country Boy" has been sung at the seventh-inning stretch of every Orioles home game.

I usually go to the games with a buddy of mine who is a die-hard Cub fan. We'd been watching Cub games in a pub in my old neighborhood on the Northwest Side of Chicago. When the Cubs were up 2–0 in Game 5 in '84, Sutcliffe on the mound, I was at home. I said, "You know what? They're gonna do it." I ran over to the hangout to see who was there and celebrate. Obviously what happened, that ball went through Durham's legs. One of my buddies who was there was a boxer and a die-hard Cub fan. When that final out was made, tears were streaming down his face, he said, "What do you gotta do to win it?" He was crying, literally bawling. He got up and walked out of the bar. The Cubs reduced a boxer down to crying.

In '03 they're up three games to one. Then, they lose Game 5 in Florida. A couple of the sportscasters, even Mark Giangreco, said, "We're going back to Chicago. We want to win it in Chicago anyway. We've got Prior and Wood, it's in the bag." I'm yelling, "No! What's the matter with you?" I'm yelling at the TV.

It was Mark Prior in Game 6 and Kerry Wood in Game 7. But Game 6 was Bartman.

To take the cake, when they gave up Game 6, I said to my wife, "For cripes sake, you know I love your sister, but I should be there." I was jealous because my sister and brother-in-law were at Game 6. The morning after Game 6, I said to my wife right before I left the house, "Even if I had tickets to go to the game tonight, Game 7, I wouldn't go. They're not going to do it. They're not going to get off the floor and come back and win it. It's just not going to happen." She said, "Oh, you're crazy!" I said, "No, I'm an optimist, but I'm just telling you the reality." I drove downtown, and my cell phone rang. It was my sister-in-law. She asked, "Hey, what are you doing tonight?" I said, "What do you think I'm doing tonight? I'm watching the game." She said, "Well, how would you like to go?" My brother-in-law had told her, "You go with him. He's more of a Cub fan." My brother-in-law is a Sox fan.

I actually hesitated. I put her on hold for a second, and for a minute I thought about it. I said I have to do it no matter what. So I was at Game 7. I'll never forget that. We were in the second row of the leftfield bleachers. When **Moises Alou** hit that home run, I was getting ready to catch it, and it went further back in the bleachers. They were up 5–3 at that point, thinking they were gonna do it, and they collapsed.

He let the bullpen blow it. That's why they lost. Poor managing.

The reason why they lost Game 7 was solely because of Dusty Baker. He used Kyle Farnsworth and Dave Veres in relief. This is Game 7, you clown. Jack McKeon brought in one of his starters in relief. Baker didn't even warm one up. You do what you need to do. If you get to the Series, who cares, somebody is going to start Game 1. He let the bullpen blow it. That's why they lost. Poor managing.

About Bartman, I've seen that replay a million times. Alou would've caught it. Bottom line is, no one says anything. Baker never went out to the mound after that play happened to talk to Prior, settle him down. You hardly ever hear anyone talking about Alex Gonzalez at shortstop. He blew a two-hopper that would have been a double play to get out of the inning and they would have still been up. If Gonzalez converted that, then nobody is even talking about Bartman because they still have the lead and they are out of the inning.

There were a lot of hands going after the Bartman ball. There were four other pairs of hands going after it. It just happened to hit his. Stroke of luck. Six inches to the left or the right, it's somebody else's hand getting it. One of my customers at that time was Hewitt Associates. He was a Hewitt employee at the time. I never met Bartman, but the people who work there said, "He's a really, really nice guy. He doesn't deserve it."

Bottom line there is some cloud or something . . . it's almost statistically impossible. They lost three straight games in '84 when all they needed was to win one. They lost three straight games in '03 when all they needed was to win one. How many teams have blown leads like that, let alone do it twice? In all those years they never won

Moises Alou: With the Expos in 1993, Moises Alou hit six consecutive home runs over a span of four games.

the Series. There's something wrong, and I just don't get it. Every year I keep coming back and coming back. If I took a whip and beat myself, it would be cheaper and less painful.

Everybody looks to Boston. Oh, poor Boston. But Boston, they lost in '86, but they were in the Series. So how could you compare a Red Sox fan's sorrows to a Cubs fan's sorrows? When the **Red Sox** won the World Series a couple years ago in 2004 and then again in 2007 . . . I'm not a Sox hater, but the fact they won it all before the Cubs just kills me.

I just love Santo. I played ball through college. High school, I wore No. 10. College, I wore No. 10. Now, I have two daughters in high school. They play basketball and softball. One is No. 10. Even my kids are wearing the numbers.

Drove by the Dusty Baker Museum of Progress today. It's still not open.

Red Sox: **The Sam Malone character in *Cheers* was patterned after former Red Sox pitcher, Bill Lee . . . Bill Lee once demanded number 337 from the Boston Red Sox because 337, upside down, spells Lee's last name.**

The Cultural Learnings of Memphis for Make Benefit Glorious Cub Nation

Fred Freres

In 1967, Fred Freres left the Milwaukee Avenue/Montrose section of Chicago for Christian Brothers College in Memphis. Over forty years later he's still there where he has been a standout teacher for decades.

For my fifth birthday, I got a Hank Sauer glove, who was the big Cub at that time. That was the year Ernie Banks broke in—1953. My grandmother had a neighbor who had a connection to the Cubs, and I got a Cubs baseball signed by all the players. I took it out one day when we couldn't find another ball and played with it and lost all the names off of it. That was a tragedy.

By the time we were nine, we were able to go to the ball games ourselves. The only Opening Day game I went to was '59 and it snowed. My buddies and I were in fifth grade. It was 32 degrees and we were drinking hot chocolate, and the Cubs actually won. We got on the bus that day, and a man asked me what the score was, and we said the Cubs won 6–1. He said, "Oh, maybe they'll be good this year." How was I to know that would become the mantra of my life?

It cost a buck to get in the bleachers and a buck a beer, so if you had a ten spot you could have a ball.

The best year to be a Cub fan was in '69. I turned twenty-one that summer, so I could drink beer legally. It cost a buck to get in the bleachers and a buck a beer, so if you had a ten spot you could have a ball. There were all kinds of gorgeous ladies out there. My buddy and I went to eighteen games, and the Cubs won seventeen of them. On the weekends only, 'cause we were working; I was in college.

One time, we were sitting in the third row of the leftfield bleachers, Houston hit a home run, and it landed right under my brother's seat. It gave Houston a one-run lead and, of course, the Bleacher Bums had already been doing that "Throw it back" stuff. I had been going fifteen years to the ball games and had never got close to a ball in my life, and here it was—my brother had one—so we wouldn't throw it back. By that time, everybody in the leftfield bleachers was throwing stuff at us.

There must have been ten or fifteen Bleacher Bums who came down and pleaded with us and threatened us. Finally, some guy asked us, "If we get you the ball back, will you throw it back?" My brother looked at me, and I told him, "Go ahead. Throw it back." So he did, and by that time Houston was in the field. It landed right behind the leftfielder. He called time-out and threw it up on a catwalk along the line. This little kid, about ten years old, got it. About twelve or fifteen Bleacher Bums assaulted this kid, grabbed the ball from him, came back down, and brought it to my brother. They said, "Thanks a lot, guys. We really appreciate it. We're sorry for all the trouble we gave you." The whole leftfield bleachers were against us. Those days, we weren't smart enough to bring another ball, like they do now.

A lot of the midweek games weren't very crowded, unlike now, when there's forty-something thousand people all the time and you can't get a ticket. We used to laugh at these old guys with their hair growing out of their ears and over their shoulders. Everyplace but their head. They'd sit there and bet on every pitch a lot of times. It was fun watching them. The vendors were hilarious. There was this one guy we called Fang. He had one tooth in his mouth, and he sold Frosty Malts.

One of the best games I ever saw was in 1977. My mom and dad, my wife, my two oldest daughters, and I were sitting in the bleachers. We'd get there two hours ahead of time so we'd get a good seat. It ended up being a five-hour game, which the Cubs won 16–15 in thirteen innings against the Reds. At that time, the Cubs were in first place with Jerry Morales and Manny Trillo. We were burnt to smithereens, and the wind was blowing at rightfield, where we were sitting in the bleachers. It was like the ball was on a conveyor belt. It would get up into that wind—it was like it was just floating out—and it would make it into the stands. It was amazing.

It was like the ball was on a conveyor belt. It would get up into that wind—it was like it was just floating out—and it would make it into the stands. It was amazing.

I would say Memphis is about ten-to-one Cardinal fans to Cub fans because it goes so deep growing up in Memphis. Harry Caray and the Cardinals, that was the only thing. In *The Painted House* by John Grisham, part of the thing the kid did all summer was sit outside and listen to the Cardinal games on radio. Cardinal fans are always nice, because they're always happy for me. When the Cardinals aren't doing well, they are always happy the Cubs are in it. It seems that usually when the Cubs are in it, the Cardinals aren't.

The year 2003 changed everything. We were sitting with friends watching that notorious sixth game, watching in disbelief as everything just fell apart in that eighth inning. There was something in my mind that said, "Well they ain't gonna do it." Just like in '84.

I still felt like they were going to be the next Atlanta Braves. With Kerry Wood and Mark Prior and Zambrano, how could they miss not being dominant over the next ten years or so in the National League? As much as I like Dusty Baker as a person, he ruined Prior and Wood. He overused them that year, and they haven't been the same since.

Chicagoans love their sports personalities. We had Ernie Banks. When I was growing up, everybody wanted to be like Ernie Banks. I told my students when we were talking about the civil rights movement, players like Ernie Banks did so much in these big northern cities to help us kids. We had grown up in basically segregated neighborhoods in Chicago, and because of people like Ernie Banks, we learned to appreciate the African Americans for who they were and what they could do.

It really disturbs me that since 2003, Cub fans boo the Cubs. I don't ever remember fans doing that. Being disgusted about the way they were playing, there was a resignation. "OK, well, that's the Cubs. What the heck are we gonna do?" I'd trade six Bulls championships for one Cub World Series. No doubt in my mind. You've heard all these stories about the lessons you learn being a Cub fan. It's a disease, to some extent. It gets in your blood early in life, because you look up to your dad and he turns you into a Cub fan. You just can't shake it. It's a part of you from the very beginning, almost. No matter how poorly they do.

Tony LaRussa's ego applied for statehood today. If approved, it would be the nation's third largest.

Wit Happens

Mike Toomey

Comedian Mike Toomey has performed on numerous television and radio programs. He's the creator of Skip Parker, the perpetual Cubs backup broadcaster. The *Chicago Tribune* has called Toomey "one of the funniest and most talented performers to ever work in Chicago." Born in Carol Stream, Toomey has lived in New Lenox for the past twenty-five years.

M y whole family was Cub fans—my dad, my mom, and their parents. I wasn't very much into sports. It was '71 when I got interested in baseball cards. The cards are what made me interested in the game, because after I knew who the players were, then I wanted to see them play.

The Cubs were always on the TV or radio. That's what my folks and everybody watched. I just got hooked very quickly. I was watching in '70 when Ernie Banks hit No. 500. I was sitting on my couch and not really understanding what the big deal was about this. It was obviously some kind of event, because everybody was going crazy. Brickhouse was screaming. I was about seven years old then. When I was eight, that's when I started getting the cards. That's when I was full-fledged hook, line, and sinker. I couldn't wait to go to Wrigley Field to see a game. The first time I ever did that and looked, it was this place that, until that moment, I had only seen on television. All of a sudden, these guys are walking around who are only on TV, and I could see them up close.

That's when I was full-fledged hook, line, and sinker. I couldn't wait to go to Wrigley Field.

I married into a family from the South Side that's Cubs fans. I don't know how it happened. I'm very fortunate that way. It's funny, cause I never understood that Cubs and Sox thing until I was in my late twenties. In the suburbs, some people are Cubs fans and some

171

Many Sox fans sprained their ankles jumping off the Sox bandwagon.

people are Sox fans. I never really knew that existed until around the time I started to live out south. Then you could just see it was such a weird take on things. It was more about hating the Cubs then it was about following the Sox.

New Lenox is Sox territory when they're winning, just like anywhere else. Like in '05, when they were doing well, Sox fans were crawling out of the woodwork. Now, I don't know where they are. There are die-hards for every team. There's a lot of bandwagons when a team does well, and that was what '05 was around here. Many Sox fans sprained their ankles jumping off the Sox bandwagon.

To me the Cubs are part of the Sox identity. All the White Sox marketing, all their commercials, they can't do anything without mentioning the Cubs. They're like, "We have this. The Cubs don't have that." "We have a scoreboard with lights, and the Cubs don't have that." "They haven't won a World Series since 1908." "The mayor likes us better." It's like they can't advertise without first identifying that they are the team in the same city as the Cubs.

One year right before the season started, the White Sox put up a big sign outside of Wrigley Field that said, "Major League Baseball, 8.1 miles south." It had the Sox logo on it. It was just low-class, bush league.

I talk Cubs in my act a little bit. I do a lot of stuff on the WGN morning news. I created a character, Skip Parker, who's been a broadcaster for the Cubs since 1977 but never got to broadcast in a game. A backup guy who's never gotten a chance. He's always waiting. Every time a broadcaster quits or is relieved of duties he always feels, "This is it now, I'm gonna get it." Something always happens. I'm on WGN a few times a month.

I still have just about every scorecard from every game I've ever gone to. I had a Cubs scrapbook. Grocery stores would give out pictures of the Cubs players; every week there would be two new players. I couldn't wait until those were available. I used to watch—and this is going to sound really nerdy—and broadcast Cubs games with my tape recorder. I would call the game in my family room like I was Brickhouse. Now those tapes would be somewhat painful to listen to by anyone other than myself. I wish I had saved those tapes.

Last year I did a bunch of pregame stuff for the Cubs. They pretty much let me have license. Basically, I interviewed fans. One day last year I talked to fans outside Wrigley about Barry Bonds. They edited it and saved it for a pregame show when the Cubs were playing the Giants. The joke was, I was trying to get people to say, "Barry Bonds." They don't even want to say it. I'd go over to people and say, "Now we're talking about home runs. If I say 'Babe,' you say . . . " and they'd go "Ruth." And I'd say "Hank" and they'd say "Aaron." And I'd say "Barry" and a woman said "Manilow." One guy said "Gordy." Another one was "Sanders." Every Barry imaginable except for Bonds. So at the end of the piece I'm just fed up, so I tell a lady, "Complete this sentence for me. Buy your savings . . . " and then she says "bonds" and gets a prize. It's an absolute thrill for me to be able to do that.

My older brother had a ball that was signed by Randy Hundley, and it was on his dresser. My friends and I were going out to play and couldn't find a ball, so we grabbed the "Hundley." Of course we ruin it, and my brother beat my #^@ over it. As a reporter for WGN, I was covering the Cubs Convention a few years ago, and I met Hundley and told him the story about the baseball. He goes, "Well, that's what a baseball is for. You're supposed to play with a baseball." Basically he was saying, "What value does my signature have? You should be out playing with the ball."

For one pregame show I wrote some new lyrics to "We Didn't Start the Fire" by Billy Joel. Instead of all the pop-culture references, it was all these players who'd played third since Ron Santo. There were over one hundred. My song probably has about seventy of them. That went over pretty well.

Where the Past Is Present

Ken Sevara

Ken Sevara is a multitalented Chicago comedian who has had national audiences laughing for years at his Harry Caray impressions.

I was the first guy in Chicago, to my knowledge, to ever do Harry's voice. I was doing him when he was still with the White Sox. I just started messing around with it. One day I was at Wrigley Field. John Caponera, a friend of mine who also does Harry Caray, and I were sitting there doing impressions and had a whole section of the bleachers watching us more than they were watching the Cubs.

I'm a White Sox fan so I started listening to Harry with the Sox. Him and Jimmy Piersall. One night I was listening to Piersall and Piersall goes "Harry, you're crazy." And Harry goes, "Jimmy, I'm crazy? You're the crazy one and you have the papers to prove it." I thought that was fantastic. I almost drove off the road, I was laughing so hard.

One night I was in a club called The Punch Line in Greenville, South Carolina, and it was very late at night. I decided I was going to do Harry.

I guess that's what attracted me to doing Harry's voice. Because, you know, he used to sit in the bleachers and take his shirt off and he had the butterfly net. And I'm going, "Man, who is this guy? This guy is insane. And he's hilarious."

We've always had great announcers in Chicago, but he was so different. He broke the mold, you know. I'm a hard-core Sox fan. A hard-core Sox fan. And I always felt that Harry actually fit in more with the White Sox crowd, the blue-collar, shot-and-a-beer crowd. So I started doing him. And it was funny because I never really had thought about doing him on stage. Then one night I was in a club called The

Punch Line in Greenville, South Carolina, and it was very late at night. I decided I was going to do Harry. I didn't care if they liked it or not. I started into this bit and it is "killing." I mean it is "killing." I think Harry had just gone over to WGN at the time. And I thought, "Oh my God, if it works here, I might be able to do this thing anywhere." I went to California shortly after that and I did a show at the Ice House in Pasadena. I closed my set there with "Harry," and it just blew the doors off the place. And I thought, well, this is incredible. I'm just going to start doing the guy everywhere. And it became a major part of my act.

When I started doing him full-time originally, I was in **Peoria, Illinois,** working a club. There was a sea of blue-haired old ladies in the club that night. It just sucked. Horrible. There were a couple of comics in the back and I just started to do "Harry Caray on acid" and had Harry Caray fall out of the booth singing "Take Me Out of the Ball Game." And it was working. These guys were just dying. I figured, well, I made the comics laugh, so I'll bring it out on stage again tomorrow night. It "killed" and I said, "Oh my God, I've really got something here." Harry never did see my act, although I met Harry on a couple occasions. Steve Stone had me do the voice for him one time and Steve said to me, "Harry never speaks that clearly."

One night I was working at the Star Plaza Theater in Merrillville, Indiana. I was working in this little comedy club that's tucked away there. The Cubs were in town doing their Caravan that night. And Jim Lefebvre, Ron Santo, Jim Bullinger, and Bruce Levine, the sports guy from radio, were there. Somebody walked up to me and said, "You're never going to guess in a million years who is here." I said, "Who?" He told me, "Lefebvre and Santo, et cetera" and I thought, "This is going to be a riot."

I'm up on stage and Lefebvre had tears coming out of his eyes, Santo is pounding the table and these guys are going nuts—Bullinger,

Peoria, Illinois: In late 1953 the Cardinals chose Jack Buck for play-by-play over Chick Hearn from Peoria. Buck had done excellent Budweiser commercials that summer while broadcasting the Rochester Red Wings, the Cardinals' AAA team in New York.

Levine, all of them. I had a radio show the next morning. I'm very disciplined when I have a radio show. I told my wife before I left I'd be home early.

Well, after I do my set before the Cubs people, Lefebvre grabs me by the arm and he goes, "Come here," and he says, "You have no idea how well you know that son of a #&%*." So they take me out and they're buying me drinks and I don't drink. And Lefebvre goes, "Come on, you want a beer?" And I said, "I really don't drink that much." And Lefebvre goes, "Ah, bull@%*&. What are you worried about? [Tribune Co. executive] Stanton Cook's paying for it."

Thank God, booze was Harry's only vice.

We start, one drink after the other, talking baseball, and I just have a passion for talking baseball. I look at my watch and it's five in the morning. I go flying out of there and I go, "Listen guys, I really appreciate it, but . . . " I get home. I put the key in the keyhole and my wife comes flying down the hall in tears, crying at the top of her lungs. She thought I got killed. She's got the state police in Illinois and Indiana looking for my car, all because I did Harry Caray.

I did a satirical look at Caray. I did him falling out of the booth. I talked about his glasses. I said, "My God, they're getting bigger every year. They're starting to look like Harry staring through an aquarium. Somebody had to be working a triple shift at LensCrafters to finish those things. You know your glasses might be a little large when in the fifth inning, guys drop down scaffolding with squeegees."

I said, "Thank God, booze was Harry's only vice. You wouldn't want to see the guy drop acid. It would have been like, 'Holy Cow, the scoreboard has lips. It's telling me the score. Steve, Heeey, the Astro-Turf guy ate Mark Grace. The leftfield bleachers are melting. Steve, holy cow, you have two heads. Why don't you sing a duet? Hey, looks like a doubleheader.'

In part of my act, I say, "It's merciful that God took Harry when he did because one more year of watching the Cubs suck and he was going to snap. It would have been like, 'Here's the wind-up and the pitch. There's a ground ball to short. Over to second. The relay . . . SON OF A ^$@&! You know, Steve, I'm getting sick of this %*$@. Two million dollars a year for that rickety-kneed son of a *^#%. This damn team couldn't hit a bull in the &*% with a banjo. You know the only person to have more trouble with a glove was **O. J. Simpson**.'"

Sometimes I would break into a Harry Caray-oke bit. You know, Harry would get a little tired of the "Take Me Out to the Ball Game" and break into Zeppelin. And it ends with Harry falling out of the booth, dangling beneath the press box with just the cord around his neck holding him up. It would have been, "Aw right, eveerybaw-dayyy, ah one, a two, a threeeeeeee . . . holy cow, pull my drunken &$#* up will you, Steve? I'm a Cub fan. I'm a Bud man. And I'm about to be a very dead man. So long, everybody."

He's been huge for me. I was to do a radio interview for the Omaha Royals. They had a rain delay. I was supposed to go up for a couple of minutes during the regular broadcast but when the rain delay hit, they said, "Let's get this guy up here and kill some time." I went up there, did Harry dropping acid and all that other stuff and these guys are just going nuts. Because of that, three other radio stations in Omaha call up this comedy club and said we got to get this guy. As a result of that, I go back every year for the College World Series. I was in Des Moines for the Iowa Cubs, actually doing play-by-play. I did an inning on the radio and an inning on TV. I'm doing Harry on acid and all these guys in the press box are absolutely falling down. This woman walks up the stairs and actually thought Harry was in the booth. What the hell would Harry be doing talking about dropping acid on a broadcast? She didn't even put two and two together that this might not actually be Harry.

O. J. Simpson: Ernie Banks and O. J. Simpson are cousins. Their grand-fathers were twin brothers.

Down at the Corner of What and If

Mark Servais

Mark Servais is the professional teams and special assignment scout for the Cubs. He is the uncle of former Cub catcher (1995–98) Scott Servais, who is now the player development director for the Texas Rangers. Both are from LaCrosse, Wisconsin. . . . . So just how do you become a scout for the Cubs?

After I got released from pro ball, I went back and started teaching and coaching and was happy doing that. A good friend of mine was scouting for the White Sox, early in the '80s. He was working up in our area of Wisconsin. He needed some help and asked me if I would be interested. He put me out as a part-time guy. I'd go out on the weekends and after school. He said they had an opening up there for the next year, so I luckily got on as a full-time guy. I don't even know if he knew I could be a good scout. He just needed somebody to give him some eyes up here in Minnesota and Wisconsin. He trusted me because he knew me.

After the White Sox, I went to Montreal for a while with Gary Hughes. We had a big shake-up at the White Sox about '85 or '86. Jerry Reinsdorf took over the whole operation, and they laid off about all the scouts. Dave Dombrowski called me up and said, "Hey, I got to let you go. I feel bad. Call Gary Hughes in Montreal. He's looking for a guy." I had a job in a half-hour. Gary was a great guy to work for. I worked for the Expos for six years, until '91. That's when most of those guys left to go to the **Marlins**. Dave Dombrowski and Gary Hughes went down there. I eventually left the Expos and went to

---

Marlins: In the '80s movie *Back to the Future, Part II*, Biff Tanner scans a sports almanac brought back from the future. Biff reads aloud, "Florida's going to win the World Series in 1997. Yeah, right." The Marlins were not a team at that time, but they did win the World Series in 1997.

Houston for five years. Then Jim Hendry got with the Cubs. The Marlins had hired him from Creighton University in Omaha, where he was the coach. I always scouted the Nebraska area and got to know Coach Hendry. My brother, Ed, is now the head baseball coach at Creighton. Every so often I had to go and see Hendry's club, so I just started talking to him about players. I got to know Jim pretty well, and when he got the job with the Cubs he said, "I'm looking for a guy." He hired me with the Cubs.

Mike Wuertz is a guy I signed. I found him in Austin, Minnesota. I liked his arm and the way he worked. I put him on my list and went back that following winter and watched him play a little basketball. Mike Restovich is another big name over there, from Rochester. I went to see them play basketball against each other, just to see how they competed. Both of the kids competed well. Sometimes it's good to see them out of their comfort zone playing another sport besides their main sport. Restovich was a big outfielder from Rochester, Minnesota. He got a little big-league time, the Twins took him. We had him a couple of years ago. He's with Washington right now. He's been up and down the last four and five years.

I haven't drafted anybody for the Cubs in quite a while. I'm a pool scout. I do minor-league and big-league teams only.

I haven't been in amateur scouting for the last eight years, so I haven't drafted anybody for the Cubs in quite a while. I'm a pool scout. I do minor-league and big-league teams only. We have certain assignments and teams to cover. I have the Brewers and Twins organizations. I cover all their clubs, from the big-league club all the way down to the short-season club. You see a wide range of talents and abilities between the short-season ball and the big leagues.

The best I ever saw was a college pitcher, Ben Christensen of Wichita State. I thought he was a lock. That's the pitcher who intentionally hit an opposing player when that player was on-deck. The Cubs drafted him. Talentwise there was no question he was a steal when we got him. He hurt his elbow, and he hurt his shoulder. He just never came back.

I look for tools. Not a whole lot different than amateur ball. Obviously the kids are at a higher level and the competition is a little better, but you just read the tools. You judge their tools and try and project what type of player this guy is going to be at the Major League level.

It's always tools. A lot of times I look how kids react to playing the game. How they handle success and failure, failure more than success. How they prepare to play a game, mentally as well as physically. How they compete in game situations, game-deciding situations. You try and paint a picture of this guy and how he can handle it emotionally, in a high-pressure situation in the big leagues. You try and tell if he's going to make your club a winning club.

Mark Grudzielanek has played for winning clubs. He's always been close to a .300 hitter. He's a defensive guy. He doesn't run like he used to because his legs are getting a little beat up now. He can hit. He's got a little power every once in a while. He's not a flashy guy. He's not a guy who's going to go out and hit 30 home runs. Sometimes we overlook this type of guy.

When these guys sign and go out and start playing, some of them got a lot bigger all of a sudden. Jose Canseco played in Madison in single-A ball. He weighed about 185 pounds, and he was just another guy. The next year when he came back, he weighed 235 or 240. We all knew something was happening but didn't know specifically what it was. We didn't talk about steroids in those days because us older guys didn't know what they were.

Mainly, I report to Jim Hendry and Tim Wilken in the Cubs organization. Tim Wilken is our scouting director, and Jim Hendry is our general manager. They are both good people. They understand how hard the scouting profession is. They appreciate our work. They respect you enough to let you do your job; they aren't critical. . . .

At a young age, all these kids are throwing breaking balls. We are worrying more about getting kids out and winning the game, rather than developing a skill. A twelve-year-old is not going to hit a breaking ball, so they throw a breaking ball. Is that developing that kid's skill? When he's fifteen, he might not be able to throw anything. . . .

Greg Maddux had great location with great movement. He wanted the pitch to draw contact. Maddux's best innings were with three ground balls getting him out of there. I never saw him when he was real young. But I've heard guys who scouted him in high school in Las Vegas say that was just who he was. He just always had it. He was a second-round pick in high school. Maybe he would get signed today, maybe he wouldn't.

Zambrano suffers from anorexia ponderosa

I'm Ready for My Close-up, Mr. Gimbel

Noel Gimbel

Noel Gimbel is the executive producer of *Hello Again Everybody,* a documentary on the life of Harry Caray. After making millions in the CD and DVD distribution business, Gimbel was looking for something to keep him busy. When he met Harry Caray's attorney one day, the light went on. Gimbel's superb DVD on Harry Caray is hilarious, poignant, and not to be missed if you are a Cub fan.

The idea actually came from my attorney, Marty Cohn . . . he was Harry Caray's attorney. After Harry passed away, he said, "There's a lot of interest in the movies. I want you to do a movie about him." As every year passed, he'd say, "Why don't you do a movie? We've had some offers."

I sold one of my companies, so I had nothing to do for a while. I was either retired or unemployed. So I thought, "Well, I will try it." I was always a Cub fan. Harry I didn't know that well because I would basically go to the games and not listen to him at home or on the radio.

I've been a Cub fan ever since I was a little kid. The ballpark wasn't too far from my high school, so I used to go over there. I would sit in the bleachers. It was about 75 cents at the time. My parents bought

Gimbel's DVD on Harry Caray

our first house from Gabby Hartnett, who was the Cubs catcher. During the summer that was the only thing you did: you played baseball. Tennis wasn't big, soccer wasn't big, and nothing like that was big.

I talked to Marty about the plan. I had never done any film before. I had done a lot of videos, DVDs where I enhanced—I added biographies; I've added animation to them, 5.1 surround sound, and additional footage. I figured I'd set up some interviews, get some Major League footage, and Marty had given me the funeral footage, in which there were testimonials to Harry. It was filled, and it was almost like a roast as opposed to a funeral. I took a look at that and said, "Gee, this is good." I decided I'd do an intro. I'd have a few interviews. I'd use the funeral footage, which was great. I'd get a lot of stuff from the Cubs, footage of him singing and other things. I thought I should think about hiring somebody to assist me, with writing a documentary and interviewing and so forth.

I decided to hire a young lady who was going to school with my son. She had worked with HBO and she was into doing documentaries for the Tennis Channel. I decided to let her write and interview some of the people . . . because I had never done it before. I'd give her the input as a baseball fan, what to look for and how to set it up. She said, "Fine." She came in and started calling some people and talking about who we could interview. She actually suggested Bob Costas and set it up.

We were going to start to film it in February or March, before the baseball season, 'cause we knew a lot of the players would be in the same place and it'd be easier to film it. Turns out that she decided to move to Spain because she was in love with someone. So all of a sudden she was in Spain and I was in *Milo Hamilton spoke out in the Chicago papers about Harry Caray and said some pretty bad things about him.* California and the baseball season was about to start. She had given me some ideas on some of the questions and people to interview. Just about the time I was about to call people for interviews, I did some PR interviews and a press release. About the same day the press release came out, Milo Hamilton spoke out in the Chicago papers about Harry Caray and said some pretty bad things about him. There was a lot of controversy.

At that particular time, Steve Stone called me up and said, "I understand you're going to do a film. If you need me to talk about anything, I'd be happy to." Pat Hughes and a couple of other people called me up too. I went to spring training in Mesa and ran into Ron Santo. I set up an interview with him and Pat Hughes. . . . Also, I called this guy in Scottsdale, this crazy, fun man. He wrote many popular sports books, and he has a great memory and many contacts. I wound up in Phoenix talking to him and getting an idea of where I'm going to film it. He gave me a lot of interesting ideas, great contacts, phone numbers, and all of them worked.

The first interview was rocky, because all of a sudden Ryne Sandberg was available and I was supposed to be doing Ron Santo in ten minutes. First, I interviewed Ryne Sandberg, then I got to Ron Santo and it didn't go real well. My phone went off a couple of times. Santo was going to leave, and he was sweating because it was almost time to get ready for his broadcast.

I did Pat Hughes right after Ron Santo. That went very well. As I started doing more and more interviews, it became easier because I wasn't nervous. I relaxed and acted like I was having a conversation with people as opposed to interviewing them. There were so many stories.

Steve Stone wanted to be interviewed at his house, so the author and I and our camera crew went and spent a couple of hours there. He was probably the most informative because he spent fifteen years or so with Harry and he learned a lot. He respected Harry. There were a lot of very interesting stories. Fewer than a third of them actually made it to the video, because there were just so many things he told me.

. . . to interview Bob Costas—the author knew him. I'd never seen anyone so professional.

After that I went to St. Louis. I interviewed Bob Costas. I had tried to set up Stan Musial and Red Schoendienst and Bob Costas. Stan Musial's manager was not very cooperative. It's interesting because it's difficult to get an interview with people, but once you get them it's usually very good.

I flew to St. Louis to interview Bob Costas—the author knew him. I'd never seen anyone so professional. I asked him a question, and he answered it. Bob had some great analysis. He said, "Here's a guy that lived well into his eighties. He celebrated life every night. He did what he wanted to do. He loved baseball and he passed away. What more could you ask for in life?" It's true. He led a good life, and all these people remember him.

People were amazed at the documentary because it was so different, and it was historical, it was entertaining, it was humorous. It was also sad. It was an opportunity to learn about him. It brought Harry back to life with rare footage and great stories told by family, friends, fans, sports lovers, broadcasters, and co-workers. He broadcast the game the way the fans felt. Everyone had a little story about him.

I'm glad I did it. You go through life. If you can do something, you leave a mark that will be around forever now . . . It was exciting in that way. It was a tremendous amount of fun, we met fabulous people and the response from Cub fans after viewing the DVD was most satisfying.

The workers at the Stockyards are complaining about the smell coming from Comiskey Park.

There Are Some That Say You Can Live among Cardinal Fans Yet Still Go On to Lead a Normal and Productive Life

Gary Sosniecki

Gary Sosniecki is the co-owner of *The Leader,* a newspaper in Vandalia, Missouri. For him, 1967 was the Summer of Love as a Cub fan. He graduated from Missouri with a degree in journalism and owns small-town newspapers with his wife, Helen, his bride of thirty-five years.

I was bred to be a Cub fan. My mom grew up a couple blocks from Wrigley Field, and the family legend is that she stood in the street and wouldn't let people park there unless they paid her. My dad went to Lane Tech for a while and went to school with Phil Cavarretta.

I was raised a Cub fan. I went to my first game in 1960. I was nine years old. It happened to be the day Don Cardwell no-hit the Cardinals 4–0, second game of a doubleheader. My very first time at Wrigley Field was a no-hitter. My brother had the chickenpox and couldn't go. My dad asked me between games if I wanted to stay for the second game, and I said, "Sure." And that was the no-hitter.

It was exciting. We were in the second row of the left-centerfield bleachers, right next to a closed-off section. After the game, people were jumping off the bleacher wall. There was no basket there in 1960. My dad walked me around to the box seats, and we walked down to the field, through the doors at the box seats. He took me to the pitcher's mound and told me to pick up some dirt and put it in my pocket. On the way home I told him, "Well, I think I need to get some more dirt next time." And he told me, "Well, son, you're not ever going to be on that field again." That was an exciting start to being a Cub fan.

I don't remember it being a big crowd. Cubs fans from that era remember that Moose Moryn made the catch for the final out, a line drive off Joe Cunningham's bat. Leftfield, Moose Moryn came running in and caught it on his shoetips. I've looked now at a Web site of the entire bottom of the ninth inning. Every ball in that ninth inning almost left the ballpark. It's amazing how Cardwell got that no-hitter.

The secondary thrill for me was nineteen years later, when I was sports editor of the daily paper in Carbondale, Illinois. I decided to call the three principals in that story—Cardwell, Joe Cunningham, and Moose Moryn, and do an interview with them about that game. I could have waited until the twentieth anniversary, but I wasn't sure I was still going to have that job. So I thought I better do it. By the twentieth anniversary, we had bought our first newspaper, so it was good timing. Cardwell was working for a Ford dealership in Winston-Salem, which is his hometown. He was leasing trucks. He was great to talk to. He sent me an autographed picture, but the picture he sent me was in a Mets uniform. Cardwell died during spring training in 2008.

Cunningham was working for the Cardinals. Moose Moryn, after he retired, was working for the Big R Discount Store on North Avenue in Lombard, which wasn't too far from where I grew up in Bensenville. They were all nice, and I got a nice column out of it. I asked Moryn, "People used to say that you held up on that ball just to make it more dramatic." He said, "Oh no, I wasn't capable of doing that."

We were at Opening Day in '69, which was when Willie Smith hit the home run in extra innings. The Cubs came from behind to beat the Phillies. That was a great year. I was there with fifteen kids from my high school World Lit class; we skipped class to go down to Opening Day. It was the only day of school I ever skipped.

We skipped class to go down to Opening Day. It was the only day of school I ever skipped.

I went to the '62 All-Star Game by myself. You didn't need a ticket. Twenty-two thousand seats were on sale the day of the game, that was the Wrigley philosophy, and as I recall there were an awful lot of seats that went unsold, even for the All-Star Game. My dad dropped me off at the bleacher entrance. This was 1962, the second All-Star Game that year. The first one was in Washington. I got a ticket for two dollars, and I sat in the centerfield bleachers, the lower centerfield bleachers. I believe that was the only game that the lower centerfield bleachers were opened up, from whenever that section was closed off in the late '40s or early '50s.

In those days about 10:30 or 11:00 we went in. Outside the park, we just stood in line, and that was typical of that era. When the Cubs started to win, which was with Durocher in '67, the lines got longer. You would have to go a little bit earlier.

I couldn't get autographs at the All-Star Game. I saw Mantle and **Maris,** I saw Rocky Colavito, Kenny Boyer, all of the big names of that era. That's fun to say that you saw those people. The National League won that game. That was during another one of those times when the National League wasn't winning a lot of All-Star Games. So I went quite a few years being able to say that I was at the last game that the National League won.

We had gone to Comiskey Park when we got free tickets. My family wouldn't have paid money to see the White Sox.

The Cubs weren't always that big. That really started in '67. Some of the best games I saw in person were in '67 when Leo Durocher really had the team going well. In June and early July they won fourteen out of fifteen games. They had a seven-game winning streak, lost one, and had another seven-game winning streak. There were some terrific games in there. There was a game when Adolfo Phillips, who Durocher said was going to be the next Willie Mays, hit four home runs in a doubleheader. He was also thrown out trying to steal home when Ted Savage, who was another outfielder, had stolen home on the prior play. That was an incredible game. The game when the Cubs

Maris: Roger Maris once held the national high school record for most kick returns for a touchdown in one game—five, at Bishop Shanley High School in Fargo, North Dakota. Maris received a full scholarship to play for Bud Wilkinson at the University of Oklahoma, but quit after two weeks.

went into first place for the first time in a generation, was against Cincinnati in 1967. Pete Rose had spiked Ernie Banks the previous day on a slide. Ernie Banks—who had played on all those terrible Cub teams—wasn't able to play on the day when they went into first place. He was sitting in the broadcast booth with Brickhouse.

The fans would not leave Wrigley Field until the flags on the scoreboard were moved. Everyone just stood there and shouted, "We're No. 1!" The players came out of the clubhouse to see what was going on. They did switch the flags on top of the scoreboard. If I had to pinpoint the most exciting day that I've been at Wrigley Field, that would be the day. I saw Don Cardwell's no-hitter, Willie Smith's home run in '69 . . . a lot of great games, but that day they went into first place in '67 was just incredible. That's when it really all started. The crowd was about 30,000. They were starting to draw by then.

The electricity was just incredible in the ballpark. The players were catching on to it. They were out on the field after the game watching all this. This was when the Bleacher Bums were being born. I just can't describe what a great atmosphere it was. This was when you could afford to go to a game every day if you could get there. We were paying two bucks for bleacher tickets back then. Cardwell's no-hitter [1960] was 75 cents to get into the bleachers, then it went to a buck and then two bucks.

You could see the fans in the bleachers becoming the Bleacher Bums. We sat in rightfield. The first group of Bleacher Bums started in leftfield, and then it spread to rightfield. We were going fairly regularly, once a week or every other week. Maybe once a month, depending on if they were in town. You would see the same guys, the same people in their twenties, sitting in the same seats and doing the same cheers.

Rightfield would wear the yellow hard hats. Leftfield wore the red hard hats. Everyone would get together on the cheers. Some of them weren't the best to be shouting. A lot of, "Rightfield sucks! Rightfield sucks! Leftfield sucks! Leftfield sucks!" Going back and forth and back and forth.

Rightfield would wear the yellow hard hats. Leftfield wore the red hard hats.

You'd have home run balls hit into the centerfield section, and you'd have guys crawling around the fence from the Bleacher Bums trying to retrieve them. Just a lot of electricity. Great times, great memories.

Sixty-nine was the magical year when we thought it was all going to happen. From the Opening Day. It was just such an incredible day, 40,000 people there. Ernie Banks hit two home runs in one of his last real impact ball games, the extra-inning win. That's when you knew all of this was going to be magical. It's unfortunate that it didn't stay that way. I was a senior in high school in '69, and often I feel like I'm still lost in '69. I'm one of those people for whom the pain from '69 just continues. It's hard to read about '69, it's hard to see pictures from '69 without getting a tear in your eye because it was going to be such a great year. It still was a great year, but we should have won.

The lead started slipping away. You pin it on so many things now, you think about the black cat at Shea Stadium. You really didn't think you were going to lose it. You thought we were going to pull it out because it was "our year." It was just so painful to lose it. I was heading to college here in Missouri, and I get down here into Missouri as we are losing it in September. That was tremendously painful to have all these Cardinal fans around, cause I'm a Cub fan. I had a Cub banner up in my dorm room. I've got big pictures of Billy Williams, Banks, hanging on my bulletin board in a dorm room. We blew it.

Then everyone thought we were going to win in '70. We blew that too. I was sitting in the bleachers at the game—you knew '70 was over—when Willie Stargell hit a home run that practically went to Lake Michigan. All terribly painful.

The Cardinal fans weren't mean to me at school in Missouri, but always joking with me. All of my friends were Cardinal fans. I've lived in Cardinal territory since then. We lived in Jackson, Tennessee, which was Cardinal territory. We live in Marion, Illinois, which is Cardinal territory. We've lived in three or four different towns in Missouri that have all been Cardinal territory. I am the token Cub fan in most of these towns. People take it pretty well.

Just last Friday, an hour before the Cub-Cardinal series started, a guy comes into the office and says, "I know you're a Cub fan. I have to take you to see my mother's kitchen." So I get in the car with this stranger and drive up to the north side of town. I go see his mother's kitchen, which is totally decorated in Cardinal stuff. This was in Vandalia. She has the Cardinal logo on every one of her kitchen cabinets, pictures of Albert Pujols, an autograph of Red Schoendienst. All this stuff hanging around her kitchen. I am a good sport about it, and she's a good sport about it. I'm writing a column about it for this week.

When they announced that the Cubs were for sale. I went into the Farber, Missouri, post office on a Wednesday. This is a small paper; my wife and I are the only full-time people here. So I'm delivering papers, too. I go into the Farber post office, and the postmaster there has a plastic jug sitting on the front counter that says, "Buy the Cubs Fund." The only thing in that jug was two Canadian pennies, and Chris, the postmaster, says, "Gary, that's all I've been able to collect. People just aren't interested in that."

Last Wednesday morning I went into the Farber post office, and he's got a sign up on his wall that has the standings. Milwaukee in first place, Cubs a half-game out, and the Cardinals just 2½ games **It's fun being the token Cub fan in town.** out and the Cardinals are underlined. He's got "the National League Central standings updated every Wednesday morning." Well, that's for my benefit, knowing that I'm going in there and he's going to have a chance to gig me on Wednesday mornings. People take it in good spirit. It's fun being the token Cub fan in town.

This is the very first Cardinal-territory town that I've met another Cub fan. I've been in the Ozarks in Missouri most of the time. I wasn't aware of any Cub fans in the Ozarks. Here there are a couple of Cub fans, because we are only half an hour from Illinois and Quincy, Illinois, carries the WGN Radio broadcast of the Cubs. The minister of the Christian church here, Roger Thomas, is a Cubs fan. That's because he did some of his seminary work in the Chicago suburbs. There's an older lady in Laddonia, Missouri, who comes in every once in a while and talks about the Cubs.

My wife grew up a Kansas City A's fan. She grew up in Clinton, Missouri, western Missouri. Her grandmother was an A's fan. So Helen has been very patient with me as a Cubs fan. We've been married since '73, so I have dragged her to game after game after game after game. Her first game was Opening Day in '72. We had just started dating, and I dragged her up to Chicago to that game. I've taken her to Atlanta for a game. I've taken her to Cincinnati for a game. We went to Montreal for a game. We've gone to Busch Stadium dozens of times to see the Cubs play.

. . . with Harry Caray singing, "The Cardinals are coming, tra-la, tra-la. The Cubbies are falling, ha-ha ha-ha."

I never accepted Harry Caray as a Cubs broadcaster. How can you accept a guy who was with the Cardinals for twenty-five years? Who actually cut a record, and I have a copy of this record, with Harry Caray singing, "The Cardinals are coming, tra-la, tra-la. The Cubbies are falling, ha-ha ha-ha." Twenty-five years with the Cardinals. We won't talk about the one year with Oakland. Then twelve years with the White Sox, and I am supposed to accept Harry Caray as a Cub fan? Harry Caray was tremendously entertaining, and he did a lot through the Superstation to make the Cubs a national team, but I couldn't accept him as a Cub fan.

Every place we've lived I have a room in my house that is devoted to the Cubs. I call it my "Ernie Banks Memorial Sports Library and Museum." I have all of the various memorabilia. I've got a '69 lithograph of the major Cubs players. It's a relatively common scene, but I've tried to collect the autographs of the various Cubs on that lithograph. I've got Banks; Fergie Jenkins signed it; I got Leo Durocher to sign it the year before he died; and Gene Oliver, whose picture isn't on it. Gene Oliver was a backup catcher who died last year. Then I've got several other Cubs from '69 who I've met. They didn't actually sign the lithograph, but I've got their signatures mounted inside the frame. The last one I got was Jimmy Hickman.

My little brother and I went to a few games back in the mid-'60s. We were very young. We sat in the bleachers this one day Jimmy Hickman was playing centerfield for the Mets. The two of us as kids were yelling, "Hickman sucks! Hickman sucks! Hickman sucks!" Later on, he's our big hero, playing for the Cubs in '69 and '70 and even making the All-Star team. So now we fast forward to four or five years ago. Helen and I are at my mother's in Sarasota, Florida, and her condo is probably a mile and a half from where the Cincinnati Reds camp is. We were there in March, and we decided to drive over to the Reds camp and see what was going on. We went over to where they were working with minor leaguers, and I notice the guy throwing batting practice had Hickman on the back of his jersey. So I asked around, "Is that Jimmy Hickman?" They said, "Yeah, he's helping out with spring training for the Reds." We waited till batting practice was over and waved Hickman over. He talked to us; the only thing I had for him to autograph was one of my business cards. I told him I still cry over '69. And he said, "So do we." I never told him the story about yelling, "Hickman sucks!" He didn't really need to know that story.

In Tennessee in '74, we got tickets to see the Cubs in Atlanta. It was a nine-hour drive for Helen and me. I don't even remember if we won the game that day. The thrill for me was when we were wandering around Fulton County Stadium after the game and Jack Brickhouse was interviewing Hank Aaron on the tenth-inning show. The broadcast booth in Fulton County Stadium was not very far from the box seating. Hank Aaron had just broke Babe Ruth's record. I just instinctively waved at Hank Aaron, and he waved back to me. Helen got the camera up just as his arm is going down. We've got a picture of his hand going down after he waved to me.

Generally, the Cardinals fans have been great. Often I've gone with friends who are Cardinal fans. I always wear a certain Cubs shirt of mine. I always manage to spill nacho cheese on it before the first pitch. That's become a tradition too. Generally, everything has been in good spirits. There was one time, not too many years ago, I got a couple smart-aleck remarks, and that was the first time anyone has done that with me. So I've been a little more careful about being as blatant as I was when I was younger about being a Cub fan. I've actually gone to Busch Stadium a couple times when the Cubs weren't playing. Someone gave us terrific seats in the third row behind home plate. They come out and cater the food for you. I saw myself applauding for the Cardinals. Then, when I realized what I was doing, I had to sit on my hands.

I've got a couple Cardinals things hanging in my room. Very select. I've got an 8-by-10 color picture of Stan Musial. I got that at a baseball card show and I stood in line for Stan's autograph, I was wearing my Cubs jacket, and I got to him and I said, "There aren't very many Cardinals whose autograph I'd stand in line for." I got a nice smile from him. I didn't talk to him in depth, but I've always admired him. He was classy. A great player as I was growing up. Plus he's Polish and I'm Polish too, so I admired that.

Another autograph story—Gene Oliver, backup catcher for the Cubs in '69. He was one of the three players who put out the record *Cubs Power*, which was one of the many things that the Cubs did to promote themselves that year. It probably distracted them from winning the pennant. On one side of the record you had Gene Oliver, Nate Oliver, and one other player singing a bunch of baseball songs, including "Hey Hey Holy Mackerel," which was the Cubs' theme song that year. "Hey Hey!" was what Jack Brickhouse shouted when there was a home run. "Holy Mackerel!" was what Vince Lloyd, the radio broadcaster, shouted when there was a home run. So there was this song, "Hey! Hey! Holy mackerel, no doubt about it, the Cubs are on their way!" I can sing the whole song.

. . . for Gene Oliver to autograph and his eyes light up and he punches Hrabosky in the arm, "Look at this!"

On the flip side of this LP is Bleacher Bum cheers. The entire flip side is cheers. "The Whole World is Watching" and just different cheers from the Bleacher Bums. I've got two copies of this LP. I go to this baseball card show, it's Gene Oliver and Al Hrabosky, the great Cardinal reliever and broadcaster. I go in wearing my Cub jacket or shirt and I'm carrying this *Cubs Power* record album for Gene Oliver to autograph and his eyes light up and he punches Hrabosky in the arm, "Look at this! Look at this! You didn't do this!" He was so excited about that, showing that to Hrabosky. That was a kick, that's in my collection, he signed it for me.

The other thing that I've got in my room is the front pages of the *Post-Dispatch* special editions that are framed when Mark McGwire broke the home-run record. I bought those at a Press Association auction. We had a lot of fun with that home-run chase, Sosa and McGwire. We owned a paper in Seymour, Missouri, back then. We had a lady on our staff who was into ceramics, and she made a hillbilly **Mark McGwire** and a hillbilly Sammy Sosa, little statues painted up in Cub colors and Cardinal colors. We had those on the front counter of our newspaper office. We had little index cards in front of them folded, and every day we would update the home-run totals. I've got those in my room.

We went to the playoffs in '89. The night that the Cubs won, I had an end roll of newsprint and some blue spray paint and I painted this big sign, CUBS WIN! HOLY COW! In the middle of the night Helen and I got up on ladders and we taped this between the first and second floors of our office outside. So when people would drive around the square of Seymour, Missouri, in the morning they would know I was bragging about the Cubs winning. Everyone's relatively good-natured about it. I try and be good-natured about it when I come to a new town. On our newspaper Web site right now we've got an interactive page called a guestbook. There's a Cardinal fan in town named Tony Teague, and on Friday he posted this message, "What? The Cardinals only 2.5 games out of first, it could be an interesting weekend with the old Cubbies." He posted that Friday morning. So Friday afternoon, after the Cubs had won the first game of the series, I put, "Cubs 2, Cardinals 1—you're right, Tony, it's going to be an interesting weekend." It's a conversation-opener to be a Cubs fan in Cardinal territory.

Mark McGwire: Mark McGwire's brother, Dan McGwire, once a starting quarterback for the Iowa Hawkeyes and a former No. 1 pick of the Seahawks, is the tallest NFL QB ever at 6 feet 8. Former NBA star and Toronto Blue Jay, Danny Ainge, is the tallest major league second baseman ever.

Outside of a Dog, a Book Is a Man's Best Friend; Inside of a Dog, It's Too Dark to Read

Gary Leibovitz

Gary Leibovitz, at the tender age of forty-three, is enjoying the leisure life since selling his highly successful kennel business. After graduating from Niles North High School, he attended Northern Illinois, Arizona State, and DePaul as part of his graduation prevention program.

My father had pretty much taken me to every Chicago sporting event since I was a toddler. In fact, one of his closest friends was Bill George, the former great Bears linebacker. We used to go into the Bears locker rooms after practices. I've been to both of the Bear Super Bowls since I've been alive. Dad used to get big-and-tall clothing for Abe Gibron and all of the coaches.

The spark that really made me into the Cubs was when I used to take the Skokie Swift when I was eleven. I'd go with my friends to Opening Day every year. I became a huge fan. My father used to take me all the time. We would sit behind the dugout and get to know the players. The first time I really felt the pain of being a Cub fan was '84. My father bet Sutcliffe every game he pitched for the Cubs. Dad was a pretty big gambler and he just rode the Sutcliffe wave to 16–1.

At San Diego in '84, I made a huge sign that said, IF YOU DON'T LOVE THE CUBBIES, YOU BELONG IN RUSSIA. CHICAGO—AMERICA'S TEAM. As soon as I walked in the stadium—it was a huge king-size sheet—my buddy and I held it up and security ran over and told us to take it down. They wouldn't let us hold the sign up. When the Cubs lost the first game in San Diego I wasn't worried. Then they lost the second game and I was a little upset. When we were winning Game 3 in the fifth inning with Sutcliffe pitching I called my father on the phone from Jack

Murphy Stadium and told him to get my tickets for the World Series.
I was a on a pay phone. I went back to my seat, and the ball went
through Durham's legs and that was it. Steve Garvey's home run was
an absolute killer. I bet 25 percent of the San
Diego crowd were Cubs fans. The San Diego
fans were pouring beer and popcorn down my
back. They weren't so nice.

Steve Garvey turns around and without hesitating, he goes, "Ah, you must be a Cub fan."

A year later, I went snow skiing in Deer
Valley out in Utah. I was over in the main lodge
having lunch, and this guy walks by in a full
white ski suit. He's walking by with this blonde woman, and I yell
out, "Garvey, you ruined my life!" Steve Garvey turns around and
without hesitating, he goes, "Ah, you must be a Cub fan."

When I opened my kennel I started taking care of the players'
dogs. I became relatively friendly with a few of them. I opened a facility called The Windy City K-9 Club. Somewhere in the first couple
of years Dr. Adams, who is the Cubs team physician—started coming
with his Rottweiler. He passed along to the players that had dogs,
that Windy City K-9 was the place to bring their dog. We started getting Kerry Wood, Shawn Estes, Ryan Dempster, Ramon Martinez, and
Moises Alou. They would call me and say, "Do you mind if we come
after hours?" I'm a huge fan so I didn't really care. Because it was
after hours they would offer to bring me something—like a signed
ball. I told them no big deal. It was my pleasure to do it. Then, midway through the 2003 season my dog passed away from cancer and
I wanted to start a charity in his name. I mentioned to Sarah Wood,
Kerry's wife, the idea of possibly having the Cubs players with their
dogs on a calendar. The proceeds of this calendar were donated to
different animal shelters. The calendar was called Players with Paws
to benefit animal charities. The cover is Kerry Wood and Mark Prior
holding Kerry's two dogs. We had a full calendar of different players
who had dogs. Since they didn't all have dogs, a few of the players
took pictures with a therapy dog or a rescued dog. They were really
cooperative. Sarah Wood said she'd take care of it and approached
the wives for me. Heather Estes and Mark Prior's fiancée at the time,

Heather, helped out as well and got all the players involved. It was in the middle of the playoff run and the Cubs had one day off the rest of the season. They came to my kennel and did the photo shoot. Mike Remlinger had a Shiba Inu—which was really cute. Kerry Wood had a Jack Russell named Toby and a pug named Stella. Shawn Estes had an English Bulldog. Ramon Martinez had a pug. Moises Alou didn't do the calendar—but he had a boxer. We initially printed 10,000. We sold them by word of mouth. The Cubs allowed us to put up a small booth toward the end of the season, right by the main entrance. Sarah Wood, Heather Prior, myself, and my brother sold them there. We had a booth at the Cubs Convention. Right during the playoffs—the Cubs were a hot topic—I sent one to Oprah Winfrey, because they were doing their Christmas gifts episode. She never replied. If she would have replied, we would have sold a million copies and there would be about $10 million for animal charities. All she had to do was say a word. The ones we didn't sell we gave away. I ended up closing the charity after about three years because it was too much work for one person to do. We gave money to different animal charities—groups that worked with pets to help people and also groups that helped to save pets' lives. I have since sold the kennel. . . .

> We gave money to different animal charities—groups that worked with pets to help people and also groups that helped to save pets' lives.

I would harass Davey Lopes from behind the dugout when I was young kid—maybe eleven. I wanted his bat. I kept on asking, "If you break your **bat,** can I have it?" I said it for five straight minutes. He was in the on-deck circle waiting for the batter ahead of him. Finally, he turns around and said, "Hey, listen kid, I haven't broken a bat in ten years. So you're not going to get my bat." He goes up to the plate and hits a broken-bat single to rightfield. He gets to first base and

---

bat: Orlando Cepeda used more bats than any player in history. He felt each bat had exactly one hit in it. When Cepeda hit safely, he would discard the bat. He had 2,364 hits in his career.

points over to the batboy to give me the bat, but the batboy wouldn't do it. He didn't know what Lopes was talking about. After the inning Lopes ran over from first base, got the bat, and gave it to me.

Right after Pete Rose's longest hitting streak, the Cubs were playing Cincinnati. My father asked Rose to autograph a program for me—my best friend and his father were with us. **Pete Rose** said, "No." This was two hours before the game when we were there for batting practice. He was a real #(@*^$. So my father and his friend put a curse on him. They started wiggling their fingers at him and giving him the curse. He went on the worst hitting period in his career. It served him right.

Ken Griffey Jr. was the most impressive visiting player. He had a bad rap for a while for having a bit of an attitude. That was later on in his career because he had been injured so much and there was a lot of talk about how he had "lost it." Two years ago I was at a game with my two godsons. There was a long fly ball out and one of the Reds players was running in with the ball. I was holding my godson in one arm and I waved to the Reds player and he threw me the ball. I jumped up to catch it because he threw it over my head. I caught my leg, fell backwards, and broke two ribs. When you break your ribs from behind instead of the front it hurts a lot more. The fan that got the ball behind me gave me the ball. I probably could have protected myself, but I didn't want to drop my godson. Griffey came trotting in behind the Reds outfielder and he saw me fall. After I got up off the ground, he came out from the dugout and waved me over. He had another ball to give the second godchild. That was a really classy move. He looked at me and shook his head, and I knew he had seen the whole thing.

The Cubs can't do a "bring your dog to the ballpark day" like the White Sox do because the Cubs don't really have an area for it. The

Pete Rose: Joe Torre was player/manager of the Mets for eighteen days in 1977. Since 1962 there have been four player/managers with Pete Rose (1984–86) being the last. . . . In 1935 there were nine player/managers.

White Sox have their centerfield bleachers and they have the whole promenade back there. The Cubs seating is so compact and close and the aisles are so small there's really nowhere to put the dogs. They would have to have an area behind the bleachers to do something like that.

Cubs fans get so comfortable with the way the team is that it's hard to find one thing that you would change. It becomes a part of your existence when you grow up the son of a huge sports fan who instills Chicago sports as an important part of your life. For me it's almost a passing of the torch. My father is almost eighty now and he hasn't seen a winner ever. There are plenty of people older than him—it's almost like a vigil—waiting for that one moment that they'll win. I will not be surprised if and when they do win the World Series if there's a slight decline in Cub fervor in terms of the fan base. It will almost be an anticlimactic end. I would hope that we don't lose some of that strong love of it when they finally win. There will be a five-year party, but it will be interesting to see what the hangover is going to be.

Kerry Wood is my favorite player. You have a relationship with some of the players when you actually get to know them a little bit. Before Shawn Estes left the Cubs, he was doing poorly and some Cubs fans were saying some nasty things on the radio about getting rid of him. When you know the players, you take it personally. I used to berate players that were lousy all the time, but the ones you know . . . you can't do it. The way Kerry Wood goes about his business as a player is very professional. When they put the weight of the world on him in his better days, he knew how to handle everything very well. He was very nice about it. He didn't have an attitude and was very approachable. Then, he was about a day away from being done and he somehow turned it around and he's back. He understands he's not the focal point of this team right now. He had no problem sitting back and doing his job and letting the team get the accolades from other areas. He goes out and doesn't show people up at all. He's more of an old-school player.

I went to a Bears game last September with Kerry Wood and his wife. It was just like going to a game with a friend. We had never hung out before. This was the first time, so I was really excited about it. We were talking about football and a little bit about baseball. The day before, he pitched two innings against Pittsburgh—and he batted for the first time in God knows how long and the fans were chanting his name. It was very much like 2003. He went up there and swung from his heels and he totally missed. When I asked him about that at-bat when we were at the football game, he said, "It was terrible!" I said, "I wasn't talking about your swings. I was talking about the fans just going nuts and chanting your name." He said, "I haven't swung a bat in quite a long time." I said, "It was reminiscent of 2003 when you hit that home run to take the lead in Game 7." I was a little buzzed at this point and said, "If Dusty would have taken you out right after that you could have had the game-winning hit." He didn't say anything. He just chuckled.

I never liked the White Sox. I was a die-hard Cub fan and hated the White Sox. When they won in 2005, the reason why it hurt a lot was because I didn't want their fans in general to have any joy. The Sox players played the game the right way. They really played baseball the way it was supposed to be played. That's why they won. I admired the way they played, but I hated the fan base. The Cubs-Sox feud has a lot more to do with just hating the other fans. It is possibly more than the team in general.

I liked Dusty Baker, but I couldn't stand the way he handled the pitchers. He got a big lead with Prior pitching. At that second game against Florida—at home—he pitched him eight innings; he was out of his mind. Those guys had been workhorses the whole year. You should be warming up the bullpen and sitting him down after five or six innings. In Game 6, the whole bullpen should have been warmed up after five innings and been waiting for any sign of a collapse. He didn't have anyone up in the bullpen until the Cubs were losing.

I do miss Mark Grace. One of my favorite things when I was at games with Mark Grace was when they'd have the fans go out to each position. Every time they did it with Grace he would keep the fan at first base and have him throw the groundballs to the infielders for warm-ups. That was really a player getting "it." I didn't like it when the Cubs got rid of Grace. Grace was getting towards the end of his career. They were doing him a favor because he finally got that World Series ring that he was looking for.

Name the Oakland manager—win valuable prizes!

Sometimes God Just
Hands Ya One

Mike Berry

Mike Berry left Des Plaines for Avondale, Arizona, in 1987. The fifty-four-year-old graduated from Maine West High School and Western Illinois University. He is a computer specialist for Wells Fargo Bank.

The first Cubs game that I went to was 1961. My dad took me to see the Milwaukee Braves at Wrigley. He spent big bucks. He popped for box seats behind the Cubs dugout. He paid five bucks a seat. That was serious money back in 1961. I got to see Dick Ellsworth play, Eddie Matthews, and a lot of the old players.

I became a Cubs fan because it seemed more like baseball. You were out in the open, it was during the day, and you were really close to the field. You felt like you were a part of it. I was a Cubs and Sox fan until high school when I realized you can't be both. There's a state law saying either-or, but not both. I started going to a lot more games. I went to a ton of games in '69. Mike Royko said it best, "Cubs fans are 98 percent scar tissue." After the '69 campaign, I can see why.

. . . it seemed more like baseball. You were out in the open, it was during the day, and you were really close to the field.

I was a Bleacher Bum. I knew most of the cheers. Me and my high school buddies would hop the bus from Des Plaines over to Evanston, hop on the el and take that to the park. If it was a weekend series we would pay the dollar for the bleacher seats. We would try and be the first in line. We'd always be the first ten or twelve in line. When they opened up the gates they'd yell, "Walk!" We would go as fast as we could to get the front row bleacher seats. If it was a Saturday-Sunday series, after the Saturday game we'd go right back outside and get in line for Sunday's game. We'd just spend the night in the street. There were usually fifteen or twenty people that would hang out from Saturday to Sunday. Early in the morning people would start lining up. In '69 . . . that was a hot year. As long as I was with a couple of my friends my parents didn't care. They never came down to check on us, but they'd see us on TV every once in awhile. We took along a sleeping bag that they'd let us take into the park. It was during the summer so it never got cold. We'd just go down to one of the stores and get some food. We would just hang out there. We talked. Sometimes we'd play catch out there. Sometimes there was a football tossed around. We'd walk around the park. There's strength in numbers. Sometimes you'd be out there by yourselves and think this wasn't the best of ideas. When more and more people started showing up, you were all Cub fans and protected each other. Never did we ever have a problem. The only time there was a problem is right before they opened up the gates. All of these people would show up early and line up orderly and try and get in and of course fifteen minutes before the ticket booth opened it was a mad rush to the front. Then, it was every man for himself. It happened every single time. You'd just get together and we never failed to get front row. We talked to a lot of the players over the course of the years. We talked to Dick Selma a lot. He was a fun guy. He used to play catch with us up in the stands. We'd throw those 6-inch footballs to him and he'd throw them back to us. A couple times he kicked them out of the park.

I never **caught a ball** in Wrigley. I've probably been there a hundred times and I've never caught a home run ball. Not even during batting practice. I just had bad luck. You'd be talking to people and they'd come rattling in the seats.

caught a ball: Actor Charlie Sheen has always dreamed of catching a home run ball. For an Angels game in Anaheim, he bought every seat in the left-field pavilion to ensure that he would get his coveted home run ball. The tickets cost him $6,000 . . . there were no home runs hit during that game.

We'd communicated with visiting players too—especially St. Louis. There was a player from the Phillies, his last name was Money. It was a doubleheader. We'd just yell, "Money! You're worth 2 cents!" We harassed him so much that he made one or two errors in that game. We never got that raunchy. We'd make fun of their names—whatever it was. The players weren't that bad back in the late '60s or early '70s.

We'd communicated with visiting players too—especially St. Louis.

Players back then cared about the game. They were ballplayers. They cared about the fans. It wasn't about contracts. It was about winning for the fans. They were pretty approachable. Leftfield Bleacher Bums had our own mentality. The players today are starting to come back to being ballplayers. The last great ballplayer was Mark Grace. He was the last really great ballplayer—dirty, grimy. Not too concerned with contracts, ego, and all that. I was really heartbroken when he came to Phoenix. I cried when they won the World Series because I was so happy for him.

A good friend of mine lives in the same subdivision in Northern California as Tony LaRussa. In fact, his wife is head of the HOA of the subdivision. LaRussa lives down the block from him. He added something to the front of his house and it violated the HOA. My buddy's wife said, "Sorry, Mr. LaRussa, you can't build that." He said, "Don't you know who I am?" She said, "Yeah, I know who you are." She said, "Don't you know who I am? I'm the head of the HOA. This is in violation; you're going to have to take it down." He refused to take it down. He said, "I'm a lawyer and you don't know who you are messing with. " Guess what? He had to take it down. There are a lot of his comments in the past ten years about being a lawyer and being educated. Many people that have bumped into him have said he is pretty arrogant. He's that way in real life too.

We really started hitting the games hard in '69. Then we went in the early '70s. For those four years we hit a lot of games. We were some of the youngest ones out there, but there were younger ones. For the most part the average age was early twenties. Of course we would try and sneak a beer here or there. It was Wrigley Field. It wasn't difficult to do. Believe it or not, we were there for the ball games. We were there to cheer the Cubs on. It wasn't about drinking.

I don't recall the exact time that I knew the Cubs blew it in '69. Certain things happen in life that you just try to block out.

I don't recall the exact time that I knew the Cubs blew it in '69. Certain things happen in life that you just try to block out. You could see in August that the team was getting tired. They only had eight players. They didn't have a lot of backup players. These guys lost 20 pounds in the regular season.

I was there for the September games. The Cubs didn't really choke until the middle of September. There was always hope, but when they were really out of it there was no electricity in the stands. With the Bleacher Bums the energy was there, but it wasn't like when they were winning. It was a party atmosphere when they were winning. Lots of energy and everybody was laughing. No one was arguing. You were family, and it was the best family you could have. You would pull together. You'd sneak the horns in, which you weren't supposed to have. It was just good times. The ushers would always yell, "Stop running!" when you were trying to get to the seats. You'd say, "If you can catch me, I'll stop running." The Andy Frains weren't too bad.

My all-time favorite Wrigley Field story happened on Billy Williams Day. In '72 it was a doubleheader against the Cardinals. In fact, Billy's bat is in the Hall of Fame. He went 7-for-8 that day. He's out there playing leftfield. There was a guy that was pretty drunk and he was dancing out on the wall. The wall out there isn't very wide. Between innings he falls out of the stands onto the field. He kind of shakes himself off and stands up. Then, here comes Billy walking over to this guy. You look toward the Cubs dugout and you see the Andy Frains coming out of the dugout. They start running out to leftfield. Picture the typical Andy Frains back then—they were probably fifty years old, 250 to 300 pounds—all from eating Chicago food. They weren't moving too quick. This guy stands up, looks up at the stands, looks at Billy, looks at the Andy Frains, and Billy walks over to this guy. He takes his glove and throws the glove off his hand. The leftfield bleachers got quiet. The

Andy Frains are getting closer. Billy looks at the Andy Frains, looks at this guy, looks up at the stands, and then puts his hands together. Billy Williams put the guy's foot in his hands and gives him a boost back up into the stands. We reached down and grabbed this guy—he didn't have a shirt on—we were grabbing him by the hair, by the arms. We pulled him into the stands and threw him back a couple rows. The ushers and cops came looking for the guy that fell out of the stands. Everybody gives Billy a standing ovation. He's smiling and does a bow. The Andy Frains go back to the dugout. The cops are still asking where the guy that fell out on the field was. Everybody is saying, "We didn't see anyone fall out on the field. Did you see anyone fall out on the field? I didn't see anyone fall out on the field." It was probably my favorite Wrigley Field moment because it was just Billy being Billy.

There was so much beer being consumed in the leftfield bleachers. What they started to do is that they started keeping the beer cups. They stacked all of the cups together. It started on the far-left side as you're looking at the bleachers. They got this big tube of empty beer cups. It was 20 feet, maybe more, of hundreds and hundreds of beer cups. It was the seventh-inning stretch when it broke. Everyone started throwing beer cups—not out on the field—but back in the stands. Beer cups were flying everywhere. When I got home my parents said, "What were you doing out in leftfield? Jack Brickhouse said the Bleacher Bums are doing something out there." I said, "Yeah, we just got a little crazy with some empty beer cups." They would take the beer cups and stick them in the chain-link fence and they would spell out words—METS SUCK or usually it was GO CUBS. . . . Andre Dawson won the MVP that year [1987] on the last-place team.

Every year a group of us guys would rent a bus and we'd get thirty or forty people to go a game. We did that up until three years ago when the Cubs stopped selling group tickets. That was almost a thirty-year tradition that came to an end. It was pretty sad.

Mets: After the first nine games in their inaugural season of 1962, the Mets were 9½ games out of first place.

My buddy, Don Rosedale, would coordinate the tickets and rent the bus. Everybody from Des Plaines—the softball teams, dads, girl-friends would get on this bus and we'd take it from Des Plaines to Wrigley Field. This one particular game my dad went. It was against St. Louis. We're watching the last home game. Dawson hit his 47th home run. The rightfield fans were bowing to him. One of the classi-est things I've seen is baseball is when Dawson dropped his glove, got on his hands and knees, and bowed back to the rightfield fans. That was one of those really treasured moments. I've met Dawson in spring training; the guy is such a class act. That's another ball-player. He deserves to be in the Hall of Fame. During the course of the game we're drinking Old Style and right behind us is a group of Cardinal fans drinking Budweiser. We started buying them Old Style, they started buying us Budweiser and it was the most fun I've had with opposing fans. The Cardinals won the division and went on to the World Series that year. We were laughing and having a good time. It's hard to say this, but I think the best fans in all sports are Cardinals fans. They love their team. They're knowledge-able. They're not rambunctious. They're just really fans. I'm always impressed with Cardinals fans.

> It's hard to say this, but I think the best fans in all sports are Cardinals fans.

My parents moved out to Arizona from Des Plaines in '84. That year the Cubs had a little run at the playoffs. They had Rick Sut-cliffe—went 16–1. He was a big guy and they called him the Red Baron because of his red beard. I'm 6-2 and I had a beard at the time and it was red. I am a spitting image of Rick Sutcliffe. When he had his beard and I had my beard after the '84 season I couldn't go out in public in Chicago without getting mobbed. Honest to goodness. I would be with my daughter and people would say, "You're Rick Sut-cliffe!" I'd say, "No, I'm not!" They'd say, "Yes, you are! How tall are you? 6-8?" I'd say, "No, I'm 6-2—a little shorter." I'd get free dinners. I would come out to visit my folks and we were sitting in the seats at Hohokam watching the game. The guy in front of me turns around and goes, "Anybody tell you that you look like Rick Sutcliffe?" I said,

"Well you're the third one today." He said, "When he pitched for Cleveland down in Tucson we used to rent our house to him. You want to meet him?" I said, "Yeah!" He said, "After the game, we can get access to the clubhouse." I said, "This is like a dream come true." Jerry Mumphrey messed up the third out in the ninth inning and the game went to extra innings. The guy had to go and I never got a chance to meet him.

At **Wrigley Field,** I yelled at Sutcliffe once and he looked at me and I said, "Who gave you permission to use my face?" He looked at me, just laughed, and nodded. Hohokam Park used to let you bring your own beer in. My dad would go with my mom to spring training in the mid-'80s. You didn't get a lot of people. He'd bring a six-pack of Bud. When he wasn't broadcasting, Harry Caray would sit next to my dad. He'd come down and they'd talk St. Louis baseball. It didn't happen a lot, but it happened several times. He would drink four or five beers and my dad would have one or two. He'd say, "Oh, I got to go! Good talking to you!" and off he went looking for more beer. There are a lot of good memories with my dad.

My son, Steve, and my nephew were out at Hohokam and Billy Williams walks right up to them and said, "What are you kids doing?" They said, "Well, we're going to watch the game." He said, "You want to be batboys?" Of course they said, "Sure." Steve was batboy for Billy and he said, "No autographs, and if I get any packages you have to check them for bombs." It was quite a game. Steve was a huge Cubs fan. In 2000, Steve moved back to Chicago. In September 2001, he got married—right after 9/11. He got sick, and in January 2002 he passed away. He passed away from pericarditis. Your heart is in a sac and the sac got infected. He passed away at the age of twenty-four. It was unexpected. When you lose a child there's not a worse pain that anybody can ever go through. We came back to Chicago to take care of the arrangements. He passed away on January 24—on the 26th I'm at his

Wrigley Field: More NFL games have been played in the Meadowlands than in any other stadium. Until 2003, Wrigley Field held the record, even though Wrigley had not hosted an NFL game since 1971.

house and getting ready to make his funeral arrangements. January 26 is also my **birthday,** so I'm thinking how for the rest of my life I will remember my birthday is the day I made funeral arrangements for my son. The emotion hit me hard and I dropped to my knees. I wept like I've never wept in my life. When I was getting ready, I could hear Steve say, "I'm sorry, Dad." I said, "Steve, it's OK." Then I had a thought right out of *Field of Dreams*. It wasn't a voice, it was a thought, but the thought was not my thought. The thought was "something incredible is going to happen to you on this day. When it happens you will know it." I went downstairs and told my wife and sister-in-law what just happened. We were driving up to make the arrangements and we are on a lot of back roads—it's about a forty-five-minute drive. My sister-in-law said, "Why do people spend so much money on funerals? Why do they spend thousands of dollars on coffins when they can take that money and donate it to a worthy cause?" As soon as she said that, it hit me. I just started saying, "Oh my God! Oh my God! That incredible thing just hit me." They said, "What is it?" I'm speechless and my sister-in-law said, "Look at the sign" and points to the street sign. For a short time we were on Route 126, which happened to be the date—January 26. They said, "What's your thing?" I said, "We have season tickets for Cubs spring training and I want to donate tickets to other fathers and sons." The times Steven and I had at Hohokam were some of the best I've ever had. It doesn't get any better than a father and son at a baseball game. I no longer have a son. I will never have that feeling again, but if I can share those seats, I can share that with somebody else. That's what Steven would want. We started getting excited and I looked at the clock and the clock was 1:05, which is first pitch for spring training. We're giddy with excitement. I'm making funeral arrangements for my son and we're laughing because we

> **birthday**: Frank and Kathie Lee Gifford have the same birthday; they're twenty-three years apart age-wise. They were married in 1986. Frank Gifford was a grandfather at the time. Their children, Cody and Cassidy, are uncle and aunt to Frank Gifford's grandchildren. . . . When told that Kathie Lee was pregnant, Don Meredith said, "I'll hunt the guy down, Frank, and I'll kill him."

found some good out of something that is tragic. We get to the funeral home and get out of the car and it's like we're going to a celebration. I called home, because at the time my mother was dying of pancreatic cancer—she would pass away a month later—my sisters both live in Arizona and I told her what had just happened. She said, "Mike, that's a miracle." I said, "You have this vision and all of a sudden it happens?" She said, "Only God grants miracles. That's confirmation Steve is in heaven. Can you think of a better birthday gift?" After the funeral we went out to dinner and we were talking about this with our family. My daughter says, "It was Steve's dream to take his son to Wrigley. Why don't you call this 'Steve's Dream?'" On January 26, 2002 Steve's Dream was born. A year ago we made it a nonprofit. This year we gave away 500 tickets to spring training baseball. We have a Web site, www.stevesdream.com. We started off with two tickets then through some donations through family we bought two more. Then, through other donations we bought two more. We have a total of six seats at spring training. The worst seats we have are sixth row behind the dugout. The first few years we would just walk up to people waiting in line to buy tickets. I would have a brochure. They would think I was a scalper. I would tell them the story and tell them I'd like to give them free tickets. I'd show them the brochure and tell them, "This is my son, Steve. He passed away in 2002, and he was a huge Cubs fan. To keep his memory and love of the game alive we'd like to treat other fathers and sons or mothers and daughters, no age or gender limitation, to a day at the ballpark. There are two conditions. First, is that you go to our Web site and you send us an e-mail and tell us how your day was. Secondly, I want the father to forget about your job and the son to forget about school. Forget about what you're doing tonight and for the next couple hours just take the time to be with each other and enjoy the day." Almost everybody wants to make a donation and I've never taken a penny. When I give away the seats, I will never accept a donation—ever. It's not about money. It's about building a bond between family. Every

> They would think I was a scalper. I would tell them the story and tell them I'd like to give them free tickets.

e-mail that we get I post on the Web site under "Letters to Steve." When we became a nonprofit, we had to change how we did our distribution, so I have to give the tickets to other nonprofits. We are working with the Phoenix Children's Hospital, Mayo Clinic, and St. Joe's of Phoenix. We give tickets to them and give them the brochures to tell them to go to the Web site. Sometimes they don't show up. It's mostly cancer patients that show up. I'm lucky enough to know the coaches. When Gene Clines was a coach with the Cubs I'd say, "Hey, Gene, can I get a ball for this kid back here?" He'd toss me a ball and I'd give it to the kid. I've probably given away a hundred baseballs to kids. We probably get a 30 percent return on the e-mails that we get back. You can't put a price tag on those e-mails. It's not about the money, it's about if you can touch a life and make a difference for one person. I think that we've done that and we are going to do it for as long as we can.

The Cubs are on national TV . . . and by that I mean WGN . . . not the NFL Channel!

Yada, Yada, Yada

I am in Iraq with "F" Battery made up of soldiers from all over Illinois. The Cubs fans in this battery listen to Pat Hughes and Ron Santo call the games on the Internet and watch the games on television when possible. This means getting up in the middle of the night to catch the games and losing some sleep, but it is worth it. I fly "win" and "loss" flags outside of my room, just like the Cubs do on the centerfield scoreboard, to let passersby know the outcomes of the games. We also have a blackboard that I use to post division standings, box scores, injury updates, Cubs stats, and trivia questions. Cubs baseball has been a nice distraction from the situation in Iraq. A World Series win would be an even better distraction.

—SSG Mark Stach,
Dixon, Illinois,
Bravo Blackhawks

I don't know if you ever did this when you were a kid. A friend of mine and I used to take our baseball cards and lay them out at the players' different positions. We would play a simulated game. We used a pencil and paper; he'd pitch the spitball wad, then I'd hit it with a pencil. If you hit it to Ernie Banks at first base, he would make the putout. Or you'd hit it to second base at Glen Beckert and he would throw over to first. We would lay it out right on the floor.

There are a lot of Cubs fans in Wisconsin. I get teased once in a while because I have vanity plates, 69 CUBS. This year, my daughters did something special for me. They had a commemorative brick program at Wrigley Field around Sheffield and Addison, so they bought a brick for me. It says, 69 NORM 69 CUBS FOREVER.

—Norm Greene, 60,
South Milwaukee

In 1945 I stayed home from school to listen to the seventh game of the World Series, but I really wasn't sick. That's the last time the Cubs played in the World Series.

In 1946, the Cubs had an exhibition in Davenport against the White Sox just a few days before they opened up the season. The interesting thing about it is, I was going to be a journalist. I wrote for the city paper, and the high school yearbook in Muscatine.

I said to the principal, "The Cubs are playing the White Sox. The city paper said I could cover it. I would like to get out of school." The principal said, "That'll be 24 eighth periods." I said, "But I'm going to be a journalist, and this is a chance to cover Major League teams." He said, "That'll be 24 eighth periods." That meant detentions. I couldn't believe this. So I went and covered the ball game. I came back and showed him the copy of the local paper. I clipped it out and said, "This is what I've done." I thought maybe he'd say, "That's a pretty good write-up." He said, "That'll be 24 eighth periods." So for being a Cub fan, I had to pay the most extreme penalty anyone could have to pay. It was well worth it.

So for being a Cub fan, I had to pay the most extreme penalty anyone could have to pay.

I wrote, "The big bats of the Chicago Cubs, National League champions, broke loose Friday afternoon at the Municipal Stadium here to lead an 11–2 victory over the Chicago White Sox at an exhibition engagement playing for a sellout crowd of eastern Iowa and western Illinois fans. The Cubs took a second-inning lead on Marv Rickert's 374-foot home run off the slants of Orval Grove and from then on were never headed." I didn't get to interview any of the players or get on the field that day. I could have, but I was a rookie. I was eighteen years old doing this. Seventeen, maybe eighteen.

I worked in the summer. Saved my money up. Took the bus to Chicago. Stayed at the White Hotel. Took the Cottage Grove streetcar to 35th Street to get to Comiskey Park. I was afraid to ride the el, because I didn't know how to get on and off it. At Comiskey Park, games were over at 10:30 or 11:00. Getting on the streetcar, everyone was black except four white guys. Nothing happened, we were safe.

When I tell people I did this, they say, "Your mother let you do that? Your father let you do that?" It was a different world. There weren't people getting murdered.

My dad worked at a radio store in downtown Davenport. He delivered a new radio to a man, and the man didn't want the old radio. This was the Depression, so now we had a radio. My mother was pregnant with me. Mother used to listen to the Cub games on that radio, and she swore that every time Hartnett would hit a home run I would leap in her stomach. I've been a Cub fan since 1933.

—Don Grensing,
Davenport, Iowa, legendary high
school baseball coach

People connected so well with Harry Caray. It was like taking an opinionated fan who had pretty good knowledge and giving him the microphone for the whole game. That was the play-by-play. That's essentially what it is. He connected with people. He had a great sense of humor. He knew the game really, really well. He had a very unique perspective and point of view.

One of my favorite things Harry used to say when people used to ask him if he played was that he was "a switch-hitter, career .300 average—.150 from the right side, .150 from the left side." I never did Harry impressions well.

> I told my buddy that I couldn't make the funeral because my son was in the hospital. The TV cameras panned the crowd. I got caught.

In 1984 the Cubs made the playoffs for the first time. I was fortunate enough to have a ticket for this playoff game. I was all set to go, and about two days prior to the game my son had an asthma attack and had to go into the hospital. Unbelievably and unexpectedly, my best pal and partner at work, his father dies. He was a very prominent person from the North Shore, and my friend wanted to have the Chicago Symphony Orchestra Choir sing at his father's funeral, and it happened to be at the same exact same time as the game. I told my buddy that I couldn't make the funeral because my son was in the hospital. Lo and behold, during the National Anthem, the TV cameras panned the crowd. I was standing there singing, and I got caught. People called me up and told me they saw me on TV. So I was sweatin', but my buddy gave me a pass. It never ends. Last year there was a Cubs special on HBO and for whatever reason there I was plain as day in the same TV shot. It's a small world . . . but I wouldn't want to paint it.

> —Al Frenzel, Chicago,
> original partner in Harry Caray's
> restaurant, University of Notre
> Dame classmate of Steve Bartman

I was talking to a good friend of mine who is a humongous Cubs fan—used to work for the Cubs—the day after they signed Soriano. I said, "How in the world are they possibly going to bat that guy lead-off just 'cause he steals 40 bases?" The guy hits home runs, but strikes out all the time. You have Derrek Lee and Aramis Ramirez to hit with him in the middle of the order, but the Cubs are going to insist on hitting him lead-off solely for the fact that the guy steals 30 to 40 bases a year. That's the only thing he does that makes him a remote fit for the lead-off spot. Because of that, the Cubs went ahead and said he was going to be their lead-off hitter instead of taking his power numbers and putting them down in the middle of the lineup that has other power hitters to surround him with. They also have other guys who could get on base and take that lead-off spot and allow Soriano to drive in runs. Instead, they've got a situation where he's going to hit 30 home runs . . . and he's hitting behind the pitcher. To me, that's shooting yourself in the foot.

Some of that goes back to the Cubs philosophy on offense, which is a little bit different than a lot of other teams. They don't quite line up with the Red Sox and the Blue Jays and the Yankees, who really believe in having disciplined hitters who only swing at strikes and wear down pitchers—make them throw a lot of pitches. It results in, over the course of a season, getting into those bullpens a lot earlier. In this day and age of baseball, that's where the big runs are scored—when you get into these bullpens before the fifth, sixth innings.

If you can get your main offensive players hitting against the back end of the opponent's bullpen, that's really where the jackpot of run scoring is.

Those are the worst pitchers in baseball. Those are the pitchers who, fifteen years ago, would have been in Triple-A. But because of expansion and teams now carrying twelve, thirteen, fourteen pitchers, those pitchers are in the Major Leagues. They still are going to face All-Star caliber hitters so if you can get your main offensive players hitting against the back end of the opponent's bullpen, that's really where the jackpot of run scoring is. It doesn't seem that the Cubs take this approach. George Castle, a Chicago sportswriter, did an in-depth piece on the same type of thing about the on-base percentage where he went and talked to a lot of other teams about why they do it. Then talked to a lot of them about what the Cubs do and what they don't do. When you read it, laid out like that, it seems hard for the Cubs to defend their philosophy. They do . . . and Jim Hendry still has a job, so . . . .

You look around the lineup on paper, for a National League lineup, it's really strong. There aren't that many National League teams that can run out three hitters the quality of Ramirez, Soriano, or Derrek Lee. They've got some complimentary pieces in there who are pretty good bats—Theriot is a pretty good bat. Murton is a pretty good bat. For a National League lineup, it's a pretty strong lineup. They've got a very poor offensive philosophy.

—Jim Walsh,
Hingham, Massachusetts, SABR
(Society for American Baseball
Research) expert

My son and I were in a sports card business in the late '80s. We thought we could attract some people to Bellevue—a small town in eastern Iowa—for a baseball card show with a Major League player. We got Shawon Dunston to agree to come and do some signings. It was my responsibility to pick him up and I arranged for him to stay at a bed-and-breakfast in Bellevue. I had him in the car and he wouldn't ride in the front seat with me. He rode in the back seat. My son and a neighbor boy were along with me. When we got to the bed-and-breakfast in Bellevue, he said, "I'm not staying there." Dunston's arrogance came across that he was too good for it. We took him back to Dubuque and got him lodging. Then I took him, my son, and a neighbor boy out to breakfast at Hardees. He wouldn't sit at the table with us. He sat a table away from us. The whole impression we got was that he was sad that he signed on with this small operation. He made us feel like we were not good people. That stuck in town for a long time. It was not just me that had that feeling. He did do the signing. He didn't dishonor that. We are good Cub fans here. (Unbeknownst to me—I never was a part of it—the Bellevue people the next season took in a sign and downgraded Shawon Dunston at Wrigley Field.)

We sold tables or space in a high school gymnasium. Dunston was going to be the attraction. Other people sold cards too. We had a pretty good card dealer—who is still a card dealer today—out of Dubuque by the name of David Orr. That was the one and only time we ever did a show, and it left a bad taste in our mouth. I was in disbelief. You're bringing in a lot of young kids. That is what card shows are for in a lot of respects. You would hope to have a player there that would be personable and inspiring. Shawon Dunston was anything but that. He was self-centered.

That was my son and his friends' first exposure to a professional player close-up and they were very disappointed. I am not the sport enthusiast in the community that a lot of people are. I did try and promote the show. I came from the point of education. I thought people who are successful could lend inspiration to kids who are trying to become successful when they grow up. I thought any player would be a good inspiration to the people that came. I was wrong!

The other day I asked my son where Shawon Dunston was now and he said, "Who cares?"

—Virgil Murray,
mayor of Bellevue, Iowa, retired
superintendent of schools

I ran into a Mets fan yesterday. Then, I backed up and ran into him again.

Hello Again Everybody

Harry Caray

Legendary Cubs announcer Harry Caray passed away over ten years ago leaving an indelible mark on the Cub Nation. Below is Harry Caray's last interview. It was with WGN Radio's Spike O'Dell just weeks before his passing. A tip of the Hatlo hat to Jim Dowdle, WGN, and Spike O'Dell for sharing this.

H arry Caray all his life has been a registered Democrat. I voted for a guy named Ronald Reagan. I voted for him because he was the first baseball announcer that ran for president of the United States. How could you deny that? Naturally I voted for him. I label myself as a registered Democrat, but I'm a more moderate Democrat. I became a little more conservative as the years went on. For a guy that didn't have a dime and was an orphan out of St. Louis, I'm pretty proud of everything I made. I made a little money, and nobody ever gave it to me. I shuddered when I first heard the amount of money that I'm going to leave to my family. All of us, what we really work for is to leave something substantial to our family. I find out when it's all over with, they're going to take it. A piece of advice, with your last living breath you should have just spent your last nickel and just have written a check that bounces for your funeral.

The first thing I remember from my childhood was the fact my father had died. I don't remember my father. Then, with my mother, I barely have an image in my mind of just getting home and the doctor had just put a mirror in front of my mother's mouth. He turned around and said, "She's dead." So for my mother and my father that's all I can remember. That's why I have such pride in the fact that I'm one of three generations all doing Major League sports and have been for quite some time. If I had only been smart enough, like Tip O'Neill, and nicknamed myself "Tip" we'd have Tip, Skip, and Chip. Who could beat that? Being an orphan, wherever I stayed was a friend of my mother's or father's and I couldn't always stay there too long. They would have obligations. Much later a woman who was my aunt through marriage—she was married to my mother's brother who passed away—took me in even though she had four kids of her own.

A woman who was my aunt through marriage took me in even though she had four kids of her own.

That's the closest thing I could ever remember of having a mother and a family. The family wasn't mine, but they were related to me, they were cousins. Shortly after that she died, but I've never forgotten or will forget to recognize all I owe to Aunt Doxie from St. Louis. . . .

I'm more convinced than ever before that the radio is baseball's partner. Baseball is a radio game, where the announcer can use his imagination, his vocabulary, his drama to build a situation up. Whereas the TV, you can see it. From the standpoint of the announcer, the radio gives him more opportunity to develop his own personality that the people will love. . . .

Now instead of drinking Budweiser I drink O'Doul's. Instead of having four, five, or six martinis before dinner I have a glass of nonalcohol wine. If anyone tells you that you can have as much fun when you don't drink as you do when you do drink, tell him he's a liar. I find myself not going to as many places now, because how many O'Doul's can you drink and not even feel a buzz? Do you think if you drank a six-pack of O'Doul's that you could get in a fake fight? How much nonalcohol wine can you drink? I'd rather drink Welch's Grape Juice.

I'm so proud of what has become my family life and why the three generations mean so much to me. You want to be successful. What you really want to do is make a lot of money so you know your kids will have something you didn't get. In my case it led to two broken marriages. Was it a woman's fault or my fault? I was too busy trying to become "Harry Caray." They did a great job raising my kids. My first wife, Dorothy, is the mother of my first three. My second wife, Marian—might have been a little bit of her fault too, but—she did a great job raising my two daughters: Michelle and Elizabeth. Elizabeth lives here in Chicago in Schaumburg where she works for American Airlines. She's married and her husband's name is Adam.

I realized what my shortcomings were. I think nothing but kindly of my ex-wives. Just like a good hitter. You strike out two or three times and then comes the occasion you hit a grand slam with the bases loaded. That's what I've got now with Dutchie. She's been wonderful . . . especially with the nonfun guy I am now that I don't have alcohol to lean on.

I wake up at about 7:30 in the morning and I go through the papers. I read every one of them. I get three: *The Tribune*, the *Sun-Times* and *USA Today*. I never have time enough to read all the papers until I get back from the ballpark. I read the sports pages first and I read the rest of the papers later. It's hard to finish reading a newspaper in a little length of time the way I do it. I like to read everything. I read the headlines, I read the continued stories. I love the editorial pages. I know which columnist is going to tell it like it really is. I only got through high school and I barely did that. I'm conscious of the fact that practically everyone is better educated than I am. Voracious reading is what got me into the radio business.

I played semi-pro baseball in **St. Louis** and I got $15 to play on Saturday and $20 to play on Sunday. That was seventy years ago; I'd be a millionaire if those pennies were today's dollars. Each year the St. Louis Cardinals would send their outstanding prospects to Decatur, Illinois, where they held this tryout camp. They put a big number on your back and you go through the paces. I lasted until the second day. The scouts called me in and said, "Son, you have a good arm, you have good hands, you have good feet, but we don't think you'll ever hit." That broke my heart, but it didn't break my heart completely because every opportunity I got I went to the ballpark and sat out

St. Louis: All six games of the 1944 World Series were played at Sportsman's Park in St. Louis. The rival managers—Luke Sewell of the Browns and Billy Southworth of the Cardinals—shared a one-bedroom apartment during the season . . . never expecting both teams to be in town at the same time.

in the bleachers. I'd listen to the broadcasts when I wasn't at the ballpark. I'd hear these announcers. You could tell they didn't enjoy the game. I had the feeling they'd rather be out playing golf. I knew they didn't have the enthusiasm within their selves that I knew I had. I wrote a letter to a guy named, Earl Jones, who later became the third man at CBS. I sent this letter to his home and I marked it "personal." I described to him why I thought I'd make a better play-by-play man for the Cardinals and Browns than the people who were doing it at that time and I was an eighteen-year-old kid. Earl Jones later told me this story. He had been wining and dining CBS executives over the weekend. He gets home on a Monday, the first time he'd ever come home inside the working hours. He picks up the mail for the first time in his life, gets to his apartment, kicks off his shoes, makes a scotch and water, is thumbing through the mail, and sees this one letter marked "personal." He drops all the rest, opens up the personal letter. He said, "I didn't know whether it was some gal I had met or some fine I might have gotten when I was loaded. I didn't know what it was, but if it had gone to the station I would have never seen it." By then, I had a job doing sales correspondence work for a manufacturing company that made school lockers, basketball backboards, and gymnastic equipment. That letter is how it all got started. Earl Jones set up an audition for me. I flopped at the audition. I had never been in front of the microphone. Earl Jones, when he set up the audition, said "Make sure I hear you after your audition." When I finished my audition I asked the program director if Mr. Jones had heard. He said, "No, he's been too busy." I said, "Well, I'm not going. Either you call him or I call him. He said he wanted to hear me after my audition." Jones told him on the phone, "Put it on again I want to hear him." Then when I went up to see him he was waiting for me with a big smile on his face, he said, "Not so easy, is it?" They gave me a regular announcer's audition with a lot of news. I said, "Who knows anything about Puccini or Beethoven or Brewsinski, I want to be a baseball announcer." He said, "I heard what I wanted to hear.

I'd hear these announcers. You could tell they didn't enjoy the game. I had the feeling they'd rather be out playing golf.

Your voice is good and exciting and that's what you're going to be making a living on. If you want to get started, I'll see to it that you get started somewhere." That somewhere was Joliet, Illinois, at WCLS. A man that had been the chief announcer at KMOX in St. Louis had been made part owner of the station and they billed me as a great sports expert. I'd never been on the air in my life. I went to Joliet and did man-on-the-street programs and high school sports, football, basketball, softball.

Everybody gets lucky one time in their life. If they're prepared they'll be ready for their one opportunity and they can become successful. If they're not lucky or they don't happen to be good or they don't happen to make recognition of themselves to other people they may never get another chance. So don't ever overlook the element of luck in anybody's career.

I've had several letters from President Clinton and I used to go to the Oaklawn **Racetrack** in Hot Springs, Arkansas. I met his mother, Virginia, down there. I knew the Budweiser distributor in Little Rock. He had a penthouse apartment and we'd go down there before going to spring training every year. I don't know that I've met the president, but I've had several letters from him. I recall talking with him and the congressman from Missouri, Dick Gephardt. They were flying to St. Louis and they called me in the hospital in Miami. Bill Clinton has been very nice to me, but I don't know him. I do know his wife, Hillary. She helped me sing "Take Me Out to the Ball Game" one day.

What's amazing to me is Skip and Chip and me being the father and grandfather. At Cooperstown in '89 when I was inducted, everybody expected me to say something about how thrilled I was. Suddenly, I couldn't say that. The only thing I could think of is my grandson

---

Racetrack: In what sport was Chris Evert the leading money winner in 1974? The answer: horse racing. The owner, Carl Rosen, named his horses after tennis players. The horse named Chris Evert won $551,063 with five wins in eight starts.

was there and my son was there and I was getting honored and they were all in the same business that I was in. Everything else pales in significance when it comes to your own flesh and blood.

Harry Caray has bad days. All you have to do is read a couple of these columns that have me dead for ten years or have me retiring every twenty-four hours. What's wrong with a man continuing to do what he so wholeheartedly loves with his whole body and soul beyond the age of twenty-five, thirty-five, or forty-five? What if he's seventy-five? If he still loves to do the work and the people he works for thinks he's doing a capable job, why should other people share their feeling, "Oh, he's too old."

What's wrong with a man continuing to do what he so wholeheartedly loves with his whole body and soul beyond the age of twenty-five, thirty-five, or forty-five? What if he's seventy-five?

I'll tell you about **Michael Jordan**. When he first came to Chicago, I met him. They brought him up to the radio booth and nobody knew Michael Jordan. I watched him develop. He may be the greatest athlete in our history. I'm sure that anything that he wanted to do he would do exceptionally well. He's never made a mistake, he's like Stan Musial and Ernie Banks. I used to call Stan Musial "the Ernie Banks of the Cardinals" and I used to call Ernie Banks "the Stan Musial of the Cubs." They never said anything wrong. They were always good to everybody. I've seen Stan wait outside the old Sportsman's Park after a doubleheader, 115 degrees with one hundred kids waiting for him. He would sign for every one of them and he never turned down an autograph, unless they had to cut it short. Unfortunately, there aren't too many people like that—Ernie is that way. I know Michael Jordan is within reason that way and Kerry Wood is learning some of the pitfalls of being a celebrity.

Michael Jordan: Michael Jordan was given his first set of golf clubs by fellow University of North Carolina classmate, Davis Love, Davis Love, Davis Love . . . The Roman Guy.

There's a handful of people I can sit down and pour my heart out to. Some of them have passed away. I don't hesitate to name Jack Barry, well-known attorney here and former star at **Notre Dame**. Now Jack is in his late 60s or early 70s. I've known him through knowing Emmet O'Neill, who is his brother-in-law. Emmitt was a force in this town; he knew everybody politically and he's a great friend of mine. In St. Louis there's a Charlie Braun, Don Hammil, and Bob Hyland from KMOX was my dear, dear friend. He's the guy that helped me get Skip into following in my footsteps. In the late '50s and early '60s everybody was rebellious, all the young guys. A young guy never wanted to follow in the footsteps of his father; he wanted to do it on his own. Mr. Hyland called me aside and said, "Harry, won't you talk to Skip?"

"I want him to be a doctor; I don't want him to be in radio." There was no television then. I used to say to Mr. Hyland, "Don't worry, he'll be successful no matter what he does." That's the way it's been. In those days I'd take Skip on road trips with me when his mother and I were no longer married. He'd come to the ballpark and say, "Hi Marty, Hi Red, Hi Stan." He knew all the ballplayers and all the ballplayers knew him. I knew if I tried to force him or encourage him, it would never happen. So Bob Hyland and I set up a trick. We tricked him and he bit the bait and he's been an announcer ever since.

The greatest thing to happen to minor-league baseball is the fact that all these guys in the Major Leagues are making so much money that the owners feel compelled to raise the price of everything. The only time that baseball is ever going to have to worry about its existence, and the time is rapidly approaching, is when a guy cannot take his wife and two little children to the ballpark because it is too expensive. Now they go to minor-league baseball. They watch baseball. They know the guy playing second base is not making $55 million.

Notre Dame: At Notre Dame, 1956 Heisman Trophy winner Paul Hornung played halfback, fullback, and quarterback; punted, kicked-off, kicked field goals; ran back punts and kickoffs; and was a starting safety. Notre Dame's schedule that year included the No. 1, No. 2, and No. 3 ranked teams, plus four others in the Top Twenty.

They can take the kids and everybody has a good time. That's really saved minor-league baseball.
. . .

The glasses certainly have become a trademark for me. It's amazing to me. I'll be riding down with somebody in another city and we come to a stop sign and three or four people will shout, "Harry Caray!" because they see through the window of the automobile. It must be the glasses. Besides that, I'm a good-looking, handsome, 6-foot-3 big hunk!

It must be the glasses. Besides that, I'm a good-looking, handsome, 6-foot-3 big hunk!

I haven't seen people out there imitating me, but they tell me for the second time on *Saturday Night Live* they had the same guy doing the bit on me. I don't know what to say about that. I know that they say imitation is the sincerest form of flattery. It seems to me that the first thing about announcers is to be yourself. If you try and copy someone else, they're going to think of the guy you're trying to copy. I've never been one to imitate anybody. I'm sure somewhere along the line I have, but I do know I didn't imitate **Phil Rizzuto** on "Holy cow!" He was playing shortstop with the Yankees when I was broadcasting baseball with both the Browns and the Cardinals in St. Louis. Rizzuto was playing short and Jerry Priddy was playing second and the only way he could have said "Holy cow!" before me is if he threw the ball to Priddy who dropped it and said, "Holy cow, Jerry, you should have held onto it!" while I was telling hundreds of thousands of people on the radio, "Holy cow!"

My home run call is about as good as it can be, because as soon as the bat is swung and you hear the crack of the bat against ball you know it might be. Then you watch the leftfielder going back, going back, and you know it could be. Then you see the fan catch it and you know it is.

Phil Rizzuto: Phil Rizzuto is the only baseball person to earn a Gold Record . . . His game-calling was in the background of Meat Loaf's "Paradise by the Dashboard Light" . . . Rizzuto was the first-ever mystery guest on *What's My Line*.

One thing I want to do before I die, and I better get around to it, . . . my father's family came from Sicily and I've never been to Italy. I've been to France, Germany, Switzerland, and other places, but I've never been to Italy and I want to make sure I make it while I'm still around.

Regrets, I've had a few. I love the country-western songs; all of them seem to tell a story. The guy that falls in love or out of love, he cheats on his girlfriend, or she cheated on him. I was just watching *An Affair to Remember* with Cary Grant and a gal, Irene Dunne I think. What a movie that was and I had to leave it just when the tears were coming out of my eyes to get here earlier than I had to be. What a lucky guy I've been.

Busch Stadium: Come see the Cubs practice for their important games.

To be continued!

We hope you have enjoyed *For Cubs Fans Only!!!* You can be in the next edition if you have a neat story. E-mail it to printedpage@cox.net (please put "Cubs" in the subject line and include a phone number where you can be reached), or call the author directly at (602) 738-5889.

For information on ordering more copies of *For Cubs Fans Only!!!* as well as any of the author's other best-selling books, call (602) 738-5889.

NOTE: There were no actual Cardinals fans harmed during the making of this book.

Photos courtesy of: Pages 1, 11, John Mocek; Page 2, Joe Bartenhagen; page 7, Rich Dozer; page 19, J. R. Russ; page 28, Doug Feldmann; page 41, Joe Drennan; pages 47, 55, Ward Tannhauser; page 48, Tony Brown; page 57, Joel Justis; page 62, George Loukas; page 66, Ted Butterman; page 72, Mark Carlson; pages 73, 117, Marty Prather; pages 87, 146, Jane Walters; page 88, Karen Kruse; page 102, Deb Kolze; page 118, Dave Stowell; page 121, Jason Myers; page 127, Alan Hartwick by Wojtek; page 133, Ray Floyd (c) PGA TOUR; page 136, Brad Zibung; page 141, Rick Phalen; page 151, John Raap; page 153, SSG Mark Stach; page 154, Spike O'Dell; page 163, Frank Mastro; page 167, Fred Freres; page 171, Mike Toomey; page 174, Ken Sevara; page 182, Noel Gimbel; page 186, Gary Sosniecki; page 196, Gary Leibovitz; page 203, Mike Berry; page 220, Harry Caray

Other Books by Rich Wolfe

Da Coach (Mike Ditka)

I Remember Harry Caray

There's No Expiration Date on Dreams (Tom Brady)

He Graduated Life with Honors and No Regrets (Pat Tillman)

Take This Job and Love It/All It Takes Is All You Got (Jon Gruden)

Been There, Shoulda Done That (John Daly)

Oh, What a Knight (Bob Knight)

And the Last Shall Be First (Kurt Warner)

Remembering Jack Buck

Sports Fans Who Made Headlines

Fandemonium

Remembering Dale Earnhardt

For Yankee Fans Only!

For Cubs Fans Only! volume 1

For Cardinal Fans Only!

For Packer Fans Only!

For Browns Fans Only!

For Mets Fans Only!

For Broncos Fans Only!

For Georgia Fans Only!

For Nebraska Fans Only!

For Notre Dame Fans Only—The New Saturday Bible

For Hawkeyes Fans Only!

For Buckeyes Fans Only!

For South Carolina Fans Only!

For Clemson Fans Only!

For Oklahoma Fans Only!

For Yankee Fans Only! volume 2

For more information on these books, call (602) 738-5889.

Sample excerpts from this book

Now instead of drinking Budweiser I drink O'Doul's. ... If anyone tells you that you can have as much fun when you don't drink as you do when you do drink, tell him he's a liar. ...How many O'Doul's can you drink and not even feel a buzz? Do you think if you drank a six-pack of O'Doul's that you could get in a fake fight? (Harry Caray, in his last interview)

The best year to be a Cubs fan was in '69. I turned twenty-one that summer, so I could drink beer legally. It cost a buck to get in the bleachers and a buck a beer, so if you had a ten-spot, you could have a ball. There were all kinds of gorgeous ladies out there.

Several years ago there was that "Got Milk" campaign. ...my friend got me a full-length Mark Grace "Got Milk" poster. At the Cubs convention we decided to tuck the life-size poster into my bed at the Hilton Towers. I didn't realize they had turn-down service.

The guy took off his T-shirt, pulled off his shorts, and stood there naked looking at the Cubs pitcher. ...Then he turned around and flashed a double bird at the broadcasting booth. Finally, security gets out there. ... They just scoop him up and drag him up the aisle. ...I'm thinking, "At least they could have covered him up." ... It's not a visual that you would want to dwell on. My dad always said, "You don't need a fence if you don't have a dog." That might explain why the guy wasn't wearing pants...